THE ASSOCIATION FOR SCOTTISH LITERARY STUDIES

NUMBER TWENTY-SIX

THE CHRISTIS KIRK TRADITION
SCOTS POEMS OF FOLK FESTIVITY

THE ASSOCIATION FOR SCOTTISH LITERARY STUDIES

The Association for Scottish Literary Studies aims to promote the study, teaching and writing of Scottish literature, and to further the study of the languages of Scotland.

To these ends, the ASLS publishes works of Scottish literature (of which this volume is an example), literary criticism in *Scottish Literary Journal*, scholarly studies of language in *Scottish Language*, and in-depth reviews of Scottish books in *SLJ Supplements*. It also publishes *New Writing Scotland*, an annual anthology of new poetry, drama and short fiction, in Scots, English and Gaelic, by Scottish writers. ASLS has also prepared a range of teaching materials covering Scottish language and literature for use in schools.

All the above publications, except for the teaching materials, are available as a single 'package', in return for an annual subscription. Enquiries should be sent to: ASLS, c/o Department of Scottish History, University of Glasgow, 9 University Gardens, Glasgow G12 8QH, telephone number 0141 330 5309 (e-mail: cmc@arts.gla.ac.uk).

A list of Annual Volumes published by ASLS can be found at the end of this book

THE ASSOCIATION FOR SCOTTISH LITERARY STUDIES

GENERAL EDITOR – C.J.M. MACLACHLAN

THE CHRISTIS KIRK TRADITION

SCOTS POEMS OF FOLK FESTIVITY

edited by

Allan H. MacLaine

GLASGOW

1996

First published in Great Britain, 1996
by The Association for Scottish Literary Studies
c/o Department of Scottish History
University of Glasgow
9, University Gardens
Glasgow G12 8QH

ISBN 0 948877 30 8

A catalogue record for this book
is available from the British Library.

The Association for Scottish Literary Studies
acknowledges subsidy from the Scottish Arts Council
towards the publication of this volume.

Typeset by Roger Booth Associates, Hassocks, West Sussex
Printed in Great Britain by Cromwell Press, Melksham, Wiltshire

In loving memory of my brother,

Robert Howard MacLaine

of Montreal and Morin Heights, Québec

1927–1992

Contents

Preface

An anthology of the most important *Christis Kirk* poems, many of which are long out of print or very hard to come by, is long overdue. This volume, I trust, will fill that gap. The original proposal to include this project in the series of annual volumes published by the Association for Scottish Literary Studies was put forward to the Association's Council, I am told, by Professor David Daiches, a man to whom all students of Scottish poetry are indebted. I am also thankful that Dr. Daiches recommended me as the editor on the basis of an extensive study of the genre that I published three decades ago. At any rate, for me the preparation of this volume has been a pleasant task.

When the project was first offered it did not seem at all daunting, but when I got well into it all kinds of unexpected complications arose, especially in the older poems like 'Sym and his Bruder' that had never been adequately glossed or edited before. What I expected would take about a year and a half to accomplish has, in fact, extended to nearly four. My aim from the beginning has been to produce the best possible texts with thorough annotations and glosses of all twenty poems in the volume. Now that the job is done I am content, and trust that the resulting book will prove useful to scholars, as well as entertaining and (by virtue of the marginal glossing) easily accessible to general readers. These are, after all, delightful poems – often undervalued or even ignored in literary histories.

For kind permission to use their texts for ten of these poems I am deeply indebted to the editors of *Longer Scottish Poems* (Edinburgh: Scottish Academic Press, 1987), specifically as follows: to Volume I, edited by Priscilla Bawcutt and Felicity Riddy, for Scott's 'Justing and Debait'; to Volume II, edited by Thomas Crawford, David Hewitt, and Alexander Law, for the pieces by Ramsay, Skinner, and Fergusson, for Mayne's 'Siller Gun', and for three of the five poems by Burns. My thanks are also due to the Scottish Text Society for permission to use Douglas Hamer's text of Lindsay's 'Justing,' and the fine transcripts of the Bannatyne, Maitland Folio, and Asloan Manuscripts, published under its auspices. My work has been advanced through the generous help of staff members at the National Library of Scotland in Edinburgh, at the Pepys Library in Magdalene College in Cambridge, and at the University of Rhode Island Library. In addition, I wish to thank three successive chairmen of the English Department at Rhode Island – David Stineback, Wilfred Dvorak, and R B Reaves, Jr. – for enthusiastic support with the typing costs for this project. Two excellent typists, Linda Hawsley Baer and Edward S. Shear provided the expertise needed for these very difficult texts, glosses, and notes. Furthermore, I owe an important debt to the Research Council of the University of Rhode Island for a timely travel grant that made possible a trip to Britain for first-hand scrutiny of the actual Bannatyne and Maitland Folio Manuscripts in Edinburgh and Cambridge.

Many individuals have assisted me with this book in various ways. Among them are Thomas Crawford, University of Aberdeen; Nancy A. Potter, Professor Emerita, University of Rhode Island; Lorraina Pinnell, Ph.D. student at Rhode Island; Dr. Harry Watson, chief editor of *DOST*; Priscilla Bawcutt (with suggestions on Dunbar's 'Justis'); Robert N. Smart, keeper of the Muniments in the University of St Andrews Library, and Geoffrey W. S. Barrow, Professor of History at the University of Edinburgh (the two last-named with information on 'Sym and his Bruder'). Very generous assistance with the thorny language problems in 'Sym' was rendered by Professor A. J. Aitken, retired chief editor of *DOST*. Professor Kenneth H. Rogers of the Department of Languages at the University of Rhode Island was immensely helpful with the Latin component of Drummond's 'Polemo-Middinia', and Dr John Strawhorn of Mauchline, Ayrshire, gave me some crucial information relating to Burns's 'The Holy Fair'. Throughout the whole of this project the General Editor for the ASLS annual volumes, Dr Christopher J. M. MacLachlan of the University of St Andrews, has been patient, knowledgeable, and most cooperative. Finally, I thank my wife, Stacy Lagerquist MacLaine, for being supportive (as always) in countless ways.

My brother, Robert Howard MacLaine, died in June of 1992, and to his memory this edition is dedicated.

Introduction

Alexander Pope was a subscriber to both editions of *Poems by Allan Ramsay* (1721, 1728); he was clearly and surprisingly an admirer of Ramsay's efforts to revive the Scots poetic tradition. In his own *Imitations of Horace* Pope made an astute comment on the universal tendency for people to become emotionally attached to their native tongues, especially as embodied in old-fashioned literary works before the pollution of new-fangled modern jargon:

> One likes no language but the Faery Queen;
> A Scot will fight for Christ's Kirk o' the Green.[1]

Certainly the *Christis Kirk* poems, beloved for so many centuries by the Scottish people, perfectly exemplify Pope's dictum. The Scots in fact have always been especially partial to traditional forms in literature. But even in Scots poetry the *Christis Kirk* genre is uniquely long lived; it is most unusual for a poetic form as specialized as this one to remain more or less in vogue for over 500 years, through many generations of changing poetic fashions. How can one explain this kind of longevity? Certainly at least part of the answer must lie in the flexible nature of the genre itself which I shall now attempt to define.

Generally speaking, the basic pattern of this type of poem as established in 'Peblis to the Play' (the earliest surviving specimen) is as follows: there is a satiric description of working-class folk (usually peasants or town tradesmen) shown on some festive occasion such as a wedding or a fair. The people are engaged in all kinds of revelry, wooing, drunkenness, horseplay, ribaldry, brawling, and bungling. This descriptive method gives a panoramic impression of the whole crowded and colourful scene by highlighting carefully chosen details. The poem is given structure and coherence through the introduction of a few rapidly-sketched characters who lend specific human interest and provide the basis for a slender thread of narrative. In most of the pieces, there is considerable use of dialogue to create an illusion of reality and immediacy. The narrative is swift-paced, with frequent transitions, full of robust movement and details.

In all cases (with the single exception of Burns's 'Ordination'), the scene is described from the point of view of an amused spectator who takes no part in the action and is presumably on a higher social and intellectual level than the merrymakers. The tone of the satire, however, is usually genial and good-natured – the narrator/observer makes fun of his clownish characters, but he also partially admires them. Only in later developments of the genre, such as Burns's 'Holy Fair' and 'Ordination', does the satiric edge become devastating. Obviously, the *Christis Kirk* genre is not folk poetry; on the contrary, these poems are the work of highly sophisticated literary artists who are satirizing folk antics. The genre, therefore, belongs to the broad category of art poetry on folk themes that is a central part of both Middle and modern Scots literature.

In verse form, most of these poems conform to a traditional and quite complex pattern: an octave of alternating iambic tetrameters and trimeters, followed by a 'bobwheel' of two lines (monometer and trimeter) at the end. The bobwheel was later simplified, reduced to a single dimeter tag-line as a closing device in each stanza. In addition, there is a very demanding rime scheme in most of the earlier poems (A B A B A B A B / C D). In 'Peblis to the Play' after the fourth stanza and in the poems of Fergusson and Burns there occurred some loosening of the rigid rimes of the octave. From the beginning many of the poems included a good deal of alliteration (consistent or sporadic) on top of the fixed patterns of rhythm and rime. This was surely not a verse form for amateurs.

This anthology is the first attempt to bring together the more important of the *Christis Kirk* poems within the covers of a single volume. To have included *all* of the poems in this voluminous genre through the six centuries of its existence would have been a thankless and impractical task. Some limits had to be set, and it was early decided (a) to end the volume with the climactic work of Burns at the close of the eighteenth century, and (b) to admit pieces of genuine literary merit only. The *Christis Kirk* tradition has, of course, continued to flourish until very recent times, as seen in such lively examples as Robert Garioch's 'Embro tae the Ploy',[2] an ironic comment on the Edinburgh International Festival of 1948. But most of the specimens of the nineteenth and early twentieth centuries are decidedly inferior in quality – not worth reprinting. Moreover, the best of them – William Tennant's *Anster Fair* – has already been well edited by Maurice Lindsay and Alexander Scott for this same series of annual volumes published by the Association for Scottish Literary Studies.[3] Of the eighteenth-century poems two – David Nicol's 'Christis Kirk on the Green, Canto IV' and Janet Little's 'Hallowe'en'[4] – have been left out simply because they are bad poems and excessively derivative. Robert Fergusson's song of

'Hallowfair' has also been excluded as a slight effort wholly overshadowed by that poet's three major poems which occupy an honoured place in this volume. On the other hand, two brief Middle Scots mock-tournament pieces that are not strictly *Christis Kirk* poems – Dunbar's 'Justis' and Lindsay's 'Justing' – are presented here as works on the fringe of the tradition that are important in the early phases of this genre.

It is not part of my purpose in this introduction to give a detailed history of the evolution of the *Christis Kirk* tradition, since such an account is available elsewhere.[5] A brief summary here, however, may give readers a helpful overview.

'Peblis to the Play', the prototype of the *Christis Kirk* genre, seems to date from about 1430 to 1450. (For some discussion of the disputed dating and authorship of this work and of 'Christis Kirk on the Grene' see the notes on these poems.) Since 'Peblis' was not printed from the Maitland Folio Manuscript until 1783, it has been assumed that it was not well known, perhaps even 'lost' for centuries before being 'discovered' by Bishop Thomas Percy, and finally printed by John Pinkerton. Two bits of evidence, however, work against this view. For one thing, 'Peblis' is mentioned in the opening stanza of 'Christis Kirk' (*c*. 1490–1510) with another poem that has perished called 'Falkland on the Green', as though they were titles familiar to the public and perhaps only representative of a fairly numerous class of poems of this kind. Furthermore, there is a line in Sir David Lindsay's *Ane Satyre of the Thrie Estaitis* (1554) that probably refers to this poem. Together, these allusions suggest that 'Peblis' was quite well known in the sixteenth century and circulated widely in manuscript. At any rate, the poem is a lively description of county folk streaming into Peebles for the annual Beltane festival, spending a boisterous and drunken day there, ending in a country dance.

This brilliant work was followed up about half a century later by a companion piece, 'Christis Kirk on the Grene', a poem of such huge popularity that it has given its name to the entire genre. 'Christis Kirk' was printed and reprinted so many times in the seventeenth century – generally a bleak period in the history of Scots poetry – that it is not too much to say it forms the main link between the older comic poetry in Middle Scots and that of the eighteenth-century revival led by Allan Ramsay and culminating in Fergusson and Burns. This crucial work is an earthy depiction of a rural celebration, including a farcical archery contest and ending up in a vivid, barbarous free-for-all.

The fifteenth century, then, saw the firm establishment of the genre with 'Peblis' and 'Christis Kirk' as prototypes. In the first half of the next century there were further developments connected with the related genre of the mock tournament. William Dunbar's 'The Justis Betwix the Talyeour and the Soutar' (*c.* 1500) is the earliest known Scots specimen of this form which also emerged in England about the same time in the 'Tournament of Tottenham'.[6] Dunbar's scatological *tour de force* shows influences from the *Christis Kirk* tradition, especially from the passages satirizing peasant cowardice in 'Christis Kirk' itself. The mock-tournament genre in general makes fun of the upper class custom of jousting as well as the bungling and craven behaviour of lower class imitators of the knightly sport. Like the *Christis Kirk* poems, the mock tournaments expose the cowardly antics of the common folk in a farcical but good-humoured way. Sir David Lindsay's 'The Justing Betwix James Watsoun and Jhone Barbour', probably written in 1539, follows this same line and shows the direct influence of both 'Christis Kirk' and the enigmatic piece called 'Sym and his Bruder' (*c.* 1530).

'Sym and his Bruder', possibly by Lindsay himself, is a full-fledged *Christis Kirk* poem in the very strict stanza form – that is a two-rime octave followed by a bobwheel, and including heavy alliteration. This piece is a hilarious satire on a pair of wholly fraudulent begging pilgrims in the town of St Andrews; the latter part of the poem describes a tournament in burlesque fashion, and is the earliest example of the *Christis Kirk* tradition combining with and absorbing the mock-tournament genre.

This trend continues and culminates a generation or so later in Alexander Scott's 'The Justing and Debait up at the Drum Betwix William Adamsone and Johine Sym' (*c.* 1560). Here the entire poem is a mock tournament treated in the *Christis Kirk* way and in the characteristic stanza. The characters are tradesmen in the neighbouring towns of Edinburgh and Dalkeith; the scenes are set on the farm of the Drum in the morning and in Dalkeith in the afternoon. Scott invents a new type of refrain in his 'wheel' lines – 'Up at the Drum that day' and 'Up at Dalkeith that day' – a device that led to a simplified form of the bobwheel in the seventeenth and eighteenth centuries when it was reduced to a single dimeter tag-line ending always with 'that day' or 'that night'. After Scott, the mock tournament died out as a poetic genre, presumably having become irrelevant when the serious sport fell into disuse with the end of the feudal Middle Ages. Not so, however, with the *Christis Kirk* tradition.

During the later sixteenth century – generally a period of gradual decline in Scots poetry – the popularity and influence of this genre were pervasive. In Sir David Lindsay's massive morality play called *Ane Satyre of the Thrie Estaitis* (1554), for example, we find many echoes of the substance and phrasing of 'Christis Kirk' itself.[7] More generally, the basic satiric method of the genre – making fun of working-class mores – is reflected in dozens of the anonymous comic works of this era, including the irresistible farce on rustic marriage called 'The Wife of Auchtermuchty'.[8]

In the seventeenth century, the removal of the Scottish court (always a source of patronage for poets) to London combined with the hostile dictates of a triumphant Calvinism to reduce the production of new poetry in Scots to an intermittent trickle. The creative bleakness was relieved almost solely by the continuing vogue of the *Christis Kirk* genre. No fewer than five printed editions of 'Christis Kirk' appeared in this period, supplemented by two new poems of some distinction. The first of these was 'Polemo-Middinia' ('The Dunghill Fight'), almost certainly the work of William Drummond of Hawthornden and composed about 1645. This is an ingenious macaronic (half Latin, half Scots) portraying a wild brawl of clownish country folk flinging cow dung at each other. All of the distinctive features of the *Christis Kirk* tradition (except for the verse form) are apparent here – the swift tempo, the dialogue, the mock heroic satire, the drunkenness, and so forth. This witty and rambunctious piece was followed later in the century by the comic song of 'The Blythsome Wedding' (*c*. 1680), using as its basic method a mock-heroic roll call of boorish heroes based on some passages in 'Polemo-Middinia'.[9] Apart from these clear extensions of the genre, there were also a few anonymous works of this era showing *Christis Kirk* influence, such as the bawdy folksong called 'Maggie Lauder', sometimes attributed to Francis Sempill of Beltrees.[10]

In the first two decades of the eighteenth century, the *Christis Kirk* genre received enormous new stimulus through the efforts of two men, James Watson and Allan Ramsay. Both Watson and Ramsay were responding to the Act of Union with England of 1707 as a betrayal of Scotland's long struggle for political and cultural independence. Watson, an Edinburgh printer, issued a remarkable anthology called *A Choice Collection of Comic and Serious Scots Poems both Ancient and Modern*, in three volumes dated 1706, 1709, and 1711, in which he gave the place of honour as the first poem in the first volume to 'Christis Kirk on the Grene'.[11] This was soon followed in the years 1718, 1720, and 1721 by Allan Ramsay's further printings of the old poem, supplemented by lengthy and impressive sequels – Cantos II and III by Ramsay himself. In these editions Ramsay took the text of 'Canto I' from Watson who had derived it from a corrupt seventeenth-century version. In 1724, however, after Ramsay had been able to borrow the magnificent Bannatyne Manuscript from a wealthy friend, he printed for the first time ever the superior Bannatyne text of 'Christis Kirk' in *The Ever Green*, his epoch-making anthology of Middle Scots poetry. This vital work of printing and publicizing 'Christis Kirk' was continued by other editors throughout the century who reprinted the poem (with or without Ramsay's sequels) at least a dozen times,[12] a sure sign of the huge popularity of this piece with Scottish readers.

More important than his pioneer editorial work were Ramsay's skilful and substantial new sequels to the old poem. In these he demonstrated convincingly that this venerable genre was still adaptable as a vehicle for Scots poets, and he reversed the late seventeenth-century tendency of the tradition to dwindle into songs of 'The Blythsome Wedding' type. His example inspired others to work along the same lines for the rest of the century.

In 1739, the Reverend John Skinner, an Episcopal minister in Aberdeenshire, produced the next ambitious poem in the genre, 'The Christmass Bawing in Monimusk', a clever and lively piece, clearly influenced by Ramsay but incorporating some local Aberdeenshire dialect and characters. With thirty-five stanzas and 315 lines Skinner's was the longest poem of its kind yet to appear. A generation later in 1766, an obscure schoolmaster, David Nicol, published his sequel to Ramsay's sequels entitled 'Christis Kirk on the Green, Canto IV'; but this is a dull and worthless performance in which Nicol's artificial English style clashes agonizingly with his trite Scots. The result is a slavish imitation of Ramsay, not fit to be reprinted.

In the long stretch of some forty years between the creative careers of Ramsay and Fergusson, no poet of comparable talent and writing in Scots appeared on the scene. Consequently, the whole movement initiated by Ramsay seemed to be in danger of disintegration because of the lack of powerful new leadership. This danger, fortunately, evaporated in the year 1772 with the sudden emergence of Robert Fergusson.

Fergusson, an obscure law clerk in Edinburgh, first achieved distinction in early 1772 as the author of lively, swift-paced satires in Scots verse, deftly portraying the follies of city life. The *Christis Kirk* genre was, therefore, an ideal medium of expression for him, and during his incredibly brief creative career in 1772 and 1773 (he died in 1774 at the age of twenty-four) he produced three major poems in this form – 'Hallow-fair', 'Leith Races' and 'The Election'. In the first two of these poems Fergusson loosened the difficult rime scheme of the traditional octave by using four instead of two rimes: A B A B / C D C D / E, an innovation Burns was to adopt in 'A Mauchline Wedding', 'Halloween', and 'The Holy Fair'. Further, in 'The Election', Fergusson compromised with three rimes, thereby linking the schemes of the two quatrains as follows: ABAB/ACAC/D.

Apart from these technical matters, all three of Fergusson's *Christis Kirk* poems extended the subject matter of the tradition in various ways – by treating town rather than rural festivities and, in 'The Election', by moving into political satire. 'Hallow-fair' describes the crowded and lively scene at an annual November fair held in the outskirts of Edinburgh; 'Leith Races' shows the goings-on at a series of horse races held every July on the sands near Edinburgh; 'The Election' is a devastating exposé of the corruption and drunkenness connected with an Edinburgh Town Council election. More important, by writing three daringly original long poems (of thirteen, twenty, and fifteen stanzas respectively) Fergusson refreshed the whole tradition and demonstrated that it was still a vital and adapable one for modern Scots poets. These works are of high quality. In vigour, gaiety, and compelling artistry, Fergusson left Ramsay and the others far behind and was the first eighteenth-century Scots poet to reveal the full potentialities of the genre. The lesson was not lost on Robert Burns.

In the very brief interval between the significantly productive careers of Fergusson and Burns, yet another Scots poet of some talent appeared in the person of John Mayne (1759-1836) of Dumfries. Mayne had met Fergusson in 1773 during the latter's visit to Dumfries, and had been deeply impressed – so much so that the youthful Mayne was inspired to begin work in 1777 on his major opus 'The Siller Gun', followed by the briefer 'Halloween' in 1780. Both of these mildly satiric accounts of working class festivities belong to the *Christis Kirk* genre, though they are not in the traditional verse form. Mayne employed instead the six-line *Habbie* stanza that was the favourite of Ramsay and Fergusson, and later of Burns. 'The Siller Gun', describing a traditional shooting competition in Dumfries, may have been known to Burns in any one of its four early versions (1777, 1779, 1780, 1783). Burns certainly was familiar with Mayne's 'Halloween' since it provided the spark for his much more ambitious poem of the same name. In the long history of the *Christis Kirk* tradition, then, John Mayne provides a bridge between Fergusson and Burns.

Finally, with the work of Robert Burns we come to the greatest achievements in this genre. Burns used the *Christis Kirk* stanza in no fewer than six of his longer poems, but one of these, 'A Dream', is a somewhat laboured satire on the British government and is totally foreign in all other respects to the *Christis Kirk* tradition. Burns's earliest experiment in the genre is 'A Mauchline Wedding', a fragment of five stanzas depicting an actual village celebration from the point of view of an amused spectator, with touches of shrewd irony and occasional brilliance. Shortly thereafter in the autumn of 1785 came a major poem of twenty-eight stanzas, 'Halloween'. Here Burns worked in the pure *Christis Kirk* vein, describing with amused tolerance the antics of country folk in Ayrshire going through the superstitious rites connected with Hallowe'en. The style is consistently lively and accomplished, but the total effect suffers from an excessive use of folklore.

From these promising beginnings Burns moved on immediately to 'The Holy Fair', written in the autumn of 1785 and unquestionably one of his supreme masterpieces. Here, as in 'Halloween', Burns adopted the looser rime scheme introduced by Fergusson – A B A B / C D C D / E. But in this great poem Burns went far beyond Fergusson (or anyone else) in extending the subject matter of the *Christis Kirk* genre to religious satire. The typical point of view of the detached observer is maintained as the narrator goes to the fair accompanied by a personified 'Fun'. Together they laugh at ordinary folk in the large congregation, but also at the fanatical and hypocritical 'Auld Licht' ministers who take turns in the pulpit. A few weeks later, in January or February of 1786, Burns followed this up with another satire in the *Christis Kirk* genre, 'The Ordination'. In this sharp-edged attack, he portrayed the vulgar gloating of the Auld Lichts in Kilmarnock at the ordination of a new minister of their own narrow-minded sort.

Finally, Burns produced in 1785-86 'Love and Liberty' (also called 'The Jolly Beggars'), the culminating masterpiece of the *Christis Kirk* tradition. In this 'cantata', Burns took the age-old commonplaces of beggar songs celebrating the beggar philosophy of 'freedom', and he combined these with the conventions of the *Christis Kirk* tradition in a rich amalgam. The cantata is written in several different verse forms, but the *Christis Kirk* stanza (pure or modified) predominates. All of the other hallmarks of the *Christis Kirk* genre are here: the point of view of the detached satirical narrator, the antics of the bawdy, brawling beggars engaged in a wild drinking party, the extensive use of dialogue (this time in the form of dramatic songs), the series of individual vignettes held together by narrative, the rapid pace, the genial irony. For sheer dramatic force and wild hilarity the *Christis Kirk* tradition in 'Love and Liberty' had reached its peak.

After Burns, the genre continued throughout the nineteenth and well into the twentieth century. Generally speaking, there was a decline in artistic quality in the post-Burnsian era, but, nevertheless, the form survived. How can we account for the astonishing longevity of the *Christis Kirk* tradition? Four or five salient characteristics in these poems can be adduced to explain this unique phenomenon.

To begin with, the *Christis Kirk* genre has proved to be surprisingly versatile, adaptable as a vehicle for social, political and religious satire, while accommodating a variety of folk themes as observed by a sophisticated narrator. Secondly, these poems are filled with a sheer energy that is universally attractive, an uninhibited exuberance in portraying the folk in festive moods – dancing, singing, brawling, wooing, eating, and drinking. These works appeal to basic instincts, to what George Orwell called humanity's 'unofficial self'.[13]

Though not of folk origin, the *Christis Kirk* poems are vibrant pictures of the lives of the common people. The poems are, of course, satirical, but always in a good-humoured way, and they become *celebrations* of the comic world they depict. There is, therefore, a strongly democratic bias in these pieces that helps to explain their remarkable popularity through several centuries. Their settings, moreover, are unmistakably Scottish, from the very beginnings in 'Peblis' and 'Christis Kirk', so that they readily became beloved as a special kind of national treasure in Scotland, an important and integral part of the specific culture that produced them. They show the hard lives of the ordinary Scots folk in an amusing and often sympathetic way.

The *Christis Kirk* poems also are marked by a species of wry irony which, if not uniquely Scottish, is at least highly characteristic of the humour of the Scots. The wild revelry in many of these scenes of brute vitality is presented by the detached narrator is such a way as to bring out the comic incongruities, irrationalities and ironies of the situations. The tone of the satire is almost always genial, however, and it enhances the tremendous overall appeal of these poems.

Finally, the high artistic quality of many of the pieces inspired emulation and reinvigorated the whole tradition. Small masterpieces like 'Peblis', the original 'Christis Kirk', Scott's 'Justing', 'Polemo-Middinia', Ramsay's 'cantos', Fergusson's 'Leith Races', and Burns's 'Holy Fair', and 'Love and Liberty' became much-admired favourites of the Scottish people, and this helps to explain why, as Pope says, 'A Scot will fight for Christ's Kirk o' the Green'.

For all of these reasons the *Christis Kirk* tradition flourished through centuries of change in literary tastes. The twenty poems included in this volume, from the fifteenth century to the end of the eighteenth century, are in themselves a delight to read; they also represent a vital major strand in the long history of Scots poetry.

Notes

1 See Pope's 'The First Epistle of the Second Book of Horace', lines 39–40, in *The Poems of Alexander Pope* (New Haven, 1939), Twickenham Ed., Vol. IV, ed. John Butt.

2 For the text, see *Scottish Verse, 1851–1951*. ed. Douglas Young (Edinburgh, 1952), pp. 253–56.

3 *The Comic Poems of William Tennant* (Edinburgh, 1989), pp. 1-100.

4 For these texts see Nicol's *Poems on Several Subjects, Both Comical and Serious* (Edinburgh, 1766), pp. 47–53; and *Poetical Works of Janet Little, The Scotch Milkmaid* (Air [sic], 1792), pp. 167–170.

5 See Allan H. MacLaine, 'The *Christis Kirk* Tradition: Its Evolution in Scots Poetry to Burns,' *Studies in Scottish Literature*, II (1964–65) 3–18, 111–124, 163–182, 234–250.

6 For the text see Thomas Percy, *Reliques of the Ancient English Poetry*, ed. H. B. Wheatley (London, 1836), II, 17–28.

7 See Allan H. MacLaine, '*Christis Kirk on the Grene* and Sir David Lindsay's *Satyre of the Thrie Estaitis*', *Journal of English and Germanic Philology*. LVI (1957), 596–601.

8 For the text see *The Bannatyne Manuscript*, ed. W. Tod Ritchie, 4 vols. (Edinburgh, 1928-34), II, 320–324.

9 For details, see Allan H. MacLaine, 'Drummond of Hawthornden's *Polemo-Middinia* as a Source for *The Blythsome Bridal*', *Notes and Queries*, N. S. I (Sept. 1954), 384–386.

10 The text of this poem is available in many anthologies, including *The Oxford Book of Scottish Verse*, ed. John MacQueen and Tom Scott (Oxford, 1966), pp. 308–9; for arguments in favour of Sempill's authorship see *The Poems of the Sempills of Beltrees*, ed. James Paterson (Edinburgh, 1849), pp. 114–119.

11 A very useful facsimile edition of Watson's work was published by the Scottish Text Society and edited by Harriet Harvey Wood, with the text in Vol. I (Edinburgh, 1977) and introduction and notes in Vol. II (1991).

12 Printings appeared in the following years: 1748, *c.* 1750, 1763, 1768, 1782, 1783 twice, 1786 twice, 1794, 1796, and 1799.

13 Orwell as cited in David Daiches, *Robert Burns* (London, 1952), p. 231. For the original context see Orwell, 'The Art of Donald McGill', in *The Collected Essays, Journalism and Letters of George Orwell* (New York, 1968), II, 163.

A Note on the Texts

The primary aim of this volume is to make these old poems accessible and enjoyable to modern readers. To this end a slight degree of modernization seemed desirable, while at the same time maintaining the basic integrity and authenticity of all the texts, with their individual linguistic flavours and spelling conventions. This modernization of the texts has been limited to the removal of certain unnecessary impediments to comprehension, as defined below.

As might be expected, the poems in Middle Scots (Nos. 1–6) have presented the most difficulties. For all but one of these (No. 5) the copy-texts are manuscripts or transcripts of manuscripts that are full of scribal abbreviations, with sporadic or eccentric capitalization, and no punctuation to speak of at all. In all of these instances the abbreviations have been silently spelled out in full, and capitals and punctuation have been provided editorially according to modern practices. The letters 'i' and 'y', which are often used interchangeably in Middle Scots, are here normalized (e.g., *Chrystis* is given as *Christis*). The same has been done with 'u', 'v', and 'w' – all three of which are confusingly interchangeable in Middle Scots. Here again these letters are given their modern values, so that MS *seruant* is given as *servant, yow* as *you, sowtar* as *soutar*, and so forth. A special case is the Scots spelling of the English adverb or preposition *over*, meaning 'overly', 'excessively', 'too', or 'above'. This word, spelled variously in Middle Scots as *owr, ower*, and *our*, is given here consistently as *owr*, to reflect actual pronunciation and to avoid confusion. In all other respects the spelling of the Middle Scots copy-texts has been faithfully retained.

The poems in modern Scots (Nos. 7–20) naturally present fewer problems. The only changes made in these texts relate to such things as non-conventional capitalization of common nouns (in Ramsay), use of small capitals (in Burns's 'Love and Liberty'), and the eighteenth-century fondness for italics in general. Since these peculiarities tend to be distracting for twentieth-century readers, they have been eliminated, and the texts normalized according to modern usage. The original spelling and punctuation of the copy-texts, however, have been reproduced exactly.

An important part of the effort to make these texts more easily readable is the marginal gloss provided for all of the poems except

Drummond's 'Polemo-Middinia' (where a complete translation into modern English seemed preferable). The marginal glossing makes for somewhat quicker comprehension than footnotes on the same page, and is far superior to a cumulative glossary at the back of the book. The glosses in this volume are not numbered; the reader's common sense should suffice to tell him which words are being defined in a particular line. In lines where more than one word is defined, the glosses are divided by semi-colons. In glosses where two alternative definitions are offered for the same word, these are separated by commas. In the texts themselves, the superscript [n] tells the reader that there is a note at the back of the book on that word or line. The editor hopes that these devices will be easily comprehensible, and will prove to be very helpful to readers struggling with the Scots vocabulary.

1. Anon., *Peblis to the Play*, c. 1430–1450

This remarkable poem is the oldest surviving specimen, and therefore the prototype, of its genre. In 1521 the historian John Major in his Latin work on the *History of Greater Britain* (Paris) attributed a comic poem called 'At Beltayne' (the opening words of 'Peblis') to King James I of Scotland (1394–1437). This is almost certainly the same poem, but the wording of Major's attribution is so ambiguous and other aspects of the authorship so dubious that it seems best to regard the poem as anonymous. King James I was more probably the author of the impressive love allegory called *The Kingis Quair*, and several of the earlier scholars cast doubt upon Major's attribution on the grounds that 'Peblis' is so very different in tone and sensibility from the love poem that they could not possibly be the work of the same poet. This is about as absurd as saying that Chaucer's *Miller's Tale* could not possibly have been written by the author of the *Knight's Tale* or *Troilus and Criseyde*. Two facts relating to Major's ascription, however, support a relatively early date of composition for 'Peblis'. In crediting the poem to James I, who died in 1437, Major clearly believed that it was close to a century old in 1521. Secondly, the linguistic evidence (including the vocabulary) corroborates a dating in the first half of the fifteenth century. The probable time of composition suggested here, 1430–1450, is an educated guess. It should be noted also that linguistic evidence in cases like this – including 'Christis Kirk' and 'Sym and his Bruder' – is never conclusive by itself, where the poem has circulated in manuscript for generations before finally being fixed in print. Such works were in a fluid condition, a state of constant revision by copyists who were naturally inclined to modernize and to modify the text according to personal preferences.

The characteristic verse form of the genre, established here in 'Peblis', is a complex one, with a very demanding rime scheme in the octave – A B A B A B A B – followed by a final 'bobwheel' device, with the last line or 'wheel' functioning as a refrain. The author maintains this rigid scheme through the first four stanzas, but thereafter introduces some rime variations in the tetrameter lines. In addition, the poet superimposes a pattern of heavy alliteration in the first couple of stanzas, though this effect becomes sporadic thereafter. The narrative structure is firm and satisfying: stanzas 1–8 describe the preparations and the antics of the country folk walking to the fair at Peebles; stanzas 9–14 give us the scene in the tavern, erupting into a general brawl; stanzas 15–19 depict the farcical episode of the 'cadger' getting into the fight; and stanzas 20–26 portray the aftermath of dancing and leave-taking at the end of a boisterous day. Despite the difficult, confining nature of the stanza form, the poet manages to achieve an admirable sense of spontaneity and freshness.

1

At Beltane,[n] quhen ilk bodie bownis	when every; gets ready
To Peblis[n] to the play,	festival, fair
To heir the singin and the soundis,	
The solace, suth to say;	truth
5 Be firth and forrest furth they found,	By wood; forth; went
Thay graythit[n] thame full gay;	dressed themselves
God wait that[n] wald thay do that stound,	knows; would; occasion
For[n] it was thair feist day,	
Thay said,	
10 Of Peblis to the play.	

2

All the wenchis of the west	
War up or the cok crew;	ere, before
For reiling thair micht na man rest,	dashing about
For garray and for glew.	uproar, commotion; sport
15 Ane[n] said, 'My curches ar nocht prest!'	kerchiefs
Than answerit Meg full blew,	dejectedly
'To get an hude I hald it best.'	hood; hold, think
'Be Goddis saull that is true!'	God's soul
Quod scho,	Said she
20 Of Peblis to the play.	

3

Scho tuik the tippet[n] be the end;	She took; cloth strip on hood
To lat it hing scho leit nocht	let; hang down; neglected not
Quod he, 'Thy bak sall beir ane bend.'[n]	shall bear; blow
'In faith,' quod scho 'We meit nocht!'[n]	meet (i.e., 'You won't catch me.')
25 Scho was so guckit and so gend	foolish; simple, foolish
That[n] day ane byt scho eit nocht.	bite; ate

Than[n] spak hir fallowis that hir kend,   *friends; knew*
   'Be still, my joy, and greit nocht,   *weep not*
     Now,
30   Of Peblis to the play!'

4

'Ever, allace!' than said scho,[n]
   'Am I nocht cleirlie tynt?   *clearly lost*
I dar nocht cum yon mercat to,[n]   *dare; market, fair*
   I am so evvil sone-brint.   *evilly sunburnt*
35 Amang[n] yon merchands my errandis do,
   Marie;[n] I sall anis mynt[n]   *once venture to, aim to*
Stand of far and keik thaim to,   *off; peek at them*
   As I at hame was wont,'   *home was accustomed*
     Quod scho,
40   Of Peblis to the play.

5

Hopcalye and Cardronow[n]   *(villages)*
   Gaderit out thik-fald;   *gathered; thick-fold*
With 'hey and how rohumbelow'[n]
   The young folkis[n] were full bald.   *bold*
45 The bagpipe[n] blew, and thai out-threw,   *thronged out*
   Out of the townis untald;   *farms unnumbered*
Lord, sic ane schout was thame amang
   Quhen thai were owr the wald,   *over the plain*
     Thair west,[n]
50   Of Peblis to the play!

6

Ane young man stert into that steid   *sprang in that place*
   Als cant as ony colt,   *lively*
Ane birken hat upon his heid,   *birch*
   With ane bow and ane bolt;   *arrow*
55 Said, 'Mirrie madinis, think not lang,   *maidens; don't be sad*
   The wedder is fair and smolt.'   *mild, fair*
He cleikit up ane hie ruf sang,   *began to sing; bold, loud*
   'Thair fure ane man to the holt,'   *went; wood*
     Quod he,
60   Of Peblis to the play.

7

Thay had nocht gane[n] half of the gait — gone; way
    Quhen the madinis come upon thame; — maidens
Ilk ane man gaif his consait — Every; gave his opinion
    How at thai wald dispone thame. — that; dispose, arrange
65 Ane said, 'The fairest fallis me; — falls to, belongs to
    Tak ye the laif and fone thame.' — rest; fondle
Ane uther said 'Wyss lat me be![n] — wise
    On, Tweddell syd,[n] and on thame — men of Tweedside
        Swyth! — swiftly
70   Of Peblis to the play.'

8

Than he to ga and scho to ga — got together
    And never ane bad, 'Abyd you.' — said, 'You wait behind'
Ane winklot fell, and her taill up, — young girl
    'Wow,' quod Malkin, 'hyd you! — cover yourself!
75 Quhat neidis you to maik it sua? — behave so
    Yon man will not owrryd you.' — mount, ride on top of you
'Ar ye owr gude,' quod scho, 'I say, — overly good, pure
    To lat thame gang besyd you, — go, walk
        Yonder,
80   Of Peblis to the play?'

9

Than thai come to the townis[n] end
    Withouttin more delay,
He befoir, and scho befoir, — in front
    To se quha wes maist gay.
85 All that luikit thame upon — looked
    Leuche fast at thair array;[n] — Laughed
Sum said that thai were merkat folk, — market
    Sum said the Quene of May
        Was cumit — Was come
90   Of Peblis to the play.

10

Than thai to the taverne hous
    With meikle oly prance;[n] — great jollity, display
Ane spak with wourdis wonder crouss, — words wonderfully elated
    'Adone with ane mischance! — Have done! Away with!

95 Braid up the burde,' he bydis tyt,   set; table; orders soon
      'We ar all in ane trance.
    Se that our napre be quhyt,   See; napery, linen; white
      For we will dyn and daunce   dine
        Thair out,   outside, in the open air
100   Of Peblis to the play.'[n]

11

    Ay as the gudwyf brocht in,   Always; hostess brought
      Ane scorit upon the wauch.   tallied; wall
    Ane bad 'Pay,' aneuther said 'Nay,   one (man) ordered
      Byd quhill we[n] rakin our lauch.'   Wait till; reckon; bill
105 The gudwyf said, 'Have ye na dreid;   'Don't worry'
      Ye sall pay at ye aucht.'   what you owe
    Ane young man start upon his feit,   jumped up; feet
      And he began to lauche,   laugh
        For heydin   scorn, derision
110   Off Peblis to the play.

12

    He gat ane trincheour in his hand   flat board (for food)
      And he began to compt;   count, reckon
    'Ilk man twa and ane happenie!   Each; two; halfpenny
      To pay thus we war wount.'   were wont, accustomed
115 Ane uther[n] stert upon his feit,   jumped up
      And said 'Thou art owr blunt   overly stupid, slow-witted
    To tak[n] sic office upoun hand!   such
      Be God thou service[n] ane dunt   By God; deserves a blow
        Of me,
120   Of Peblis to the play.'

13

    'Ane dunt,' quod he, 'Quhat devil is that?   the devil
      Be God, you dar not du'd!'   dare; do it
    He stert till ane broggit stauf,   leaped to; pointed staff
      Wincheand as he war woode.   Wincing; mad, insane
125 All that hous was in an reirde: uproar
      Ane cryit, 'The halie rude!   holy cross!
    Help us, Lord, upon this erde,   earth
      That thair be spilt na blude   blood
        Heir in,   Herein

130   Of Peblis to the play!'

14

Thay thrang out at the dure at anis,   *crowded; door; once*
    Withouttin ony reddin.   *separating (of brawlers)*
Gilbert in ane gutter glayde –   *gutter slid*
    He gat na better beddin.
135 Thair wes not ane of thame that day
    Wald do ane utheris biddin:
Thair by lay thre and threttie sum   *Thereby; three and thirty*
    Thrimland in ane midding   *struggling; rubbish pile*
        Off draff,   *brewer's waste*
140   Of Peblis to the play.

15

Ane cadgear on the mercat gait[n]   *peddlar; market street*
    Hard thame bargane begin;   *Heard; to fight*
He gaif ane schout, his wyff came out;
    Scantlie scho micht owr hy him.   *Scarcely; overtake him*
145 ....
    ....
He held, scho drew; for dust that day   *pulled*
    Micht na man se ane styme   *Might; see; glimpse*
        To red thame,   *separate*
150   Of Peblis to the play.

16

He stert to his greit gray meir,   *ran; mare*
    And of he tumblit the creilis.   *off; baskets*
'Alace!' quod scho, 'Hald one, gud man!'[n]   *'Hold on, husband!'*
    And on hir kneis scho knelis.
155 'Abyd,' quod scho; 'Wy, nay,' quod he;   *'Wait'*
    In till his stirrappis he lap;   *Into; stirrups; leaped*
The girding brak, and he flew of,   *girthing broke; off*
    And upstert bayth his heilis   *up shot both; heels*
        At anis,   *once*
160   Of Peblis to the play.

17

His wyf come out, and gaif ane schout,
    And be the fute scho gat him;   *by the foot*

All be dirtin drew him out;   dirtied, soiled
    Lord God, richt weil that sat him!   well; became him
165 He said, 'Quhare is yon culroun knaif?'   low-born scoundrel
    Quod scho, 'I reid ye lat him   advise
Gang hame his gaites.' 'Be God,' quod he,   Go home his ways
    'I sall anis have at him   once
        Yit,
170 Of Peblis to the play.'

18

'Ye fylit me, fy for schame!' quod scho;   soiled, defiled
    'Se as ye have drest me!   See; treated me
How fell[n] ye, schir?' 'As my girdin brak,   girthing (saddle strap)
    Quhat meikle devill may lest me,   great; hinder
175 I wait weill nocht[n] quhat it wes,   know not
    My awin gray meir that kest me,   own; cast, threw
Or gif I wes forfochtin faynt,   if; weary with fighting
    And syn lay doun to rest me   then
        Yonder,
180 Of Peblis to the play.'

19

Be that the bargan was all playit;   By the time that; battle
    The stringis stert out of thair nokkis;   notches (of arrows)
Sevinsum that the tulye maid   Sevensome; fight started
    Lay grufling[n] in the stokkis.   grovelling; stocks
185 John Nicksoun of the nether warde   lower district (of town)
    Had lever have giffin an ox[n]   rather; given
Or he had cum[n] in that cumpanie,   Ere (before)
    He swore be Goddis cockkis[n]   cocks
        And mannis bayth,   man's also
190 Of Peblis to the play.

20

With that Will Swane come sweitand out,   sweating
    Ane meikle millar man;   large
'Gif I sall dance have doun, lat se,   have done, stop; let's see
    Blaw up the bagpyp than!
195 The schamous dance[n] I mon begin,   pipe dance; must
    I trow it sall not pane.'   believe; cause pain
So hevelie he hochit about,   fidgeted, hotched

To se him, Lord, as thai ran   see; how they ran
          That tyd,   time
200   Of Peblis to the play!

21

Thay gadderit out of the toun,   gathered
And neirar him thai dreuche;   nearer; drew
Ane bade, 'Gif the daunsaris rowme!   Give; room
Will Swane makis wounder teuche.'   makes it very lively
205   Than all the wenschis 'Te he!' thai playit.   Then; girls
Bot, Lord, as Will Young leuche!   laughed
'Gude gossep, come hyn your^n gaitis,   woman; hence your ways
For we have daunsit aneuche   enough
          At anis   once, one time
210   At Peblis at the play.'

22

Sa ferslie fyr heit wes the day   So fiercely fire hot
His face began to frekill.   freckle
Than Tisbe tuik him by the hand,   Tibbie took
Wes new cuming fra the heckill.   flax comb
215   'Allace!' quod scho, 'Quhat sall I do?
And our doure hes na stekill!'   door; latch
And scho to ga as hir taill brynt,^{n} went with (him); burned
And all the cairlis to kekill   men; cackle
          At hir,
220   Of Peblis to the play.

24

The^n pyper said, 'Now I begin
To tyre for playing too,^{n}
Bot yit I have gottin na thing
For all my pyping to you.
225   Thre happennis for half ane day,   Three halfpennies
And that will nocht undo you;
And gif ye will gif me richt nocht   nothing at all
The meikill devill gang with you!'   great; go
          Quod he,
230   Of Peblis to the play.

24

Be that[n] the daunsing wes all done,   By the time that
   Thair leif tuik les and mair;   leave; lesser; greater
Quhen the winklottis and the
                wawarris twynnit   wenches; wooers parted
   To se it wes hart sair.   see; heart-breaking
235 Wat[n] Atkin said to fair Ales,
   'My bird, now will I fayr.'   sweetheart; go, leave
The devill a wourde that scho micht speik,
   Bot swownit that sweit of swair[n]   swooned; sweet necked one
      For kyndnes,
240   Of Peblis to the play.

25

He fippillit lyk ane faderles fole;   fidgeted; fatherless foal
   'And be still, my sweit thing!'
'Be the halyrud of Peblis   By; holy cross
   I may nocht rest for greting.'   weeping
245 He quhissillit and he pypit bayth   whistled; piped both
   To mak hir blyth that meiting: meeting
'My hony hart, how sayis the sang,
   "Thair sall be mirth at our meting,"   shall be
      Yit,
250   Of Peblis to the play.'

26

Be that the sone was settand schaftis,[n]   sun; setting rays, beams
   And neir done wes the day.
Thair men micht heir schukin of chaftis[n]   shaking of jaws (tongue
   Quhen that thai went thair way.   [wagging?]
255 Had thair bein mair made of this sang   more
   Mair suld I to you say.   should, would
At Beltane ilka bodie bownd   every; got ready
   To Peblis to the play.

2. Anon., *Christis Kirk on the Grene, c.* 1490–1510

This poem, though certainly much later than 'Peblis', became enormously popular in Scotland and so has given its name to the entire genre. George Bannatyne, in his great manuscript anthology of 1568, credited this piece to King James I of Scotland (1394–1437); but some later editors, beginning with Bishop Edmund Gibson in 1691, have given it to James V (1512–1542). Neither of these attributions to royal authors seems probable. The linguistic evidence (see Notes for details) strongly suggests a date of composition after 1450 and perhaps as late as the first decade of the sixteenth century, though, as with 'Peblis', this kind of evidence is far from conclusive in a poem that circulated widely in manuscript. Nevertheless, the language seems to rule out James I. On the other hand, the mature years of James V (the 1530s) seem too late for this poem. Bannatyne, after all, in naming James I as the author, clearly believed the work to be about 140 years old in 1568; it is hard to believe that he could have been so far out as to grossly misdate a relatively recent poem in this way. It seems best, therefore, to consider the poem as an anonymous work of about 1500.

In its verse form, 'Christis Kirk' follows the difficult rime scheme established in 'Peblis', but superimposes a consistent pattern of heavy alliteration as well. The result is a *tour de force* of technical virtuosity even more remarkable than 'Peblis', while creating the same kind of illusion of naturalness. Though it lacks the unifying narrative line of the earlier piece, 'Christis Kirk' compensates with a greater degree of sheer energy in its successive vignettes, achieving tremendous momentum and a cumulative vividness.

1

Was nevir in Scotland hard nor sene	heard; seen
Sic dansing nor deray,	Such; disorder
Nowthir at Falkland on the grene[n]	Neither
Nor Peblis at the play,[n]	
5 As wes of wowaris, as I wene,	wooers; think
At Christ Kirk[n] on ane day.	
Thair come our kitteis[n] weschin clene	young girls washed clean
In thair new kirtillis of gray,	gowns

Full gay,[n]
10　At Christis Kirk of the grene.[n]

2

To dans thir damysellis thame dicht,　　　those damsels; prepared
　Thir lassis licht of laitis,　　　Those; lively of manners
Thair gluvis wes of the raffell rycht,　　　gloves; skin of roe deer
　Thair schone wes of the straitis;　　　shoes; coarse woollen cloth
15　Thair kirtillis wer of lynkome licht,[n]　　　linen light
　Weill prest with mony plaitis.　　　pleats
Thay wcr so nyss quhen men thame nicht　　　giddy when; nighed, camc near
　Thay squeilit lyk ony gaitis,　　　squealed like; goats
　　So loud,
20　At Christis Kirk of the grene that day.[n]

3

Of all thir madynis myld as meid[n]　　　mead
　Wes nane so gympt as Gillie;　　　trim, slender
As ony ross hir rude wes reid,　　　rose; cheek; red
　Hir lyre wes lyk the lillie;　　　skin, complexion
25　Fow yellow yellow wes hir heid,　　　Full
　Bot scho of lufe wes sillie;　　　smitten, made foolish
Thocht all hir kin had sworn hir deid　　　Though
　Scho wald haif bot sweit Willie　　　would have only
　　Allone,
30　At Christis Kirk of the grene.

4

Scho skornit Jok and skraipit at him,　　　scoffed
　And murionit[n] him with mokkis;　　　made faces at
He wald haif luvit, scho wald nocht lat him,　　　loved, made love
　For all his yallow loikkis:　　　locks
35　He chereist hir, scho bad ga chat him;　　　cherished; go hang himself
　Scho compt him nocht twa clokkis;　　　counted; beetles
So schamefully his schort gown set him,　　　became him, fitted him
　His lymmis wes lyk twa rokkis,　　　legs; distaffs
　　Scho said,
40　At Christis Kirk of the grene.

5

Thome Lular wes thair menstrall meit;[n]　　　well qualified

O Lord! as he coud lanss;	leap, spring
He playit so schill, and sang so sweit	shrill
Quhill Towsy tuke a transs.	Until; went into a trance
45 Auld lychtfute[n] thair he did forleit,	'light-foot' dances; forsake
And counterfutit Franss;	imitated France (in dance style)
He use him self as man discreit	behaved
And up tuke moreiss danss,[n]	morris dance
Full loud,[n]	
50 At Christis Kirk of the grene.	

6

Than Stevin come stoppand in with stendis;	stepping; strides
No rynk mycht him arreist.	man; stop
Platfute he bobbit up with bendis;	'Flat-foot' (name of dance); leap
For Mald he maid requeist.	
55 He lap quhill he lay on his lendis;	leaped until; buttocks
Bot rysand he wes preist	rising; ready for action
Quhill that he oistit at bath the endis	Until; coughed; both
For honour of the feist,	
That day,	
60 At Christis Kirk of the grene.	

7

Syne Robene Roy begowth to revell,	Then; began
And Dowie[n] till him druggit;	to; dragged
'Lat be,' quod Jok; and cawd him javell[n]	called him ruffian
And be the taill him tuggit.	
65 The kensy[n] cleikit to the cavell,	scoundrel grasped; low fellow
Bot Lord! than gif thay luggit,	if; grabbed ears
Thai partit thair play thane with a nevell,[n]	separated; then; blow
God wait gif hair wes ruggit	knows if; pulled
Betwix thame,	
70 At Christis Kirk of the grene.	

8

Ane bent a bow, sic sturt coud steir him;[n]	such wrath did move him
Grit skayth wesd to haif skard him;	harm it was; scared
He chesit a flane as did affeir him,	chose; arrow; did suit
The toder said 'Dirdum Dardum'.[n]	other; 'Big Noise' (contemptuou
75 Throw[n] baith the cheikis he thocht to cheir him,	Through; cheeks; pierce
Or throw the erss haif chard him;	arse; pierced

Bot be ane akerbraid it come nocht neir him,   by an acre's breadth
   I can nocht tell quhat mard him,[n]   marred
     Thair
80 At Christis Kirk of the grene.

9

With that a freynd of his cryd 'Fy!'
   And up ane arrow drew;
He forgit it so fowriously   bent
   The bow in flenders flew.   splinters
85 Sa wes the will of God, trow I,
   For had the tre bene trew,   tree, wood (of bow); sound
Men said that kend his archery   knew
   That he had slane anew,   enough
     That day,
90 At Christis Kirk on the grene.

10

Ane hasty hensure[n] callit Hary,   idle young fellow?
   Quha wes ane archer heynd,   Who; dexterous
Titt up a taikle withowttin tary,   Snatched; tackle; delay
   That torment so him teynd.   enraged
95 I wait nocht quhidder his hand coud vary,   know; whether; did waver
   Or the man wes his freynd,
For he eschaipit throu michtis of Mary   escaped through powers of Mary
   As man that no ill meynd,   As a man; intended
     Bot gud,
100 At Christis Kirk of the grene.

11

Than Lowry as ane lyon lap,
   And sone a flane coud fedder;   soon; arrow did feather
He hecht to perss him at the pap,   promised; pierce; breast
   Thair on to wed a weddir.[n]   wager; wether (castrated ram)
105 He hit him on the wame a wap,   belly; knock
   It buft lyk ony bledder;   made puffing sound; bladder
Bot swa his fortoun wes and hap   so; luck
   His doublet wes maid of ledder,   jacket; leather
     And saift him,   saved
110 At Christis Kirk of the grene.

12

[The baff so boustuousle abasit him[n]   blow; strongly downed him
    To the erd he duschit down;   earth; fell heavily
The tother for dreid he preissit him   fear; exerted himself
    And fled out of the town.
115 The wyffis come furth and up thay paisit him wives; lifted
    And fand lyff in the loun;   found life; fellow
And with thre routis thay raisit him,   shouts; roused
    And coverit him of swoune.   revived; swoon
            Agane,
120   At Christis Kirk of the grene.]

13

A yaip yung man that stude him neist   eager; next
    Lowsd of a schot with yre;   loosed off; ire
He ettlit the bern in at the breist;   aimed at; man
    The bolt flew owr the byre.   over the cowshed
125 Ane cryit 'Fy! he had slane a preist
    A myll beyond ane myre';   mile; bog
Than bow and bag fra him he keist   Then; quiver; cast
    And fled as ferss as fyre   fiercely, swiftly
            Of flynt,
130   At Christis Kirk of the grene.

14

With forkis and flailis thay lait grit flappis,   struck great blows
    And flang togiddir lyk friggis;   flung themselves; stout lads
With bowgaris of barnis thay beft blew kappis   rafters; beat blue caps
    Quhill thay of bernis maid briggis.   Until; men made bridges
135 The reird raiss rudly with the rappis,   uproar rose; blows
    Quhen rungis wes layd on riggis;   cudgels; backs
The[n] wyffis come furth with cryis and clappis,
    'Lo quhair my lyking liggis!'   where; love lies
            Quod thay
140   At Christ Kirk of the grene.

15

Thay girnit and lait gird with granis,   looked angry; struck blows; groa
    Ilk gossep uder grevit;   Each; vexed the other
Sum straik with stingis, sum gadderit stanis,   struck; poles; stones
    Sum fled and evill eschewit;[n]   avoided

145 The menstrall wan within twa wanis, *dwellings*
    That day full weill he previt, *proved*
For he come hame with unbirsed banis, *unbruised bones*
    Quhair fechtaris wer mischevit *fighters; injured*
        For evir,
150   At Christis Kirk of the grene.

16

Heich Hucheoun, with a hissill ryss, *Tall; hazel branch*
    To red can throu thame rummill; *separate; through; rush*
He mudlet thame down[n] lyk ony myss, *knocked; mice*
He wes no baty bummill.[n] *bungling oaf*
155 Thocht he wes wicht he wes nocht wyss *Though; strong; wise*
    With sic jangleris to jummill, *wranglers; meddle*
For fra his[n] thowme thay dang a sklyss, *thumb; struck; slice*
    Quhill he cryd 'Barla fummyll![n] *Until; 'A truce!'*
        I am slane,
160   At Christis Kirk of the grene.

17

Quhen that he saw his blude so reid,
    To fle micht no man lat him; *flee; prevent*
He wend it bene for auld done feid, *thought; feud*
    The far sarar it set him. *more sorely; afflicted*
165 He gart his feit defend his heid, *made, caused*
    He thocht ane cryd, 'Haif at him!' *Have*
Quhill he wes past out of all pleid *Till; strife*
    He suld bene swift that gat him *would have been*
        Throu speid, *Through*
170   At Christis Kirk of the grene.

18

The toun sowtar in greif wes bowdin,[n] *shoemaker; anger; swollen*
    His wyfe hang in his waist; *hung at*
His body wes with blud all browdin, *stained*
    He granit lyk ony gaist. *groaned; ghost*
175 Hir glitternad hair that wes full goldin *glittering*
    So hard in lufe him lest *tied, laced*
That for hir saik he wes nocht yoldin, *yielded*
    Sevin myll quhill he wes chest, *miles while; chased*
        And mair, *more*

180   At Christis Kirk of the grene.

19

The millar wes of manly mak;
  To meit him wes na mowis;   joke
Thair durst nocht ten cum him to tak,
  So nowit he thair nowis.   knocked; heads
185 The buschment haill about him brak   ambush whole; broke
  And bikkerit him with bowis,   assailed; bows
Syne tratourly behind his bak   Then treacherously
  Thay hewit him on the howiss   hacked; hocks
        Behind,
190 At Christis Kirk of the grene.

20

Twa that wes heidmen of the heird   headmen; herd
  Ran upoun utheris lyk rammis;   rams
Than followit feymen rycht on affeird,[n]   doomed men quite unafraid
  Bet on with barrow trammis.   Beat; shafts
195 Bot quhair thair gobbis wes ungeird   mouths; unprotected
  Thay gat upoun the gammis,   got blows; mouths (gums)
Quhill bludy berkit wes thair beird   Until; clotted (barked); beard
  As thay had wirreit lammis,   worried (mangled) lambs
        Maist lyk,   Most likely
200 At Christ Kirk of the grene that day.

21

The wyvis kest up ane hiddouss yell   cast; hideous
  Quhen all thir yunkeris yokkit;   those young men set to (yoked)
Als ferss as ony fyrflaught fell   fiercely; flash of lightning
  Freikis to the feild thay flokkit;   stout fellows
205 Tha cairlis with clubbis coud uder quell, men; did each other
  Quhill blud at breistis out bokkit;   Till; spurted
So rudly range the Commoun bell,
  Quhill all the stepill rokkit
        For reird,   noise, din
210 At Christis Kirk of the grene.

22

Quhen thay had berit lyk baitit bulis,   roared; bated bulls
  And branewod[n] brynt in bailis,   madmen(?) burned in bonfires

Thay wer als meik as ony mulis   meek; mules
    That mangit wer with mailis.   worn out; burdens
215 For fantness tha forfochin fulis   faintness those exhausted fools
    Fell down lyk flawchtir failis,   turfs cut with spades
And freschmen come in and held thair dulis,[n]   held their ground(?)
    And dang thame down in dailis   knocked; heaps
        Be dene,   At once, soon
220   At Christ Kirk of the grene.

23

Quhen all wes done, Dik with ane aix   ax
    Come furth to fell a fidder.   wagon load
Quod he, 'Quhair ar yone hangit smaix   mean wretches
    Rycht now wald slane my bruder?'   would have killed
225 His wyfe bade him, 'Ga hame, gud glaikis!'[n]   you silly fool
    And sa did Meg his muder.
He turnd and gaif thame bayth thair paikis,   pokes, blows
    For he durst ding nane udir,   strike none other
        For feir,
230   At Christ Kirk of the grene that day.

3. William Dunbar, *The Justis Betwix the Talyeour and the Soutar* (also called *The Turnament*), c. 1500.

William Dunbar (*c.* 1460 – *c.* 1520) is generally ranked together with Robert Henryson and Gawain Douglas as one of the three greatest of the Middle Scots poets. Apart from its unusually wide range and variety in subject matter, Dunbar's work is noted for dazzling stylistic virtuosity, and extravagant imagination. This mock-tournament poem well illustrates the latter two qualities. It is part of a three-poem series comprising 'The Dance of the sevin deidly Synnis' (beginning 'Off Februar the fyiftene nycht'), 'The Justis', and 'The Amendis to the Telyouris and Soutaris for the Turnament Maid on Thame' (beginning 'Betwix twell houris and ellevin'). These pieces were probably composed at separate times in Dunbar's career, but are clearly linked by transitional passages.

Though not strictly a *Christis Kirk* poem, Dunbar's scatological mock tournament is closely akin to the genre: not only is it a satiric view of town tradesmen by an outside observer, it also shows some influence from the stanzas making fun of peasant cowardice and bungling in 'Christis Kirk on the Grene' itself. The rollicking verse form of six-line stanzas, combining tetrameter and trimeter lines with a demanding rime scheme, is quite similar in effect to the *Christis Kirk* formula. The sheer energy, the grossness, the swift movement, and the outrageous farce in this poem – so typical of Dunbar's extravagant genius – all relate closely to our genre.

1

Nixt at a tornament was tryit	After that; tournament; tried,
That lang befor in hell was cryit	proclaimed [contested
In presens of Mahoune;[n]	Mahomet (the devil)
Betwix a talyeour & a soutare,	tailor; cobbler
5 A priklouss and a coble cloutare;[n]	prick-louse (tailor); shoe mender
Thar barrass was maid boune.	Their lists (enclosure); ready

2

The talyeour baith with speire & scheld	
Convoyit was unto the feld	Convoyed; field
With mony a lymmere loune	thieving rogue
10 Of seme bytaris & best gnapparis,[n]	seam-biters; animal hide snappers

18

Of stomok stelaris & cat knapparis——[n]   cloth fragment stealers;
A graceless garisoun.   company, troop [cat killers

3

His banere borne was him before
Quharin war cloutis a hundreth score,   Wherein; patches
15 Ilkane of diverss hew,   Each one; hue (colour)
And all stollyn out of syndry webbis;   various cloths
For quhill the se flude fillis & ebbis[n]   while; sea tide rises; ebbs
Talyeouris will never be trewe.   honest

4

The buthman[n] on the barrass blent;   shopkeeper (booth-man); glanced
20 Allace, he tynt all hardyment,   Alas; lost; courage
For feir he changit hew;   colour
Mahoune come furth[n] & maid him knycht——   dubbed him a knight
No ferly thocht his hart was licht   No wonder though; light
That to sic honour grew.   such

5

25 He hecht hiely befor Mahoune   promised highly
That he suld dyng the soutar doun   should strike
Thocht he war wicht as mast;[n]   Though; strong; ship's mast
Bot quhen he on the barrass blenkit   glanced, looked
The talyeouris corage a litill schrenkit,   shrank
30 His hart did all owr cast.   was overcome

6

And quhen he saw the soutar cum,
Off all sic wordis he was dum,   such; dumb
Full sair he was agast.   sorely; aghast
For he in hart tuke sic a scunner   such a shrinking back from fear
35 A rak of fartis lyk ony thunnere   storm, rush of wind; thunder
Went fra him, blast for blast.

7

The soutar to the feld him drest;   made ready
He was convoyit out of the west
As a defendour stout.
40 Suposs he had no lusty verlot,   varlet, attendant on a knight
He had full mony lousy harlot   rascal, knave

Fast rynnand him about.   running

8

His baner was a barkit hyd   banner; tanned hide
Quharin Sanct Girnyga[n] did glyde   Wherein St Girnega (a devil); glide
45 Befor that rebald rout;   licentious crowd
Full soutarlyk he was of laitis   demeanour, manners
For ay betwene the harnas platis   always; armour plates
The oyly bristit out.   oil bursted

9

Apon the talyeour quhen he did luke
50 His hart a litill dwalmyng tuke,   fainting fit
Uneiss he mycht upsit;[n]   Not easily; sit up
In till his stomok was sic a steire,   commotion, upset
Of all his dynere that cost him deire   dinner; dearly
His brest held never a bit.

10

55 To comfort him or he raide forther   before he rode
The devill of knychthed gaf him order;   knighthood gave
For stynk than he did spit;   Because of the stench
And he about the devillis nek
Did spewe agane a quart of blek—   black (bile)
60 So knychtlie he him quyt.   in a knightly way; paid back

11

Than forty tymis the fend cryit, 'Fy!'   fiend, devil
The soutar furth affraitlye   forth in panic
Unto the feld he soucht.   went
Quhen thai war servit with thair speris,   served, handed; spears
65 Folk had a feile be thar efferiss   sense, feeling; by their manners
Thar hartis was baith on flocht.   in a flutter

12

Thai spurrit apon athir syd,   spurred; both sides
The horss attour the grene did glyd,   horses across; glide
And tham togidder brocht.   together brought
70 The talyeour was no thing wele sittin,   not well seated
He left the sadill all beschittin,   saddle soiled with excrement
And to the ground he socht.   went

13

His birnes brak[n] and maid a bratill, breastplate broke; clatter
The soutaris horss scarrit[n] with the rattill was scared; rattle
75 And round about did reile; run wildly
This beist, that was affrayit full evill, terrified to an extreme degree
Ran with the soutar to the devill
And thar revardit him wele. there he punished him

14

Sumthing fra him the fende eschewit— Some distance; drew back
80 He trowit agane to be bespewit believed (feared); vomited upon
So stern he was in stele.[n] in steel (armour)
He thocht he wald agane debait him; would defend himself against it
He torned his erss and all bedrait him, arse; fouled with excrement
Quyte owr fra nek to hele. Quite over; heel

15

85 He lowsit it with sic a rerd let it go; roar
Baith horss and man flawe to the erd, flew; earth, ground
He fart with sic a feire. blast, force
'Now haf I quyt ye,' quod Mahoun. paid you back
The new maid knycht lay in to swoun in a swoon
90 And did all armes forswere. weapons renounce (swear off)

16

The devill gart thaim to dungeoun dryf had them driven to
And tham of knychthed to depryf, knighthood; deprived
Discharging tham all weire; Dismissing them from all battle
And maid tham harlotis agane for ever, churls, low fellows; forever
95 Quhilk style to kepe thai had fer levire Which; far rather
Na ony armes beire. Nor; bear

17

I had mair of thar werkis writtin more; their doings
Had nocht the soutar bene beschittin not
With Belialis[n] arss unblist; Belial's arse unblest
100 Bot that sa gud a bourd me thocht, joke, merry tale it seemed to me
Sic solace to my hart thar socht,[n] Such; there went
For lauchter neir I brist. laughter; burst

18

Quharthrow I walkinnit of my trauns.	As a result of which; wakened
To put in to rememberans	remembrance
105 Micht no man me resist	Might; prevent
To dyte how all this thing befell	put in writing
Befor Mahoune the heir[n] of hell:	lord
Schirris, trow it gif ye list.[n]	Gentlemen; if you please

Heir endis the soutar and tailyouris war maid be the nobill poyet Maister
William Dunbar.[n]

4. Anon., *Sym and his Bruder,* c. 1530

This fascinating and enigmatic poem has survived in only one very corrupt text in the Bannatyne Manuscript of 1568. Between stanzas 8 and 9 there seems to be at least one stanza missing, and the rest of the text is littered with scribal errors, indicating that Bannatyne was transcribing this piece from a very bad copy. The language suggests a date of about 1530. The author must have had an intimate knowledge of the town and environs of St Andrews, and he may well have been Sir David Lindsay of the Mount (see Notes for analysis of the evidence). At any rate, this poem is a hilarious satire on the antics of a pair of charlatans who pretend to be religious pilgrims begging for support to enable them to travel to sacred shrines in Europe and the Holy Land. Sym's brother marries a rich widow, and there is a wild wedding party in St Andrews.

A very interesting feature of this piece is that it combines for the first time the *Christis Kirk* tradition with the genre of the mock tournament. The later part of the poem depicts a farcical 'justing' scene with the usual bungling ineptness. In all other respects 'Sym' is in the pure vein of 'Christis Kirk' and confirms strictly to the traditional stanza form – a two-rime octave followed by a 'bobwheel', with a heavy pattern of alliteration.

1

Thair is no story that I of heir,[n]	
Of Johine nor Robene Hude,[n]	[Little] John; Robin Hood
Nor yit of Wallace wicht but weir,[n]	Wallace strong without doubt
That me thinkis half so gude,	good
5 As of thir palmaris[n] twa but peir,	those pilgrims; without peer
To heir how thay conclude;	end up
In to begging, I trow, fyve yeir	believe
In Sanct Andris[n] thay stude	Saint Andrews; stood
Togidder,	together
10 Bayth Sym and his bruder.	Both; brother

2

Thocht thay war wicht, I warrand you,	Though; strong; warrant
Thay had no will to wirk;	work
Thay maid thame burdounis nocht to bow,	stout staffs unbending
Twa bewis of the birk,	boughs; birch

23

15 Weill stobbit with steill, I trow,   *pointed with steel*
    To stik in to the mirk;   *in the darkness, secretly*
  Bot sen thair bairdis grew on thair mou,[n]   *since; beards; mouth*
    Thay saw nevir the kirk   *church*
      Within,   *Inside*
20 Nowthir Sym nor his bruder.   *Neither*

3

  Syne schupe thame up to lowp owr leiss,[n]   *Then prepared; dash over*
    Twa tabartis of the tartane;   *Two overcoats; tartan [meadows*
  Thay comptit nocht quhat thair cloutis weis,   *cared; rags weigh*
    Wes sewit thairon incertane.   *sewn thereon insecurely*
25 Syne clampit up Sanct Peteris keiss,[n]   *Then patched together; keys*
    Bot of ane auld reid gartane;   *Just; red garter*
  Sanct James schellis[n] on the tothir syd slevis,   *shells; other long sleeves*
    As pretty as ony pertane[n]   *crab ('partan')*
      Ta,   *Toe (claw)*
30 On Sym and his bruder.

4

  Thus quhen thai had reddit thair ragis,   *when; readied; rags*
    To rome[n] they war inspyrit;   *roam, wander*
  Tuk up thair jaipis and all thair jaggis,   *trinkets; rags, tatters*
    Fure furth as thay war fyrit[n]   *Went forth; fired, inspired*
35 And ay the eldest bure the baggis,   *always; bore, carried*
    Quhenn that the yungest tyrit;   *grew tired*
  Tuk counsall at Kinkellis craggis,[n]   *Took counsel; cliffs*
    Come hame as thay war hyrit[n]   *home; as if paid to do so*
      Agane,
40 Bath Sym and his bruther.

5

  Than held thay houss, as men me tellis,   *they held open house*
    And spendit of thair feis;   *spent their winnings*
  Quhen meit wes went, thay flew owr fellis[n]   *food was gone; over hills*
    Als bissy as ony beis;   *As; bees*
45 Syne clengit Sanct Jameis schellis,   *Then [they] cleaned up*
    And pecis of palme treis,[n]   *pieces; trees*
  To se quha best the pardone spellis.[n]   *see who; reads*
    'I schrew thame that ay leiss   *curse; at all times lives*
      But lauchter,'   *Without laughter*

50 Quod Syme to his bruder.

6

Quhen thay wer welthfull in thair wynning,
Thay puft thame up in pryde;
Bot quhair that Symy levit in synnyng,   where; lived in sin
His bruder wald haif ane bryd;   would have; bride
55 Hir wedoheid fra the begynning   widowhood from
Wes neir ane moneth tyd;   month's time
Gif scho wes spedy ay in spynning,   If; always
Tak witness of thame besyde,   them nearby, who were there
Ilk ane,   Each one
60 Baith Sym and his bruder.

7

The carlis thay thikkit fast in cludis,   men; gathered; clouds, swarms
Agane the man wes mareit,   In preparation for the time; wed
With breid and beif, and uthir budis,   other gifts
Syne[n] to the kirk thay kareit;   Then; went
65 Bot or thay twynd him and his dudis,[n]   before; separated; rags
The tyme of none wes tareit: noon meal; tarried, delayed
'Wa worth this wedding, for be thir widis,   Curse; and also these fine clothes
The meit is all miskareit   feast; miscarried, ruined
To day!'
70 Quod Sym to his bruder.[n]

8

Owr all the houss, be lyne and levall,[n]   Over; with methodical accuracy
The ladis come to luk him;[n]   lads; inspect him (sexually)
To tak a justing of that javell,[n]   copulation with that low fellow
The bryd wount nocht to bruk him;   was unaccustomed to enjoy him
75 Thay maneist him with mony nevell,   menaced; blow
Than Symme raiss and schuk him,   rose; shook himself
'I cleme to clergy,'[n] quod the cavell,   claim benefit of clergy; fellow
'How dar thou cum to luk him   inspect
Yondir!'
80 Quod Sym and his bruder.

9

With that the carle begowth to crak,[n]   man (Sym) began to boast
Glowrit up and gaf a glufe;[n]   glowered; gave a startled glance

His beird it wes als lang and blak   beard; as
  That it hang owr his mouf;[n]   over his muffler, scarf
85 He wes als lang upoun the bak,   as long
  As evir wes Angus Dufe;[n]   Black Angus(?)
He sayis, 'This justing I undirtak,
  My coit is of gud stuffe,   coat (of armour)
    Call to,'[n]   'Drive on!'
90 Quod Sym and his bruder.

10

He hoppit sa mycht na man hald him,   jumped; hold
  Said 'Blame me bot I bind him;   unless I tie him up
I sall owrtak him, and that I tald him,   shall overtake, catch
  In yone feild gife I fynd him.'   if
95 On his gray meir fast furth thay cald him,   forth; drove
  The flokis flew furth behind him;   crowds; forth
Thay daschit him doun, the dirt ourhaild him,   flung; covered, overpowered
  Than start thay to and bind him[n]   they leaped in
    Tycht,   Tight
100 Baith Sym and his bruder.

11

Than brak he lowss, the horss that bair him   broke; loose; bore
  Ran startling to Stratyrum,[n]   wildly; Strathtyrum
And he gat up, and Symme swair him,   swore to himself   [... bemir
  'Ye meit nocht[n] bot ye myr him!'   'You won't catch him unless
105 Off that fowll courss for to declair him   charge; proclaim his intent
  The cairlis come to requyr him,   men
Than all the laddis tryd with a lairrum   Then; lads; alarm bell
  To flud him and to flyr him[n]   scare; mock
    Bayth,
110 Bayth Symme and his bruder.[n]

12

This was no bourdene to Brown Hill,[n]   joke, sport
  That gatt betwene the browis,[n]   got [a blow]; eyebrows
And had no thing ado thairtill,   had nothing to do with it
  As mony uder trowis;   others believe
115 Bot come furth on his awin gud will,   came forth; own
  To Squyar Johine of Mowis;[n]

He gatt ane sit up in the schill,[n]   seat; hut for shepherds
    And that the laddis allowis   lads
      Ilk ane,   Each one
120   To Sym and his bruder.

13

Yob Symmer was the stirrepman,[n]   stirrupman, second
    Was nolthird of the toun;   cattle herd
He said 'I will just as I can,   'joust as well as I can'
    Sen he is strickin doun.'   Since
125 He gatt twa plaitis of ane auld pan,   flat sheets; old
    Ane breistplait maid him boun;   breastplate; ready
The first rynk raif his mouth a span,[n]   attack tore; handsbreadth
    And thair he fell in swoune   swoon
      Almaist,   Almost
130   By Sym and his bruder.[n]

14

Doun fra the luggis quhen he wes laist,[n]   ears; laced up, bandaged
    He maid a peteouss panting,   pitiful, piteous
He swownit and he swelt almaist,   swooned; died
    For gaping and for ganting;   yawning
135 'Abyd,' quod the leich, 'I se a waist;[n]   Wait; doctor; a gap, void
    His wrangtwch is in wanting';   crooked tooth; missing
'God saif him, and the Haly Gaist,[n]   save
    And keip the man fra manting   from stuttering
      Mekle,'   Much
140   Quod Sym[n] and his bruder.

15

His mouth wes schent, and sa forschorne,   ruined; so torn
    Held nowdir wind nor watter;   neither
Fair weill all blast of blawing horne,   Farewell
    Hc mycht nocht do bot blatter;   except blabber
145 He endis the story with harme forlorne,   serious injury
    The nolt begowth till skatter,[n]   cattle began to
The ky ran startling to the corne,   cows; wildly; wheat field
    'Wa worth the tyme thou gat hir   Cursed be; got her
      Now!'
150   Quod Symme till his bruder.   to

5. Sir David Lindsay, *The Justing Betwix James Watsoun and Jhone Barbour, c.* 1539

Sir David Lindsay of the Mount (*c.* 1486 – *c.* 1555) was a distinguished functionary of the Scottish court during the reign of James V (1513–1542) and later, serving in various capacities – as tutor to the young king, as diplomat, finally in the prestigious heraldic post of Lord Lyon King of Anns, and, most important, as the official court poet. In his poetic function Lindsay produced an impressive corpus of works, including everything from witty entertainments to political, social, and religious satires, culminating in *The Monarchie* (a long political allegory for the instruction of the king), and his masterpiece *Ane pleasant Satyre of the Thrie Estaitis*, a massive morality play.

In the *Thrie Estaitis* and in some of his other writings Lindsay attacked the deep corruption of the church in Scotland, and later was hailed as a kind of morning star of the Scottish Reforrnation. Because he was on the side of the future in Scotland Lindsay became revered as a poetic national hero until superseded by Burns two and a half centuries later.

Lindsay's 'Justing' belongs in the category of pure entertainment, and was probably based on an actual comic tournament put on for the amusement of King James V and his queen, Marie de Lorraine, at St Andrews in May of 1539. In one passage at least this lively mock-tournament poem contains echoes of 'Sym and his Bruder',which may also have been the work of Lindsay. Though written in pentameter couplets, Lindsay's 'Justing' is clearly akin to the *Christis Kirk* genre; it shows the direct influence of 'Christis Kirk on the Grene' itself, as well as of 'Peblis', 'Sym' and Dunbar's 'Justis'. The satire in Lindsay's mock tournament, however, is gentler and more good-natured than in any of these earlier poems.

In Sanctandrois on Witsoun Monnunday,[n]	St. Andrews; Whitsunday
Twa campionis thare manheid did assay,	champions their courage
Past to the barres,[n] enarmit heid and handis.	enclosure for jousting; armed
Wes never sene sic justing in no landis,	jousting
5 In presence of the kingis grace and quene,	
Quhare mony lustie lady mycht be sene.	Where

28

Mony ane knicht, barroun, and banrent,[n] — *baron; knight with vassals*
Come for to se that awfull tomament.
The ane of thame was gentill James Watsoun,[n]
10 And Johne Barbour the uther campioun:
Unto the king thay war familiaris, — *personal servants*
And of his chalmer boith cubicularis. — *bed-chamber; attendants*
James was ane man of greit intelligence,
Ane medicinar, ful of experience; — *layman skilled in medicine*
15 And Johne Barbour, he was ane nobill leche, — *physician*
Crukit carlingis he wald gar thame get speche. — *Deformed men; make them*
Frome tyme they enterit war in to the feild. — *were*
Full womanlie thay weildit speir and scheild,
And wichtlie waiffit in the wynd thare heillis, — *stoutly waved; heels*
20 Hobland lyke cadgeris rydand on thare creillis:[n] — *Moving clumsily; peddlers riding*
Bot ather ran at uther with sic haist, — *each; haste*
That thay could never thair speir get in the reist. — *spear; rest, resting place*
Quhen gentil James trowit best with Johne — *believed it*
  to meit,
His speir did fald amang his horssis feit. — *bend*
25 I am rycht sure gude James had bene undone,
War not that Johne his mark tuke be the mone. — *Were it not; aim; moon*
(Quod Johne) 'Howbeit thou thinkis my — *Although; distaffs, thin sticks*
  leggis lyke rokkis,[n]
My speir is gude: now keip the fra my knokkis.' — *keep thee from*
'Tary' (quod James) 'ane quhyle, for, be my thrift, — *while; by my prosperity*
30 The feind ane thing I can se bot the lift.' — *devil a thing (nothing); see; sky*
'Nor more can I' (quode Johne), 'Be goddes — *By God's bread*
  breid:[n] — *(communion bread)*
I se no thing except the steipill heid. — *steeple top*
Yit thocht thy braunis be lyk twa — *Yet though; limbs;*
  barrow trammis,[n] — *barrow shafts*
Defend the, man.' Than ran thay to, lyk rammis. — *thee; rams*
35 At that rude rink, James had bene strykin doun,[n] — *fierce onset; stricken*
Wer not that Johne for feirsnes fell in swoun; — *fierceness; swoon*
And rychtso James to Johne had done greit deir, — *just so; injury*
Wer not amangis his hors feit he brak his speir.[n]
(Quod James) to Johne, 'Yit for our ladyis saikis, — *sakes*
40 Lat us to gidder straik thre market straikis.'[n] — *together strike; counted blows*
'I had' (quod Johne) 'that sall on the be — *hold (believe); shall;*
  wrokin;'[n] — *avenged*
But or he spurrit his hors, his speir wes brokin. — *before*

From tyme with speiris none could his — *From that time on;*
    marrow meit, — *opponent*
James drew ane sweird, with ane rycht
    awful spreit, — *spirit, vigour*
45 And ran til Johne, til haif raucht him ane rout. — *to have dealt him a blow*
Johnis swerd was roustit, and wald no way — *rusted*
    cum out.
Than James leit dryfe at Johne with boith — *let drive;*
    his fystis;[n] — *fists*
He mist the man, and dang upon the lystis, — *hit; lists, barriers*
And with that straik, he trowit that John — *stroke; believed*
    was slane,
50 His swerd stak fast, and gat it never agane. — *stuck*
Be this gude Johne had gottin furth his swerd, — *By this time*
And ran to James with mony awfull word:
'My furiousnes forsuith now sall thow find.' — *for sooth, in truth*
Straikand at James, his swerd flew in the wind. — *Striking*
55 Than gentill James began to crak greit wordis, — *speak big*
'Allace' (quode he) 'this day for falt — *for lack, failure*
    of swordis.'[n]
Than ather ran at uther with new raicis, — *each; charges, attacks*
With gluifis of plait thay dang at utheris facis. — *gloves of plate (sheet metal)*
Quha wan this feild, no creature could ken, — *Who; know*
60 Till, at the last, Johne cryit, 'Fy, red the men.'[n] — *separate the men*
'Ye, red' (quod James), 'for that is my desyre, — *Yes, separate*
It is ane hour sen I began to tyre.' — *since; tire*
Sone be thay had endit that royall rink, — *As soon as; charge, battle*
Into the feild mycht no man stand for stink.[n]
65 Than every man that stude on far cryit, fy, — *stood at a distance*
Sayand, adew, for dirt partis cumpany.[n] — *Saying, adieu; filth breaks up*
Thare hors, harnes, and all geir was so gude, — *Their; harness; equipment*
68 Lovyng to God, that day was sched no blude.[n] — *Thanks to God's love; shed*

6. Alexander Scott, *The Justing and Debait up at the Drum Betwix William Adamsone and Johine Sym*, c.1560

Alexander Scott (*c.* 1515–1583), one of the last of the Middle Scots poets or 'makaris', is chiefly remembered as the author of a slim but intense body of courtly love poems, most of which, like those of Burns, were written to fit pre-existing musical compositions. In these, the best known of which is probably the poignant 'To luve unluvit', Scott was following in a fresh and individual style the patterns of the great English and French love poetry of the Renaissance. The longest and most original of his poems, however, is the 'Justing and Debait',where Scott moves into an entirely different field – the native and earthy tradition of *Christis Kirk*, a genre that is a far cry indeed from the rarefied world of courtly love.

The characters in the 'Justing and Debait' are ordinary tradesmen of Dalkeith and Edinburgh, engaged in the first part of the poem in a farcical tournament that degenerates into a drunken free-for-all in the evening in Dalkeith. The poem conforms strictly to the *Christis Kirk* formulas and is written in the traditional stanza, except that Scott has reduced the bobwheel to a single trimeter tag-line functioning as a refrain – 'Up at the Drum that day' or 'Up at Dalkeith that day'. The Drum was the name of a farm in the open country between Edinburgh and Dalkeith, and this piece may well have been based on a real incident. Scott probably derived his 'that day' refrain idea from the fact that three of the stanzas in the original 'Christis Kirk' (2, 20, and 23) have that phrase added to the final line: 'At Christis Kirk of the grene that day'.

In all other respects Scott's poem is in the pure vein of its genre, while incorporating in the first ten stanzas the idea of the mock tournament. One notable feature is the consistent use of mock-heroic style from the beginning to the end. In this impressive poem the *Christis Kirk* tradition includes and absorbs the mock tournament, with the final drunken brawl epitomizing the satire on lower-class life styles.

1

The grit debait and turnament   great conflict
    Of trewth no toung can tell,   Truly
Wes for a lusty lady gent[n]   beautiful; graceful
    Betwix twa freikis fell.   Between two warriors fierce

5   For Mars, the god armipotent,   *mighty in arms*
       Was nocht sa fers him sell,   *not so fierce himself*
      Nor Hercules, that aikkis uprent[n]   *oaks tore up*
      And dang the devill of hell   *struck*
         —With hornis—   *horns*
10   Up at the Drum that day.[n]

2

  Doutles wes nocht so duchty deidis   *there were not; courageous*
      Amangis the dousy peiris,[n]   *Among; 12 peers (of Charlemagne)*
  Nor yit no clerk in story reidis   *learned man; reads*
      Of sa triumphand[n] weiris;   *so triumphant wars*
15   To se so stoutly on thair steidis   *see; bravely; steeds*
      Tha stalwart knychtis steiris,   *Those; steer*
  Quhill bellyis bair for brodding bleidis *Until bellies bare; pricking*
      With spurris als scherp as breiris   *spurs; sharp; briars*
        And kene,   *keen*
20   Up at the Drum that day.

3

  Up at the Drum the day wes sett,   *was set*
      And fixt wes the feild   *field (of battle)*
  Quhair baith thir noble chiftanis mett, *Where both those; chieftains*
      Enarmit undir scheild.   *Armed; shield*
25   Thay wer sa haisty and sa hett   *so; hot*
      That nane of thame wald yeild,   *none of them*
  Bot to debait or be doun bett   *But; fight; down struck*
      And in the quarrell keild   *killed*
        Or slane,[n]
30   Up at the Drum that day.

4

  Thair wes ane bettir and ane wors,
      I wald that it wer wittin: *would; known*
  For William wichttar wes of cors   *stronger; body*
      Nor Sym, and bettir knittin.   *Than; built*
35   Sym said he sett nocht by his fors,   *set no store by; strength*
      Bot hecht he sould be hittin   *promised; should be hit*
  And he micht counter Will on hors;   *If; might encounter*
      For Sym wes bettir sittin   *better sitting (on horseback)*
        Nor Will,   *Than*

40   Up at the Drum that day.

5

To se the stryfe come yunkeirs stout   see; young men brave
    And mony galyart man;   many a gallant
All denteis deir wes thair, but dout;   delicacies expensive; doubtless
    The wine on broich it ran.   wine on tap
45 Trumpettis and schalmis[n] with a schout   shawms (oboes); shout
    Playid or the rink began,   Played before; attack
And eikwall juges satt about   impartial judges
    To se quha tint or wan   see who lost; won
        The field,
50   Up at the Drum that day.

6

With twa blunt trincher speiris squair,   blunt-pointed spears sturdy
    It wes thair interpryis   their undertaking
To fecht with baith thair facis bair[n]   fight; both; bare (unprotected)
    For lufe, as is the gyis.   love; custom
55 Ane freynd of thairis, throu hap, come thair   friend; by chance; came
    And hard the rumor ryis,   heard; circulate
Quha stall away thair stingis bath clair   Who stole; spears both
    And hid in secreit wyis,[n]   secretly
        For skaith,   For mischief
60   Up at the Drum that day.

7

Strang men of armes and of micht   Strong; might
    Wes sett thame for to sinder,[n]   appointed; to part them
The harraldis cryd: 'God schaw the richt!'   heralds; show; right
    Syne bad thame go togidder.   Then; attack one another
65 'Quhair is my speir?' sayis Sym the knicht,   Where
    'Sum man go bring it hidder!'   hither
But wald they tary thair all nicht   would they linger; night
    Thair lancis come to lidder   lances; too sluggishly
        And slaw,   slow
70   Up at the Drum that day.

8

Syme flew als fery as a fowne;[n]   as nimble as a fawn
    Doun fra the hors he slaid,   Down; slid

Sayis: 'He sall rew my stalf hes stowin,   rue who has stolen my spear
    For I salbe his deid!'   shall be; death
75 William his vow plicht to the powin[n]   plighted; peacock
    For favour or for feid: good or ill (hostility)
    'Als gude the tre had nevir growin   As good; tree
      Quhairof my speir wes maid   Whereof
        To just,   joust
80 Up at the Drum that day.'

9

Thir vowis maid to syn and mone,   Their; sun; moon
    Thay raikit baith to rest,   proceeded both
Thame to refres with thair disjone,   refresh; lunch (déjeuner)
    And of thair armour kest,   off; cast
85 Nocht knawing of the deid wes done   deed that was done
      Quhen thay suld haif fairin best: When; should have been served
The fyre wes pischt out lang or none   fire; pissed out; before noon
      Thair dennaris suld haif drest   dinners should have cooked
        And dicht,   prepared
90 Up at the Drum that day.

10

Than wer thay movit out of mind   angered beyond reason
    Far mair than of beforne.   more; before
Thay wist nocht how to get him pynd   knew not; punished
    That thame had drevin to skorne.   subjected to scorn
95 Thair wes no deth mycht be devynd,   death might; devised
      Bot ethis haif they sworne   But oaths have
He suld deir by, be thay had dynd,   dearly pay; by the time; dined
      And ban that he wes borne   curse
        Or bred,
100 Up at the Drum that day.

11

Than to Dalkeith[n] thay maid thame boun,   made ready to go
    Reidwod of this reproche.   Furious at; affront
Thair wes baith wine and vennisoun
    And barrellis ran on broche.   on tap
105 Thay band up kindnes in that toun,   vowed friendship; town
    Nane fra his feir to foche,   from his comrade; depart
For thair wes nowdir lad nor loun   neither; fellow

Micht eit ane baikin loche,[n]   Might eat; baked loach (fish)
    For founes,   fullness (drunkenness)
110 Up at Dalkeith that day.

12

Syne eftir denner rais the din   Then after; rose; noise
    And all the toun on steir.   astir
William wes wyis and held him in,   wise; restrained himself
    For he wes in a feir;   afraid
115 Sym to haif bargan could nocht blin   have a fight; not cease
    Bot bukkit Will on weir,   incited; to battle
Sayis: 'Gif thou wald this lady win,   If thou would
    Cum furth and brek a speir   break
      With me.'
120 Up at Dalkeith that day.

13

This still for bargan Sym abyddis,   Thus; a fight; waits
    And schouttit Will to schame.   shouted; shame
Will saw his fais on bath the syddis;   foes; both; sides
    Full sair he dred for blame.   sorely; feared; censure
125 Will schortly to his hors he slydis,   slips
    And sayis to Sym be name: by
'Bettir we bath wer byand hyddis[n]   buying hides
    And weddir skinnis at hame   wether skins; home
      Nor heir.'   Than here
130 Up at Dalkeith that day.

14

Now is the growme that wes so grim   man; fierce
    Richt glaid to leif in lie.   live in peace (idleness)
'Fy, theif, for schame!' sayis littill Sym,
    'Will thou nocht fecht with me?   fight
135 Thou art moir lerge of lyth and lym   more large; joint
    Nor I am, be sic thre.'   Than; by three times
And all the feild cryd, 'Fy on him!'   crowd (of fighting men)
    Sa cowartly tuk the fle,   cowardly took flight
      For feir,
140 Up at Dalkeith that day.

15

Than every man gaif Will a mok		mocked Will
And said he wes owr meik.		too meek
Sayis Sym, 'Send for thy broder Jok!		
I sall nocht be to seik,		need to be sought for
145 For were ye foursum in a flok		four together; body
I compt you nocht a leik,		reckon you; worth a leek
Thocht I had richt nocht bot a rok		Though; but a distaff
To gar your rumpill reik		make; backside burn
Behind!'		
150 Up at Dalkeith that day.		

16

Thair wes richt nocht but haif and ga;[n]		but to have at it; let go
With lawchter loud thay lewche		laughed
Quhen thay saw Sym sic curage ta		When; such courage take
And Will mak it sa tuche.		be so reluctant
155 Sym lap on horsbak lyk a ra		leaped; roe (deer)
And ran him till a huche;		rode; steep hill
Sayis: 'William, cum ryd doun this bra,		hillside
Thocht ye suld brek ane buche,		break; shoulder
For lufe.'		love
160 Up at Dalkeith that day.		

17

Sone doun the bra Sym braid lyk thunder		Soon; hill; sprang
And bad Will fallow fast;		follow
To grund for fersnes he did funder		ground for fierceness; fall
Be he midhill had past.		By the time that; half way
165 William saw Sym in sic a blunder;		such
To ga he wes agast,		go; terrified
For he affeird – it wes na winder—		afraid; no wonder
His cursour suld him cast		horse should; throw
And hurt him,		
170 Up at Dalkeith that day.		

18

Than all the yungkeiris bad Will yeild		young men; give up
Or doun the glen to gang.		into the valley; go
Sum cryd: 'The koward suld be keild!'		should be killed
Sum doun the hewche he thrang,		steep hill; stormed

175 Sum ruscht, sum rummyld, sum reild,   rushed; rumbled; whirled
  Sum be the bewche he hang.   by the (horse) shoulder; hung
 Thair avairis[n] fyld up all the feild,   cart horses fouled
  Thay wer so fou and pang   full; packed
   With drafe,   swill
180 Up at Dalkeith that day.

19

 Than gelly Johine[n] come in a jak   pleasant; leather jerkin
  To feild quhair he wes feidit;   the field where; challenged
 Abone his brand ane bucklar blak—   Above; sword; shield
  Baill fell the bern that bedit.   Misery befell; man; struck it
185 He slippit swiftly to the slak   valley
  And rudly doun he raid it;   roughly; rode
 Befoir his curpall wes a crak,   crupper (rear); explosive sound
  Culd na man tell quha maid it,   who made
   For lawchter,   laughter
190 Up at Dalkeith that day.

20

 Be than the bowgill gan to blaw,   bugle began; blow
  For nicht had thame owrtane.   overtaken
 'Allais,' said Sym, 'for falt of law   for lack of flame (torchlight)
  That bargan get I nane.'   fight; none
195 Thus hame with mony crak and flaw   home; a break and defect
  Thay passid every ane,
 Syne pairtit at the Potter Raw,[n]   separated; Potterrow
  And sindry gaitis ar gane   various ways; gone
   To rest thame
200 Within the toun that nicht.

Lenvoy

21

 This Will was he begyld the may[n]   (who) deceived; maid
  And did hir marriage spill.   spoil
 He promeist hir, to lat him play,   let
  Hir purpos to fulfill.
205 Fra scho fell fou he fled away   From when she; pregnant
  And come na mair hir till;   no more to her
 Quhairfoir he tynt the feild that day   Wherefore; lost; victory

And tuk him to ane mill	took himself
To hyd him,	hide
210 As coward fals of fey.	false of faith

7. William Drummond of Hawthornden, *Polemo-Middinia inter Vitarvam et Nebernam, c.* 1645

This scintillating piece of macaronic verse – in Latin and Scots – was first attributed to William Drummond (1584–1649) by Edmund Gibson who published the text together with 'Christis Kirk on the Grene' in 1691. In so doing Gibson clearly understood the link between the two poems and saw 'Polemo-Middinia' as a special development of the *Christis Kirk* genre, one that shared with the older poem the boisterous satire of the rustic mores. Drummond was almost certainly the author, since he was intimately acquainted with both of the Fifeshire families involved in the dispute over a right of way depicted in the poem – specifically, the Scots of Scotstarvit and the Cunninghams of Newbarns. In his youth Drummond had been engaged to marry the beautiful daughter of Cunningham of Newbarns, a young woman who died unexpectedly; in his mature years Drummond was a close friend, political ally, and brother-in-law of Sir John Scot of Scotstarvit. The poem was probably written in about 1645, though the earliest printing of it states that it was 'reprintat' in Edinburgh in 1684. In all likelihood, 'Polemo-Middinia' was a facetious work of Drummond's late years, one that circulated in ephemeral broadsides that have perished, before it was permanently recorded in the editions of 1684 and 1691.

At any rate, this is an ingenious and witty satire on peasant cowardice, with the women of Newbarns finally defeating the men of Scotstarvit in a battle that surely owes something to the 'midden' brawl in 'Peblis' and the archery contest in 'Christis Kirk' and contains also an echo of Lindsay's 'Justing' The poem also is remarkable for two burlesque roll calls of clownish 'heroes' and 'heroines'. Its coarseness is partially masked by the Latin vocabulary, the hilarious Latinized Scots phrasing, and the hexameter rhythms, all of which add to the sophistication and intellectual appeal of a *Christis Kirk* poem obviously intended for a highly educated readership.

Because of the many difficulties in the vocabulary of this work, instead of a marginal gloss a full literal translation of the text into modern English has been provided.

Nymphae quae colitis highissima monta *Fifaea*,[n]
Seu vos *Pittenwema*[n] tenent seu *Crelia* crofta,
Sive *Anstraea* domus, ubi nat haddocus in undis,
Codlineusque ingens, & fleucca & sketta pererrant
5 Per costam, et scopulis lobster mony-footus in udis
Creepat, & in mediis ludit whitenius undis;
Et vos skipperii, soliti qui per mare breddum[n]
Valde procul lanchare foris, iterumque redire,
Linquite scellatas[n] bottas shippasque picatas,
10 Whistlantesque simul fechtam[n] memorate bloodaeam,
Fechtam terribilem, quam marvellaverit omnis
Banda Deum, & Nympharum Cockelshelleatarum,
Maia ubi sheepifeda atque ubi solgoosifera *Bassa*[n]
Suellant in pelago, cum Sol boottatus *Edenum*[n]
15 Postabat radiis madidis & shouribus atris.
Quo viso, ad fechtae noisam cecidere volucres,
Ad terram cecidere grues, plish plashque dedere
Sol-goosi in pelago prope littora *Bruntiliana*;[n]
Sea-sutor[n] obstupuit, summique in margine saxi
20 Scartavit[n] praelustre caput, wingasque flapavit;
Quodque magis, alte volitans heronius ipse
Ingeminans clig clag[n] shyttavit in undis.
Namque in principio (storiam tellabimus omnem)
Muckrellium[n] ingentem turbam *Vitarva*[n] per agros
25 *Nebernae* marchare fecit, & dixit ad illos:
Ite hodie armati greppis,[n] dryvate caballos
Crofta[n] per & agros *Nebernae*,[n] transque fenestras:
Quod si forte ipsa *Neberna* venerit extra,
Warrantabo omnes, & vos bene defendebo.
30 Hic aderant *Geordie Akinhedius*, & little *Johnus*,[n]
Et *Jamie Richaeus*, & stout *Michael Hendersonus*,
Qui jolly tryppas ante alios dansare solebat,
Et bobbare bene, & lassas kissare bonaeas;
Duncan Oliphantus valde stalvartus, & ejus
35 Filius eldestus joly boyus, atque *Oldmoudus*,[n]
Qui pleugham[n] longo gaddo[n] dryvare solebat,
Et *Rob Gib* wantonus homo, atque *Oliver Hutchin*,
Et plouky-fac'd[n] Wattis Stranq, atque inkne'd Alshinder[n] Atkin,
Et *Willie Dick* heavi-arstus homo, pigerrimus omnium,

Ye nymphs who cultivate the highest mountains of Fife,
Or if you hold farms at Pittenween or at Crail,
Or have your home at Anstruther, where the haddock swims in the waves,
And the huge codling, and the fluke and skate wander
5 Along the coast, and in the rocks the many-footed lobster in the wet
Creeps, and in the midst of the waves the whiting plays;
And ye skippers, who are accustomed through the broad sea
Very far away to launch forth, and to come back again,
Leave your shell-like boats and ships covered with pitch,
10 And whistling at the same time call to mind the bloody fight,
The terrible fight, at which will marvel all
The band of the Gods, and of the nymphs of the cockleshells,
Where the sheep-feeding Isle of May and where the
    solan-goose-bearing Bass Rock
Rise in the sea at the same time that the Sun in boots to Edinburgh
15 Was sending wet rays and stormy showers.
At which sight, at the noise of the fight birds fell,
To earth fell cranes, and 'plish plash' solan geese
Gave themselves up in the sea near the shore of Burntisland;
The cormorant was stupified, and on the edge of the highest rock
20 Scratched his very illustrious head, and flapped his wings;
And something more: the heron itself flying high
Increasingly shat 'clig clag' into the waves.
For in the beginning (we shall tell the whole story)
The lady of Scotstarvit made a large disorderly crowd of
    dungbasket carriers
25 To march through the fields of Newbarns, and she said to them:
'Today go armed with pronged forks, drive horses
Through the farm and fields of Newbarns, and past the windows:
But if by chance the lady of Newbarns herself will come outside,
I warrant you all, and I will protect you well.'
30 Here were present Geordie Akinhead, and little John,
And Jamie Richy, and stout Michael Henderson,
Who was accustomed to dance jolly capers before the others,
And to bob up and down well, and to kiss the bonny lasses;
Duncan Oliphant very stalwart, and his
35 Eldest son, a jolly boy, and also Oldmouth [sagacious in speech],
Who the plough was accustomed to drive with a long stick,
And Rob Gib, the wanton fellow, and also Oliver Hutchin,
And pimply-faced Wattie Strang, and knock-kneed Alexander Atkin,
And Willie Dick, the heavy-arsed man, the laziest of all,

40   Valde lethus pugnare, sed hunc Corn-greivus[n] heros
     Nout-headdum[n] vocavit, & illum forcit ad arma.
     In super hic aderant *Tom Tailor* & *Tom Nicolsonus*,
     Et *Tamie Gilchristus*, & fool *Jockie Robinsonus*,
     Andrew Alshinderus, & *Jamie Thomsonus*, & alter
45   (Heu pudet, ignoro nomen) slaveri-beardus homo,
     Qui pottas dightabat,[n] & assam[n] jecerat[n] extra.
     Denique prae reliquis *Geordium* affatur,[n] & inquit,
     Geordie, mi formanne, inter stoutissimus omnes,
     Huc ades, & crooksaddeliis,[n] heghemisque,[n] creilisque,
50   Brechimmisque[n] simul cunctos armato jumentos;
     Amblentemque meam naiggam,[n] fattumque magistri
     Curserem, & reliquos trottantes simul averos,[n]
     In cartis yockato[n] omnes, extrahito muckam
     Crofta per & agros *Nebernae* transque fenestras,
55   Quod si forte ipsa *Neberna* contra loquatur,
     In sidis tu pone manus, et dicito, *fart, iade.*
     Nec mora, formannus cunctos flankavit[n] averos,
     Workmannosque ad workam omnes vocavit, & illi
     Extemplo cartas bene fillavere gigantes:
60   Whistlavere viri, workhorsosque ordine swieros[n]
     Drivavere omnes, donec iterumque iterumque
     Fartavere omnes, & sic turba horrida mustrat,[n]
     Haud aliter quam si cum multis *Spinola* trouppis[n]
     Proudus ad *Ostendam* marchasset fortiter urbem.
65   Interea ipse ante alios piperlaius heros
     Praecedens, magnam gestans cum burdine pyppam,
     Incipit *Harlaei* cunctis sonare Batellum.[n]
     Tunc *Neberna* furens, foras ipsa egressa vidensque
     Muck-creilleos transire viam, valde angria facta,
70   Haud tulit affrontam tantam, verum, agmine facto
     Convocat extemplo horsboyos atque ladaeos,
     Jackmannum,[n] hyremannos, pleughdryv'sters atque pleughmannos,
     Tumblentesque simul ricoso[n] ex kitchine boyos,
     Hunc qui gruelias scivit bene lickere plettas,
75   Hunc qui dirtiferas tersit cum dishcloute dishas;
     Et saltpannifumos,[n] & widebricatos[n] fisheros,
     Hellaeosque[n] etiam salteros eduxit ab antris
     Coalheughos nigri grinnantes more divelli;
     Life-guardamque sibi saevas vocat improba lassas

40 Very loath to fight, but this foreman hero
   Called him a blockhead, and forced him to fight.
   In addition here were Tom Tailor and Tom Nicolson,
   And Tamie Gilchrist, and the fool Jockie Robinson,
   Andrew Alexander, and Jamie Thomson, and another
45 (Alas, it is a shame, I do not know his name) slobbery-bearded man,
   Who wiped the pots, and threw out the ashes.
   At last in front of the rest Geordie is spoken to, and she says,
   'Geordie, my foreman, the stoutest of all,
   Come hither, and with crook-saddles, and hames, and creels,
50 And horse-collars, and at the same time prepare all the beasts of burden
       for battle;
   And my ambling nag, and the master's fat
   Racer, and at the same time, the remaining trotting cart-horses;
   To carts harness them all, draw out the dung
   Through the farms and fields of Newbarns and past the windows;
55 But if by chance the lady of Newbarns herself speaks against it,
   You place your hand on your hip and say, "Fart, you jade!"'
   Without delay, the foreman harnessed all of the cart-horses
   And called all of the workmen to work, and they
   Immediately filled well the gigantic carts;
60 The men whistled, and with the lazy workhorses set in order
   They drove off all of them, until again and again
   They all farted, and such a terrible uproar is displayed,
   Exactly as if Spinola with many troops
   The proud man marched bravely to the city of Ostend.
65 Meanwhile, the same bagpiping hero before the others
   Went ahead, carrying as a burden the great pipes,
   He began to play the 'Battle of Harlaw', for everyone.
   Then the lady of Newbarns, raging, and having come out herself, seeing
   The dung baskets cross the road, became very angry;
70 Not at all did she tolerate so great an affront; in truth, she a throng does
   Call together immediately of horseboys and laddies [servants],
   The retainer, hired men, plough drivers and ploughmen,
   And at the same time boys tumbling out of the smoky kitchen,
   This one who knew well how to lick gruel from the plates,
75 That one who wiped off the dirty dishes with a dishtowel;
   And smoky salt-panners, and wide-breeked fishermen,
   And hellions once saltmen she led out from caves,
   Coalhewers grinning in the way of the wicked devil;
   And she boldly calls to her the lifeguard and the wild girls:

80 *Magaeam* magis doctam milkare cowaeas,
Et doctam sweeppare fleuras, & sternere beddas,
Quaeque novit spinare, & longas ducere threedas;
Nansaeam claves bene quae keepaverate omnes,
Yellantemque *Elpen*, & longo bardo *Anapellam*,[n]

85 Fartantemque simul *Gyllam*, gliedamque[n] *Ketaeam*
Egregie indutam blacco caput suttie clutto,[n]
Mammaeamque etiam vetulam, quae sciverat aptè
Infantum teneras blande oscularier[n] arsas,
Quaeque lanam cardare solet olifingria *Beattie*.

90 Tum vero hungraeos ventres *Neberna* gruelis
Farsit, & guttas rasuinibus[n] implet amaris,[n]
Postea newbarmae[n] ingentem dedit omnibus haustum:
Staggravere omnes, grandesque ad sidera riftos[n]
Barmifumi[n] attollunt, & sic ad praelia marchant.

95 Nec mora, marchavit foras longo ordine turma,
Ipsa prior *Neberna* suis stout facta ribauldis,[n]
Roustaeam manibus gestans furibunda goulaeam,[n]
Tandem muckcreilios vocat ad pellmellia[n] fleidos.[n]
Ite, ait, uglei felloes, si quis modo posthac

100 Muckifer has nostras tenet crossare fenestras,
Juro ego quod ejus longum extrahabo thrapellum,[n]
Et totam rivabo[n] faciem, luggasque[n] gulaeo hoc
Ex capite cuttabo ferox, totumque videbo
Heart-blooddum fluere in terram. Sic verba finivit.

105 Obstupuit *Vitarva* diu dirtfleyda,[n] sed inde
Couragium accipiens, muckcreilleos ordine cunctos
Middini[n] in medio faciem turnare coegit.
O qualem primo fleuram[n] gustasses[n] in ipso
Batalli onsetto! pugnat muckcreillius heros[n]

110 Fortiter, & muckam per posteriora cadentem
In creillis shoollare[n] ardet: sic dirta[n] volavit.
O qualis feire fairie[n] fuit, si forte vidisses
Pypantes arsas, & flavo sanguine breickas[n]
Dripantes, hominumque heartas ad praelia fantas!

115 O qualis hurlie burlie fuit! namque alteri nemo
Ne vel foot-breddum yerdae[n] yeeldare volebat:
Stout erant ambo quidem, valdeque hard-hearta caterva.
Tum vero è medio mukdryv'ster prosilit unus,

80   Maggie who was well instructed to milk the cows,
     And taught to sweep the floors and make the beds,
     And who knew how to spin and draw out long threads;
     Nancy who had kept all the keys well,
     And yelling Elpen, and Anabel, with the long beard [?],
85   And quick-farting Gill, and squint-eyed Katie
     Excellently dressed with her black head in a sooty rag,
     And Mammie, already somewhat old, who had known appropriately
     How to kiss tenderly the soft arses of children,
     As well as greasy-fingered Bettie who is used to carding the wool.
90   Then indeed the hungry bellies the lady of Newbarns with gruel
     Stuffed full and filled up their guts with bitter [unripe] grapes
     Afterwards, she gave to all a huge draught of new beer:
     All of them were staggered, and great belches to the stars
     They sent up, inflamed with beer, and so they march to battle.
95   Without delay, the throng marched forth in a long line,
     The lady of Newbarns herself first, strengthened by her clowns,
     Carrying furiously in her hands a rusty gully [large knife],
     At last she calls to the dungbasketers who were frightened and in
         utter confusion
     'Go,' she says, 'You ugly fellows. If in the future
100 Any dungcarrier even tries to cross past our windows,
     I swear that I shall cut out his long throat
     And tear up his whole face, and his ears with this gully
     I shall cut ferociously from his head, and I shall see all
     Of his heart's blood flow into the earth.' So she finished speaking.
105 The lady of Scotstarvit was stupified and frightened shitless for a
         long while, but
     Taking courage, the whole of the dungcarts in line
     In the middle of the dung heap she forced to turn in a fashion.
     O what a smell you would have experienced in the very first
     Onset of battle! The dungbasket hero fights
110 Bravely, and falling dung next in order
     He is eager to shovel in basketfuls; so the shit flew.
     O what an angry tumult there was! If by chance you had seen
     The piping arses, and the breeks with yellow blood
     Dripping, and the faint hearts of men in the fight!
115 O what a hurly burly there was! For no one or other
     Was willing to yield a single footbreadth of ground;
     Both sides indeed were stout, and very hard-hearted troops.
     Then in truth out of the midst springs one muckdriver,

Gallantaeus homo, & greppam minatur in ipsam
120 *Nebernam*, quoniam misere scaldaverat[n] omnes,
Dirtavitque totam petticottam gutture[n] thicko,
Perlineasque[n] ejus skirtas, silkamque gownaeam,
Vasquineamque[n] rubram mucksherdo[n] begariavit.[n]
Sed tamen ille fuit valde faint-heartus, & ivit
125 Valde procul, metuens shottum woundumque profundum;
At non valde procul fuerat revengda, sed illum
Extemplo *Gyllaea* ferox invasit, & ejus
In faciem girnavit[n] atrox, & tigrida facta,
Bublentem[n] grippans bardum,[n] sic dixit ad illum:
130 Vade domum, filthaea nequam, aut te interficiabo.
Tum cum Herculeo[n] magnum fecit Gilliwyppum,[n]
Ingentemque manu sherdam[n] levavit, & omnem
Gallentey hominis gash-beardum[n] besmiriavit.
Sume tibi hoc (inquit) sneezing[n] valde operativum
135 Pro praemio, swingere,[n] tuo. Tum denique fleido
Ingentem Gilliwamphra[n] dedit, validamque nevellam,[n]
Ingeminatque iterum, donec bis fecerit ignem
Ambobus fugere ex oculis: sic *Gylla* triumphat.
Obstupuit bumbasedus[n] homo, backumque repente
140 Turnavit veluti nasus bloodasset, & *O fy!*
Ter quater exclamat, & O quam saepe nizavit![n]
Disjuniumque[n] omnem evomuit valde hungrius homo
Lausavitque[n] supra & infra, miserabile visu,
Et luggas necko imponens, sic cucurrit absens,
145 Non audens gimpare[n] iterum, ne worsa tulisset.
Haec *Vitarva* videns, yellavit turpia verba,
Et *fy, fy!* exclamat, prope nunc victoria losta est.
Elatisque hippis magno cum murmure fartum
Barytonum emisit, veluti Monsmegga[n] cracasset:
150 Tum vero quaccare[n] hostes, flightamque repente
Sumpserunt, retrospexit *Jackmannus*, & ipse
Sheepheadus metuit sonitumque ictumque buleti.
Quod si King Spanius, *Philippus* nomine, septem[n]
Consimiles hisce habuisset forte canones
155 Batterare *Sluissam, Sluissam* dingasset[n] in assam;
Aut si tot magnus *Ludovicus* forte dedisset[n]
Ingentes fartas ad moenia *Montalbana*,
Ipsam continuo tounam dingasset in yerdam.[n]

A gallant man, and threatens with his pitchfork
120 The lady of Newbarns herself, since she had scolded all of them
         violently,
     And he soiled all of her petticoat with thick mud,
     And her skirts trimmed with perlin [lace], and her silk gown,
     And her red petticoat was bespattered with pieces of cow dung.
     But for all that he was very faint-hearted, and went
125 Very far off, fearing a shot and a deep wound;
     But at least not long after she [Neberna] was avenged, for that man
     The fierce Gill assailed immediately and in his face
     She snarled horribly and looked like a tigress;
     Gripping his snotty beard, she spoke to him thus:
130 'Go home, you filthy good-for-nothing, or else I shall kill you.'
     Then, when like Hercules she struck a great hard blow,
     She lifted up in her. hand a huge patch of cow-dung and all of
     The protruding beard of the gallant man she besmeared.
     'Take upon yourself,' (she said) 'this very effective snuff
135 For your reward, you rascal.' Then at last to the frightened one
     She gave a tremendous blow, and a powerful blow,
     And redoubled again, until twice she made fire
     To escape from both his eyes: in this way Gill is victorious.
     The bewildered man was stupified, and suddenly backwards
140 He turned just as if his nose had been bloodied, and 'O fy!'
     Three, four times he exclaims, and O how often he sneezed [snorted?]!
     And he vomited up his whole breakfast and the very hungry man
     Let loose above and below, a miserable sight,
     And putting his ears to his neck he ran away in such a fashion,
145 Not daring to scoff for a second time, and he would not suffer worse.
     Seeing this, the mistress of Scotstarvit yelled filthy words,
     And 'fy, fy!' she exclaims, 'Now the victory is nearly lost.'
     And from elevated hips with a massive murmur a baritone fart
     She let fly, such as would have cracked Mons Meg:
150 Thereupon truly the enemies quaked, and suddenly to flight
     They took; the retainer looked back, and that same
     Sheepheaded man was afraid of the sounds and the blows of a bullet.
     And if by chance the Spanish King, by the name of Philip, seven
     Exactly equal cannons had made to open their mouths
155 To batter Sluys, he would have smashed Sluys to ashes;
     Or if great Louis had given by chance so many
     Enormous farts to the fortifications of Montauban,
     That same town he would have instantly smashed to the ground.

Exit Corngreivus, wracco[n] omnia tendere videns,
160 Consiliumque meum si non accipitis, inquit,
Formosas scartabo facies, & vos wirriabo.[n]
Sed needlo per seustram[n] broddatus,[n] inque privatas
Partes stobbatus,[n] greittans,[n] lookansque grivatè,
Barlafumle[n] clamat, & dixit, *O Deus, O God*!
165 Quid multis? Sic fraya fuit, sic guisa[n] peracta est,
Una nec interea spillata est dropa cruoris.[n]

The foreman left, seeing everything covered with debris;
160 'And if you do not accept my advice,' she [Gill] said,
     'I shall scratch your beautiful faces, and I shall strangle you.'
     But pierced with a needle by the seamstress, and in private
     Parts stabbed, weeping, and looking aggrieved,
     He cried, 'Truce,' and said 'O God, O God!'
165 What further? In this way the fray ended, in this way the affair was
        acted out,
     Nevertheless, not one drop of blood was spilled.

8. Anon., *The Blythsome Wedding*, *c.*1680

This amusing piece has sometimes been credited to Francis Sempill of Beltrees (died 1682), but the attribution is based solely on family oral tradition. Since there is absolutely no solid evidence of Sempill's connection with this work, it seems best to regard it as anonymous. The model for the first six stanzas was certainly Drummond's 'Polemo-Middinia' with its two comic roll calls of 'heroes' from which several names with the same adjectives attached were taken. The latter part of the song, in which the good things to eat and drink on this occasion are listed, is a delightful earthy burlesque, with cheap peasant dishes and drinks treated as though they were gourmet delicacies. The basic setting of a country wedding celebration is a wholly typical *Christis Kirk* milieu, and equally characteristic is the lively mockery of the wedding guests.

1

Fy let us all to the briddel,	bridal, wedding
For there will be lilting there;	singing
For Jockie's to be marry'd to Maggie,	
The lass with the gauden-hair:	golden
5 And there will be lang-kail and pottage	purplish cabbage; porridge
And bannocks of barley-meal;	round cakes
And there will be good salt-herring	
To relish a kog of good ale.	wooden drinking vesssel
Fy let us all to the briddel,	
For there will be lilting there,	
For Jockie's to be marry'd to Maggie,	
The lass with the gauden hair:	

2

And there will be Sandie the sutor,[n]	cobbler, shoemaker
10 And Willie with the meikle mow,	big mouth
And there will be Tom the ploutter,	trimmer of nap on woollen cloth
And Andrew the tinkler I trow;	believe
And there will be bow-legged Robbie,	
And thumbless Kettie's good-man,	husband
15 And there will be blue cheeked Dallie	
And Lawrie the laird of the land.	landowner
Fy let us all, &c.	

3

And there will be sow-libber Peatie,	sow-gelder
And plouckie fac'd Wat[n] in the mill,	pimply
Capper-nos'd Gibbie and Francie	with copper-coloured nose
20 That wins in the how of the hill,	lives; hollow
And there will be Alaster Dougal	
That splee-fitted Bessie did woo,[n]	splay-footed
And sneevling Lillie and Tibbie,	whining
And Kirstie that belly-god sow.[n]	gluttonous pig
Fy let us all, &c.	

4

25 And Crampie that married Stainie	
And coft him breeks to his arse,	bought; trousers
And afterwards hanged for stealing,	
Great mercy it hapned na warse;	no worse

And there will be fairnticklld Hew,[n]	freckled
30 And Bess with the lillie white leg;	
That gat to the south for breeding,[n]	education, manners
And bang'd up her wame in Mons-Meg	belly
Fy let us all, &c.	

5

And there will be Geordie McCowrie,	
And blinking daft Barbra and Meg,	ogling silly
35 And there will be blencht Gillie-whimple[n]	pale, white faced
And peuter fac'd flitching Joug,	pewter, leaden; wheedling
And there will be happer-ars'd Nanzie[n]	hopper-arsed (with bony hips)
And fairie-fac'd Jeanie be name,	
Gleed Kettie[n] and fat lugged Lizie	squint-eyed; eared
40 The lass with the gauden wame.	golden belly
Fy let us all, &c.	

6

And there will be girn-again Gibbie	ill-humoured
And his glaked wife Jennie Bell,	crazy
And mizlie-chin'd flyting Geordie	measly, blotched; scolding
The lad that was skipper himsell;	
45 There'll be all the lads and the lasses	
Set down in the midst of the ha,	hall
With sybows, and rifarts and carlings,[n]	scallions; radishes; buttered peas
That are both sodden and ra.	boiled; raw
Fy let us all &c.	

7

There will be tartan, dragen and brachen,[n]	cabbage meal; soaked meal; gruel
50 And fouth of good gappoks of skate,	plenty; mouthfuls
Pow-sodie, and drammock, and crowdie,	sheephead soup; watered meal; [raw watered oatmeal
And callour nout-feet in a plate;	fresh calves' feet
And there will be partons, and buckies,	crabs; whelks (sea snails)
Speldens, and haddocks anew,	dried salt haddocks; enough
55 And sing'd sheep-heads and a haggize[n]	haggis
And scadlips to sup till ye're fou.	thin broth (scald-lips); full
Fy let us all &c.	

8

There will be good lapper'd milk kebbucks,[n]   curdled; cheeses
    And sowens,[n] and farles,[n] and baps,   porridge; oatcakes; rolls
And swatts, and scraped paunches,   oat-hust broth; bellies (tripe)
60   And brandie in stoups and in caps;   tankards; wooden bowls
And there will be meal-kail and castocks,   oatmeal cabbage; cabbage stalks
    And skink[n] to sup till you rive,   thin, wishy-washy drink; burst
And rosts to rost on a brander,   roasts; gridiron
    Of flouks that was taken alive.   flounders
Fy et us all, &c .

9

65 Scrapt haddocks, wilks, dilse and tangles,   periwinkles; dulse; seaweeds
    And a mill of good sneezing to prie,   box; snuff; try, sample
When weary with eating and drinking,
    We'll rise up and dance till we die.
Fy let us all to the Bridel,
    For there will be lilting there;
For Jockie's to be marry'd to Maggie,
    The lass wi th the gauden hair.

9. Allan Ramsay, *Christ's Kirk on the Green,*
Cantos II and III, 1715, 1718

Allan Ramsay (1684–1758) was a man of remarkable talent and energy who, almost singlehandedly, launched the revival of Scots poetry in the eighteenth century. Rising from very humble beginnings, Ramsay gradually became a successful bookseller, publisher, editor, original poet and songwriter in Edinburgh – the central figure of a reborn national literature.

During the long winter of the seventeenth century the brilliant poetry in Middle Scots had been largely forgotten, and what little new work in Scots continued to be written was sporadic and limited to comic treatments of low life. Inheriting this situation, Ramsay naturally started out as a comic poet in Scots, working in the still popular tradition of *Christis Kirk,* and establishing other genres like the comic elegy and verse epistle, before moving on to experiments with Scots song, pastoral elegies, and finally to his masterpiece *The Gentle Shepherd,* a full blown pastoral drama. At the same time Ramsay was engaged in pioneer editorial work, producing an enormously successful collection of Scots songs, *The Tea-Table Miscellany.* This was followed by *The Ever Green* (1724), the first anthology of Middle Scots poetry, taken mostly from the Bannatyne MS of 1568, and making accessible to eighteenth-century readers for the first time the great Scottish poetry of the past. In all of these endeavours Ramsay was laying the essential foundations for the revival of the native poetic tradition, creating a reading public that welcomed the later, more dazzling work of Fergusson and Burns.

Ramsay's two continuations of the original 'Christis Kirk', composed (as he tells us) in 1715 and 1718, are the finest achievement of the first phase of his career (1712–1721). Not only did Ramsay give vital publicity to the genre by publishing the old poem as 'Canto I', he also, and more importantly, gave the tradition a whole new impetus by virtue of his own impressive sequel – Cantos II and III. Each of these represented the longest *Christis Kirk* poems to appear since Alexander Scott's 'Justing and Debait', and together they demonstated that the venerable genre was still adaptable for modern purposes. In these cantos Ramsay adopted the truncated bobwheel, the dimeter tag-line ending in 'that day' as he found it in Watson's *Choice Collection* (1706) and in the corrupt broadside printings of the seventeenth century, and in so doing he established this form of the stanza as the standard for the eighteenth century and beyond. It is true that Ramsay's cantos are occasionally weakened by a self-concious antiquitarianism as seen in the old-fashioned marriage customs, such as the 'bedding of the bride' and the 'riding of the stang', of which he makes too much; but these are minor faults in an otherwise lively and brilliant piece of work.

Canto II

Ramsay's headnote: 'The King having painted the rustick squabble with an uncommon spirit, in a most ludicrous manner, in a stanza of verse the most difficult to keep the sense complete, as he has done, without being forced to bring in words for crambo's [rime's] sake, where they return so frequently: Ambitious to imitate so great an original, I put a stop to the war; called a congress, and made them sign a peace, that the world might have their picture in the more agreeable hours of drinking, dancing, and singing. The following cantos were wrote, one in 1715, the other in 1718, about 300 years after the first. Let no worthy poet despair of immortality; good sense will always be the same in spite of the revolution of words.'

1

But there had been mair blood and skaith,	more; harm
Sair harship and great spulie,	Severe devastation; plundering
And mony a ane had gotten his death	
By this unsonsie tooly:	unfortunate fight
5 But that the bauld good-wife of Braith[n]	bold
Arm'd wi' a great kail gully,	cabbage knife
Came bellyflaught,[n] and loot an aith,	swooping down; let forth; oath
She'd gar them a' be hooly[n]	make; quiet
Fou fast that day.	Very (full) fast

2

10 Blyth to win aff sae wi' hale banes	Happy; off so; whole bones
Tho mony had clowr'd pows;	battered heads
And dragl'd sae 'mang muck and stanes,	dragged; stones
They look'd like wirry-kows:	scarecrows
Quoth some, who 'maist had tint their aynds,	almost; lost; breath
15 'Let's see how a' bowls rows:[n]	all bowling balls roll
And quat this brulyiement at anes,	quit; broil; once
Yon gully is nae mows,	knife; no joke
Forsooth this day.'	In truth

3

Quoth Hutchon,[n] 'I am well content,
20   I think we may do war;   worse
   Till this time toumond I'se indent   twelvemonth I'll promise
      Our claiths of dirt will sa'r: clothes; smell (savour)
   Wi' nevels I'm amaist fawn faint,   punches; almost fallen
      My chafts are dung a char;'   jaws; beaten out of shape (ajar)
25 Then took his bonnet to the bent,   field
      And daddit aff the glar,   knocked off; mud
         Fou clean that day.

4

Tam Taylor, wha in time of battle
   Lay as gin some had fell'd him;   as though
30 Gat up now wi' an unco' rattle,   Got; awful, unseemly
   As nane there durst a quell'd him: have beaten
   Bauld Bess flew till him wi' a brattle,   Bold; to; fury
   And spite of his teeth held him
   Closs by the craig, and with her fatal   Close; throat
35   Knife shored she would geld him,   threatened; castrate
         For peace that day.

5

Syne a' wi' ae consent shook hands,   Then; one
   As they stood in a ring,
Some red their hair, some set their bands,   combed
40   Some did their sark tails wring: shirt
Then for a hap to shaw their brands,   hop (dance); calves of legs
   They did there minstrel bring,   their
Where clever houghs like willi-wands,   thighs, legs; willow wands
   At ilka blythsome spring   each
45   Lap high that day.   Leaped

6

Claud Peky was na very blate,   shy
   He stood nae lang a dreigh;   not long at a distance
For by the wame he gripped Kate,   belly
   And gard her gi'e a skreigh: made; give a squeal
50 'Had aff,' quoth she, 'ye filthy slate,   Hold off; sloven
   Ye stink o' leeks, O figh!
Let gae my hands. I say, be quait,'   quiet

And wow gin she was skeigh,	if; skittish
And mim that day.	affectedly modest

7

55 Now settl'd gossies sat, and keen	gossips
Did for fresh bickers birle;[n]	drinks contribute
While the young swankies on the green	young fellows
Took round a merry tirle:	twirl, dance
Meg Wallet wi' her pinky een,	winking eyes
60 Gart Lawrie's heart-strings dirle,	Made; tingle
And fouk wad threep, that she did green	folk; allege; long for
For what wad gar her skirle	make her yell
And skreigh some day.	screech

8

The manly miller, haff and haff,[n]	half tipsy
65 Came out to shaw good will.	show
Flang by his mittens and his staff,	Flung off
Cry'd, 'Gi'e me *Paty's-Mill,*'	(title of tune)
He lap bawk-hight,[n] and cry'd, 'Had aff,'	leaped joist-high; Hold off
They rus'd him that had skill;	praised
70 'He wad do't better,'quoth a cawf,	fool (calf)
'Had he another gill	drink measure
Of usquebae.'	whisky

9

Furth started neist a pensy blade,	Forth; next; conceited
And out a maiden took,	
75 They said that he was Falkland bred,[n]	
And danced by the book;	
A souple taylor to his trade,[n]	supple
And when their hands he shook,	
Ga'e them what he got frae his dad,	Gave; father
80 *Videlicet* the yuke,	Namely; itch
To claw that day.	

10

Whan a' cry'd out he did sae weel,	well
He Meg and Bess did call up;	
The lasses bab'd about the reel,	bobbed, danced
85 Gar'd a' their hurdies wallop,	Made all; buttocks

And swat like pownies whan they speel   sweated; ponies; climb
    Up braes, or when they gallop,   hills
But a thrawn knublock hit his heel,   cursed small stone
    And wives had him to haul up,
90   Haff fell'd that day.   Half

11

But mony a pauky look and tale   sly
    Gaed round whan glowming hous'd them,[n] Went; twilight brought them in
The ostler wife brought ben good ale,   in
    And bade[n] the lasses rouze them;   stir themselves
95 'Up wi' them lads, and I'se be bail   I'll guarantee
    They'll loo ye an ye touze them:'   love; if; rumple them
Quoth Gawssie, 'this will never fail
    Wi' them that this gate woes them,   way woos
       On sic a day.'   such

12

100 Syne stools and furms were drawn aside,   Then; forms
    And up raise Willy Dadle,
A short hought man, but fou o' pride,   legged; full
    He said the fidler play'd ill;
'Let's ha'e the pipes,' quoth he, 'beside;'   have
105   Quoth a', 'That is nae said ill;'   all
He fits the floor syne wi' the bride   foots; then
    To *Cuttymun* and *Treeladle*,[n]   (names of tunes)
       Thick, thick that day.

13

In the mean time in came the laird,   landowner
110   And by some right did claim,
To kiss and dance wi' Masie Aird,
    A dink and dortie dame: neat; conceited
But O poor Mause was aff her guard,
    For back gate frae her wame,   backward from; abdomen
115 Beckin she loot a fearfu' raird,   Curtsying; let; fart
    That gart her think great shame,   made
       And blush that day.

14

Auld Steen led out Maggie Forsyth,

He was her ain good-brither;   own brother-in-law
120 And ilka ane was unco' blyth, everyone; extremely
  To see auld fouk sae clever. old folk
Quoth Jock, wi' laughing like to rive, burst
  'What think ye o' my mither?'
Were my dad dead, let me ne'er thrive
125   But she wa'd get anither would
    Goodman this day.' Husband

15

Tam Lutter had a muckle dish, large drinking bowl
  And betwisht ilka tune, between
He laid his lugs in't like a fish, ears
130   And suckt till it was done;
His bags were liquor'd to his wish, guts, belly
  His face was like a moon:[n]
But he cou'd get nae place to pish piss
  In, but his ain twa shoon, own two shoes
135   For thrang that day. Because of the crowd

16

The latter-gae of haly rhime,[n] giver out; holy hymns
  Sat up at the boord-head, head of the table
And a' he said was thought a crime all
  To contradict indeed:
140 For in clark-lear he was right prime, clerical learning
  And cou'd baith write and read,[n]
And drank sae firm till ne'er a styme blink
  He cou'd keek on a bead,[n] look at a rosary bead (pray)
    Or book that day.

17

145 When he was strute, twa sturdy chiels, drunk; fellows
  Be's oxter and be's coller, By his arm pit; collar
Held up frae cowping o' the creels[n] falling head over heels
  The liquid logic scholar.
When he came hame his wife did reel, rush about
150   And rampage in her choler, anger
With that he brake the spining-wheel,
  That cost a good rix-dollar,[n] silver coin
    And mair some say. more

18

Near bed-time now ilk weary wight   *each; person*
155   Was gaunting for his rest;   *yawning*
For some were like to tyne their sight,   *lose*
    Wi' sleep and drinking strest.   *overcome*
But ithers that were stomach-tight,   *others; had a good appetite*
    Cry'd out, it was nae best
160 To leave a supper that was dight,   *prepared*
    To Brownies,[n] or a ghaist,   *spirits; ghost*
       To eat or day.   *before, ere*

19

On whomelt tubs lay twa lang dails,   *turned upside down; planks*
    On them stood mony a goan,   *wooden porridge bowl*
165 Some fill'd wi' brachan, some wi' kail,   *oatmeal gruel; broth*
    And milk het frae the loan.   *hot; village common*
Of daintiths they had routh and wale,   *delicacies; plenty; choice*
    Of which they were right fon;   *fond, desirous*
But nathing wad gae down but ale
170   Wi' drunken Donald Don
       The smith that day.

20

Twa times aught bannocks in a heap,   *eight thick oatcakes*
    And twa good junts of beef,   *joints*
Wi' hind and fore spaul of a sheep,   *shoulder*
175   Drew whitles frae ilk sheath: *knives (whittles); each*
Wi' gravie a their beards did dreep,   *all; drip*
    They kempit with their teeth;   *combed*
A kebbuck syn that 'maist cou'd creep   *cheese then; almost*
    Its lane pat on the sheaf,[n]   *By itself to crown the meal*
180   In stous that day.   *slices*

21

The bride was now laid in her bed,
    Her left leg ho was flung;[n]   *stocking*
And Geordie Gib was fidgen glad,   *excitedly*
    Because it hit Jean Gun:
185 She was his jo, and aft had said,   *sweetheart; often*
    'Fy Geordie, had your tongue,   *hold*
Ye's ne'er get me to be your bride:'

But chang'd her mind when bung,   tipsy
    This very day.

22

190 'Tehee,' quoth Touzie, when she saw
    The cathel coming ben,   hot alcoholic punch; in
It pypin het gae'd round them a',   piping hot went
    The bride she made a fen,   made an effort
To sit in wylicoat sae braw,   underpetticoat; fine
195   Upon her nether en;   lower end
Her lad like ony cock did craw,   crow
    That meets a clockin hen,   hen sitting on eggs
        And blyth were they.

23

The souter, miller, smith and Dick,   shoemaker
200   Lawrie and Hutchon bauld,   bold
Carles that keep nae very strict   Fellows
    Be hours, tho they were auld;   By; old
Nor cou'd they e'er leave aff that trick,   off
    But whare good ale was sald,   where; sold
205 They drank a' night, e'en tho auld Nick   (the Devil)
    Shou'd tempt their wives to scald   scold
        Them for't neist day.   next

24

Was ne'er in Scotland heard or seen[n]
    Sic banqueting and drinkin,   Such
210 Sic revelling and battles keen,
    Sic dancing, and sic jinkin,   frolicking
And unko wark that fell at e'en,   strange doings
    Whan lasses were haff winkin,   half closing their eyes
They lost their feet and baith their een,   both their eyes
215   And maidenheads gac'd linkin   slipping off quickly
        Aff a' that day.   Off all

Canto III

Ramsay's headnote: 'Curious to know how my bridal folks would look next day after the marriage, I attempted this third canto, which opens with a description of the morning. Then the friends come and present their gifts to the new married couple. A view is taken of one girl (Kirsh) who had come fairly off, and of Mause who had stumbled with the laird. Next a new scene of drinking is represented, and the young good-man is creel'd. Then the character of the smith's ill-natured shrew is drawn, which leads in the description of riding the stang. Next Maggy Murdy has an exemplary character of a good wise wife. Deep drinking and bloodless quarrels makes an end of an old tale.'

1

Now frae East Nook of Fife[n] the daw'n	
Speel'd westlines up the lift,	climbed westwards; sky
Carles wha heard the cock had craw'n,	Men; crowed
Begoud to rax and rift:	Began; stretch; belch
5 And greedy wives wi' girning thrawn,	grumbling sullen
Cry'd 'Lasses up to thrift';	work
Dogs barked, and the lads frae hand	immediately
Bang'd to their breeks like drift,	threw on; trousers with speed
Be break of day.	By

2

10 But some wha had been fow yestreen,	drunk yesterday evening
Sic as the latter-gae,	Such; church precentor
Air up had nae will to be seen,	Early
Grudgin their groat[n] to pay.	four pence (for drunkenness)
But what aft fristed's no forgeen,	oft trusted to pay; forgiven
15 When fouk has nought to say;	folk
Yet sweer were they to rake their een[n],	reluctant; open; eyes
Sic dizzy heads had they,	
And het that day.	hot

3

Be that time it was fair foor days,[n]	By; broad daylight (late in day)
20 As fou's the house cou'd pang,	full's, squeeze in
To see the young fouk or they raise,	before; rose
Gossips came in ding dang,	in rapid succession
And wi' a soss aboon the claiths,[n]	thump above; clothes
Ilk ane their gifts down flang:	Each one; flung
25 Twall toop horn-spoons down Maggy lays,	Twelve ram
Baith muckle mow'd and lang,	Both wide-mouthed; long
For kale or whey.	broth; skim milk

4

Her aunt a pair of tangs fush in,   tongs fetched in
   Right bauld she spake and spruce,   boldly; smartly
30 'Gin your goodman shall make a din,   If; husband; noise
   And gabble like a goose,
Shorin whan fou to skelp yer skin,   Threatening; drunk; smack
   Thir tangs may be of use;   These tongs
Lay them enlang his pow or shin,   along; head
35   Wha wins syn may make roose,   then; take the commendation
     Between you twa.'

5

Auld Bessie in her red coat braw,   handsome
   Cam wi' her ain oe Nanny,   Came; own grandchild
An odd like wife, they said that saw,   odd kind of woman
40   A moupin runckled granny,   nibbling (toothless) wrinkled
She fley'd the kimmers ane and a',   frightened; gossips
   Word gae'd she was na kanny;[n]   went around; was uncanny, weird
Nor wad they let Lucky awa,   would; the old woman away
   Till she was burnt wi' branny,   with brandy
45   Like mony mae.   many more

6

Steen fresh and fastin 'mang the rest   among
   Came in to get his morning,   strong drink before breakfast
Speer'd gin the bride had tane the test,[n]   Asked if; taken
   And how she loo'd her corning?   loved; love-making
50 She leugh as she had fun a nest,   laughed; found; nest of eggs
   Said, 'Let a be ye'r scorning,'   Leave off all
Quoth Roger, 'Fegs I've done my best,   Faith!
   To ge'er a charge of horning,[n]   give her; writ requiring payment
     As well's I may.'

7

55 Kind Kirsh was there, a kanty lass,   lively
   Black-ey'd, black-hair'd, and bonny;
Right well red up and jimp she was,   dressed; slender
   And wooers had fow mony: very (full) many
I wat na how it came to pass,   know not
60   She cutled in wi' Jonnie,   cuddled
And tumbling wi' him on the grass,

Dung a' her cockernonny   Knocked; coiffure
    A jee that day.   Awry

8

But Mause begrutten was and bleer'd,   tear-stained; inflamed
65   Look'd thowless, dowf and sleepy;   listless; sad
Auld Maggy kend the wyt, and sneer'd,   knew; source of blame
    Caw'd her a poor daft heepy: Called; silly hypochondriac
'It's a wise wife that kens her weird,   knows; fate
    What tho ye mount the creepy;[n]   stool of repentance (in church)
70 There a good lesson may be lear'd,   leamed
    And what the war will ye be   worse
        To stand a day.

9

'Or bairns can read, they first maun spell,   Before children; must
    I learn'd this frae my mammy,
75 And coost a legen-girth[n] my sell,   cast a bottom hoop (from tub)
    Lang or I married Tammie: before
I'se warrand ye have a' heard tell,   I'll guarantee
    Of bonny Andrew Lammy,
Stifly in loove wi' me he fell,   Strongly; love
80   As soon as e'er he saw me:
        That was a day.'

10

Hait drink, frush butter'd caiks and cheese,   Hot; fresh; cakes
    That held their hearts aboon,   kept their hearts up
Wi' clashes mingled aft wi' lies,   gossip; often
85   Drave aff the hale forenoon: Drove off; whole
But after dinner an ye please,   if
    To weary not o'er soon,
We down to e'ning edge wi' ease   evening
    Shall loup, and see what's done   leap
90   I' the doup o' the day.   butt end

11

Now what the friends wad fain been at,
    They that were right true blue;   staunchly devoted, genuine
Was e'en to get their wysons wat,   throats wet
    And fill young Roger fou:[n]   full, drunken

95 But the bauld billy took his maut,	bold fellow; malt (drink)
And was right stiff to bow;	hard to bend
He fairly ga'e them tit for tat,	gave
And scourd aff healths anew,	drank off; enough
Clean out that day.	

12

100 A creel[n] bout fow of muckle stains	full to the brim; big stones
They clinked on his back,	fastened
To try the pith o's rigg and reins,	strength; back; loins
They gart him cadge this pack.	made; carry
Now as a sign he had tane pains,	taken
105 His young wife was na slack,	
To rin and ease his shoulder bains,	run; bones
And sneg'd the raips fow snack,	cut; ropes; full nimbly
We'er knife that day.	With her

13

Syne the blyth carles, tooth and nail,	Then; men
110 Fell keenly to the wark;	work
To ease the gantrees of the ale,	barrel stand
And try wha was maist stark;	most sturdy
'Till boord and floor, and a' did sail,	table; all; swim
Wi' spilt ale i' the dark;	
115 Gart Jock's fit slide, he like a fail,	Made; foot; turf
Play'd dad, and dang the bark	Fell with heavy thud; knocked
Aff's shins that day.	Off his

14

The souter, miller, smith and Dick,[n]	cobbler, shoemaker
Et cet'ra, closs sat cockin,	close; drinking
120 Till wasted was baith cash and tick,	both; credit
Sae ill were they to slocken;	So difficult; quench
Gane out to pish in gutters thick,	Gone; piss
Some fell, and some gae'd rockin,	went staggering
Sawny hang sneering on his stick,	Sandy (Alexander)
125 To see bauld Hutchon bockin	bold Hugh vomiting
Rainbows that day.	

15

The smith's wife her black deary sought,

	And fand him skin and birn:[n]	found; burn (brand mark)
	Quoth she, 'This day's wark's be dear bought.'	work will be
130	He ban'd, and gae a girn;	cursed; gave a groan
	Ca'd her a jade, and said she mucht	Called; might
	Gae hame and scum her kirn;	Go home; butter churn
	'Whisht ladren, for gin ye say ought	Hush lazy lout; if
	Mair, I'se wind ye a pirn[n]	More, I'll; bobbin
135	To reel some day.'	

16

	'Ye'll wind a pirn! Ye silly snool,	coward
	Wae-worth ye'r drunken saul,'	Woe befall; soul
	Quoth she, and lap out o'er a stool,	leaped
	And claught him be the spaul:	grabbed; shoulder
140	He shook her, and sware 'Muckle dool	Great sorrow
	Ye's thole for this,[n] ye scaul;	You will suffer; scold
	I'se rive frae aff ye'r hips the hool,	I'll tear from off; skin
	And learn ye to be baul	bold
	On sic a day.'	such

17

145	'Your tippanizing, scant o' grace,'	drinking two-penny ale
	Quoth she, 'gars me gang duddy;	makes; go about in rags
	Our nibour Pate sin break o' day's	neighbour; since
	Been thumpin at his studdy,	anvil
	An it be true that some fowk says,	If; what; folk
150	Ye'll girn yet in a woody;'	snarl; gallows rope
	Syne wi' her nails she rave his face,	Then; tore
	Made a' his black baird bloody,	beard
	Wi' scarts that day.	scratches

18

	A gilpy that had seen the faught,	lively young man; fight
155	I wat he was nae lang,	know; took not long (time)
	Till he had gather'd seven or aught	eight
	Wild hempies stout and strang;	rogues
	They frae a barn a kaber raught,	rafter reached
	Ane mounted wi' a bang,	with speed
160	Betwisht twa's shoulders, and sat straught	Between; straight
	Upon't, and rade the stang[n]	rode; pole
	On her that day.	

19

The wives and gytlings a' span'd out	children; spread
O'er middings, and o'er dykes,	rubbish heaps, stone walls
165 Wi' mony an unco skirl and shout,	wild shriek
Like bumbees frae their bykes;	bumble-bees; hives
Thro thick and thin they scour'd about,	rushed
Plashin thro dubs and sykes,	Splashing; puddles; streams
And sic a reird ran thro the rout,	such a roar; crowd
170 Gart a' the hale town tykes	Made all; entire; dogs
Yamph loud that day.	Bark

20

But d'ye see foun better bred	how
Was mens-fou Maggy Murdy,	well-behaved
She her man like a lammy led	lamb
175 Hame, wi' a well wail'd wordy:	Home; chosen word
Fast frae the company he fled,	
As he had tane the sturdy;[n]	become dizzy
She fleech'd him fairly to his bed,	coaxed
Wi' ca'ing him her burdy,	With calling; sweetheart
180 Kindly that day.	

21

But Lawrie he took out his nap	
Upon a mow of pease,	heap
And Robin spew'd in's ain wife's lap;	in his own
He said it ga'e him ease.	gave
185 Hutchon wi' a three lugged cap,	eared (handled) wood cup
His head bizzin wi' bees,	buzzing
Hit Geordy a mislushios rap,	malicious
And brake the brig o's neese	broke; bridge; nose
Right sair that day.	sore

22

190 Syne ilka thing gae'd arse o'er head,	Then every; went
Chanlers, boord, stools and stowps,	Candlesticks; table; flagons
Flew thro' the house wi' muckle speed,	great
And there was little hopes,	
But there had been some ill done deed,	
195 They gat sic thrawart cowps;	got such perverse tumbles
But a' the skaith that chanc'd indeed,	harm

Was only on their dowps,   backsides
    Wi' faws that day.   falls

23

    Sae whiles they toolied, whiles they drank,   So sometimes; fought
200   Till a' their sense was smor'd,   smothered
And in their maws there was nae mank,   stomachs; lack
    Upon the furms some snor'd: wooden seats
Ithers frae aff the bunkers sank,   Others; benches
    Wi' een like collops scor'd: eyes; minced meat
205 Some ram'd their noddles wi' a clank,   heads; resounding blow
    E'en like a thick scull'd lord,
        On posts that day.

24

    The young good-man to bed did clim,   husband; climb
    His dear the door did lock in;
210 Crap down beyont him, and the rim   Crept; beyond
    O'er wame he clapt' his dock on: her belly; buttocks
She fand her lad was not in trim,   found
    And be this same good token,
That ilka member, lith and limb,   every; joint
215   Was souple like a doken,   supple; dock (a soft plant)
        'Bout him that day.

10. John Skinner, *The Christmass Bawing of Monimusk*, 1739

The Reverend John Skinner (1721–1807) was the highly esteemed Episcopal minister of Langside, Aberdeenshire, during most of his long life. He also pursued as an avocation a career as a talented poet and songwriter. He was greatly admired by Burns, who especially liked his song of 'Tullochgorum' (the 'best Scotch song ever Scotland saw'), and who corresponded with him in 1787 and 1788. Burns certainly knew 'The Christmass Bawing' as well since there is an echo of it in 'Tam o' Shanter'.

This poem, inspired by Skinner's admiration of both the old 'Christis Kirk' and Ramsay's sequels, is a major effort produced very early in the poet's life (1739) when he was only about eighteen years old and serving as assistant schoolmaster at Monymusk, Aberdeenshire. Skinner is said to have known the original 'Christis Kirk' by heart before he was twelve years of age. At any rate, his own work is a very substantial one (315 lines) that apparently circulated in manuscript until 1788 when it was finally printed in the *Caledonian Magazine*. For his verse form Skinner followed in the octave the extremely difficult two-rime pattern with heavy alliteration of 'Christis Kirk', while adopting the later simplified tag-line used by Ramsay and ending in 'that day'. The poem was probably based on an actual game at Monymusk (eighteen miles west of Aberdeen) while Skinner was there, and it includes several Aberdeenshire dialect words and pronunciations. Skinner goes farther than Ramsay in using very colloquial diction for an old-fashioned effect in this entertaining piece.

1

Has never in a' this country been   — Such shouldering; falling
  Sic shoudering and sic fawing,
As happent twa, three days senseen,   — since
  Here at the Christmass Ba'ing: — Football game
5 At evening syne the fallows keen,   — then; fellows
  Drank till the neist day's dawing   — next; dawning
Sae snell that some tint baith their een,   — keenly; lost use of both; eyes
  And coudna pay their lawing   — could not; bill
    For a' that day.

2

10 Like bumbees bizzing frae a bike,[n]   bumble bees buzzing; hive
        Whan hirds their riggins tirr,   herds; roofs strip off
    The swankies lap thro' mire and slike,   agile fellows leaped; mud
        Wow! as their heads did birr: were confused
    They yowph'd the ba' frae dike to dike,   swiped; ball; stone wall
15   Wi' unco' speed and virr,   amazing; vigour
    Some baith their shoulders up did fyke,   hitch
        For blythness some did flirr   grind
            Their teeth that day.

3

    Rob Roy,[n] I wot, he was na dull,
20   He first loot at the ba',   aimed
    And wi' a rap clash'd Geordy's skull,   struck
        Hard to the steeple wa':   wall
    Wha was aside but auld Tam Tull,   close by; old
        His frien's mishap he saw,
25 Syne brein'd like ony baited bull,   Then bellowed
        And wi' a thud dang twa   knocked two
            To th' yird that day.   earth, ground

4

    The hurry-burry now began,   excited bustle
        Was right well worth the seeing,
30 Wi' bensils bauld tweish man and man,   violent blows; between
        Some getting fa's, some gieing,   falls; giving
    And a' the tricks o' foot and hand,
        That ever were in being:
    Sometimes the ba' a yirdlins ran,   along the ground
35   Sometimes in air was fleeing
            Fou heigh that day.   Full high

5

    The tanner was a primpit bit,   conceited prig
        And light like ony feather,
    He thought it best to try a hit,
40   Ere a' the thrang shoud gather: all the crowd
    He flew wi' neither fear nor wit,
        As fou' o' wind's a bladder,   full
    Unluckily he tint the fit   lost his footing

Aud tann'd his ain bum-leather	own behind
45 Fell well that day.	Very

6

Syne Francy Winsy steppit in,	Then; stepped
A sauchin slav'ry slype,[n]	flabby drooling lout
Ran forrat wi' a fearfu' din,	forward
And drew a swingeing swype,	sweeping blow
50 But hieland Tammy thought nae sin	highland
T' come o'er him wi' a snype,	sharp blow
Levell'd his nose maist wi' his chin,	almost
And gart his swall'd een sype	made; swollen eyes leak
Sawt tears that day.	Salt

7

55 Bockin red bleed the fleip mair cawm,	Gushing; blood; oaf more calm
Ran to the house to mammie,	
'Alas,' co' Katie when she saw him,	quoth, said
'Wha did you this, my lammie?'	little lamb
'A muckle man,' co' he, 'foul fa' him,	large; foul befall
60 They ca' him hieland Tammie,	call
Rax'd me alang the chafts a whawm	Dealt; jaw; blow
As soon as ever he saw me,	
And made me blae.'[n]	cry, bleat (like a lamb)

8

'Waeworth his chandler chafts,' co' Kate,	Curse; lantern jaws
65 'Deil rax his saul a whang,	The Devil deal; soul; blow
Gin I had here the countra skate	If; country lout
Sae beins I shoud him bang.'	That being so
The gilpy glowr'd and leuk'd fell blate	fellow stared; very sheepish
To see'r in sic a sang,	see her; such a fuss
70 He squeel'd to her like a young gyte,	goat
But wadna mird to gang	would not dare to go
Back a' that day.	

9

Stout Steen gart mony a fallow stoyt	made; fellow stagger
And flang them down like faill,	flung; turf
75 Said he'd nae care ae clypit doyt[n]	a clipped small coin
Tho' a' should turn their taill,	

	But wi' a yark Gib made his queet,	hard knock; ankle
	As dwabill as a flail,	flexible
	And o'er fell he, maist like to greet,	most; weep, cry
80	Just at the westmost gaill	gable end-wall
	O' th' kirk that day.	church

10

	In came the inset dominie,[n]	substitute teacher
	Just riftin frae his dinner,	belching
	A young Mess John as ane cou'd see,	Minister
85	Was neither saint nor sinner:	
	A brattlin band unhappilie,	noisy
	Drave by him wi' a binner,	Drove; rumbling noise
	And heels-o'er-gowdie cowpit he,	head over heels fell
	And rave his guid horn penner	broke; pen box
90	In twa that day.	two

11

	Leitch lent the ba' a lounrin lick,	heavy wallop
	She flew fast lik a stane,	like a stone
	Syne lightit whare faes were maist thick,	Then landed; foes; most
	Gart ae gruff grunshy grane:	Made one; big fellow groan
95	The cawrl whoppit up a stick,	fellow whipped
	I wot he was na fain,	not happy
	Leitch wi's fit gae him sic a kick,	with his foot gave; such
	Till they a' thought him slain	
	That very day.	

12

100	Was nae ane there coud Cowley bide,	no one; stand, tolerate
	The gryte gudman, nor nane,	big farmer; nor anyone
	He stenn'd bawk-height[n] at ilka stride,	leaped joist-high; every
	And rampag'd thro' the green:	
	For the Kirk-yard was braid and wide,	Churchyard; broad
105	And o'er a knabliech stane,	large lumpy stone
	He rumbled down a rammage glyde,	uneven opening
	And peel'd the gardie-bane	arm bone
	O' him that day.	

13

	His cousin was a bierly swank,	well-built fellow

110 A stier young man heght Robb,   sturdy; called
     To mell wi' twa he wadna mank   brawl; would not fail
       At staffy-nevel job: a fight with clubs and fists
     I wat na fow,[n] but on a bank,   know not how
       Whare thrangest was the mob,   Where thickest
115 The cousins bicker'd wi' a clank,   fought; loud noise
       Gart ane anither sob   Made one another
         And gasp that day.

14

     Tho' Rob was stout, his cousin dang   knocked
       Him down wi' a gryte shudder,   great
120 Syne a' the drochlin hempy thrang   Then; dawdling roguish mob
       Gat o'er him wi' a fudder: Got; sudden rush
     Gin he shou'd rise, an' hame o'er gang,   If; home; go
       Lang was he in a swidder,   Long; state of indecision
     For bleed frae's mou and nize did bang,   blood; mouth; nose; burst
125   And in braid burns did bludder   broad streams; make bloody
         His face that day.

15

     A huddrin hynd came wi' his pattle,   slovenly ploughman; staff
       As he'd been at the pleugh,   plough
     Said there was nane in a the battle,   no one; all
130   That broolzied bend aneugh.   fought bravely enough
     But i' the mids' o's windy tattle,   of his chatter
       A chiel came wi' a feugh,   fellow; sharp blow
     Box'd him on 's arse wi' a bauld brattle,   bold noisy onset
       Till a' the kendlins leuch   youngsters laughed
135   At him that day.

16

     A stalwart stirk in tartain claise,   sturdy young man; clothes
       Sware mony a sturdy aith,   Swore; oath
     To bear the ba' thro' a' his faes,   ball; all his foes
       And nae kepp muckle skaith: not suffer much harm
140 Rob Roy heard the frieksome fraise,   wild bragging talk
       Well browden'd in his graith,   adorned; clothes
     Gowph'd him alang his shins a blaise,   Struck; along; blow
       And gart him tyne his faith   made; lose
         And feet that day.

17

145 His neipor[n] was a man o' might,   neighbour
    Was few there cou'd ha quell'd him,
He didna see the dreary sight,
    Till some yap gilpy tell'd him: eager young fellow
To Robin syne he flew outright,   then
150   As he'd been gawing to geld him,   going
But suddenly frae some curst wight,   fellow
    A clammyhowat fell'd him   severe blow
        Hawf dead that day.   Half

18

The prior's man, a chiel as stark   fellow; strong
155   Amaist as giant cou'd be,   Almost
Had kent afore o' this day's wark,   known before; work
    For certain that it wou'd be:
He ween'd to drive in o'er the park,   intended
    And ilkane thought it shou'd be: everyone
160 What way it was he miss'd the mark,
    I canna tell, but fou'd be[n]   however it be (was)
        He fell that day.

19

Ere he wan out o' that foul lair,   Before; escaped; mire
    That black mischance had gi'en him,   given
165 There tumbl'd a mischievous pair
    O' mawtent lolls aboon him: lazy idlers on top of him
It wad ha made your heart fou sair,   would have; very sore
    Gin ye had only seen him,   If
An't had na been for Davy Mair,   If it had not
170   The rascals had ondane him,   undone, ruined
        Belyve that day.   Quickly

20

But waes my heart for Petry Gibb,   sad is my heart
    The carlie's head was scawt,   fellow's; scabby
It gat a fell uncanny skib,   got; severe, violent crack
175   That gart him yowl and claw't: made; howl
So he took gate to hodge to Tibb,   started off to hobble
    And spy at hame some fawt;   home; fault (in his wife)
I thought he might ha' gotn a snib,   have gotten; cut

Sae thought ilk ane that saw't   So; everyone
180   O' th' green that day.   On the

21

The Taylor Hutchin he was there,
    A curst illtrickit spark,   mischievous
Saw Pate had caught a camshuch care   unlucky hurt
    At this unsonsy wark: treacherous business
185 He stood na lang to seek his lare,[n]   not long; his learning (?)
    But wi' a yawfou' yark,   awful whack
Whare Pate's richt spawl by hap was bare,   right leg by chance
    He derfly dang the bark   roughly knocked
        Frae 's shin that day.   From his

22

190 Poor Petry gae a weary winch,   wince
    He coudna do but bann;   swear, curse
The taylor baith his sides did pinch,
    Wi' laughing out o' hand:
He jee'd na out o' that an inch,   budged not
195   Afore a menseless man,   Before; boorish
Came a' at anes athort his hinch   all at once across; haunch
    A sowph, and gart him pran   blow; made; bruise
        His arse that day.

23

The town sutor like Laury lap[n]   shoemaker like the Fox leaped
200   Three fit at ilka stenn,   feet; every jump
He didna miss the ba' ae chap,   ball one (single) stroke
    Ilk ane did him commenn: Everyone; commend, praise
But a lang trypal there was snap,   one tall thin fellow; eager
    Came on him wi' a benn,   bound
205 Gart him ere ever he wist cry clap   Made; dash noisily down
    Upon his nether end,
        And there he lay.

24

Sanny soon saw the sutor slain,   Sandy (Alexander); cobbler
    He was his ain hawf-brither;   own half-brother
210 I wat mysell he was fou' brain,   very angry
    And how cou'd he be ither?   otherwise

He ran to help wi' might and main,
   Twa buckl'd wi'm the gether,   with him together
Wi' a firm gowph he fell'd the t'ane   punch; the one
215   But wi' a gowph the tither   blow the other
       Fell'd him that day.

25

The millart lad, a souple fallow,   miller; supple
   Ran 's he had been red wood,   demented
He fether'd fierce like ony swallow,   flew
220   Cry'd hegh at ilka thud: Panted noisily; every
A stiblart gurk wi' phiz o' yellow   sturdy young lad; face
   In youthit's sappy bud,   youth's (youth-head's)
Nae twa there wadha gart him wallow,   would have made
   Wi' fair play i' the mud
225   On's back that day.

26

Tam Tull upon him kiest his ee,   cast his eye
   Saw him sae mony foolzie,   trample down
He green'd again some prott to pree,   longed; trick; try
   An' raise anither bruilzie: another broil
230 Up the kirk-yard he fast did jee,   move
   I wat he was na hooly,   not slow
And a' the ablachs glowr'd to see   good-for-nothings stared
   A bonny kind o' toolzie   fight
       Atween them twae.   Between; two

27

235 The millart never notic'd Tam,   miller
   Sae browden'd he the ba',   So intent was he on
He rumbl'd rudely like a ram,
   Dang o'er whiles ane, whiles twa: Knocked over sometimes
The traitor in afore him came,
240   Ere ever he him saw,
Rawght him a rap o' the forestamm,   Struck; forehead
   But hadna time to draw
       Anither sae.

28

Afore he cou'd step three inch back,

245 The millart drew a knife,
    A curst-like gully and a snack,   large knife; a sharp one
        Was made, fowk said, in Fife: folk
    The lave their thumbs did blythely knack,   rest; snap
        To see the sturty strife,   contentious, quarrelsome
250 But Tam, I ken, wadha gien a plack,   would have given 4 pennies
        T' ha been safe wi' his wife   To have
            At hame that day.   home

29

The parish-clerk came up the yard,
    A man fou' meek o' mind,   very
255 Right jinsh he was and fell well fawr'd,   spruce; very well favoured
        His claithing was fou' fine: clothing; very
    Just whare their feet the dubs had glaar'd   puddles; muddied
        And brew'd them a' like brine,   stained
    Daft Davy Don wi' a derf dawrd,   fierce, violent dash
260   Beft o'er the grave divine   Knocked
            On 's bum that day.

30

When a' were pitying sic mishap,   such
    And swarm'd about the clark,   clerk
    Wi' whittles some his hat did scrap,   knives; scrape
265   Some dighted at his sark: wiped; shirt
    Will Winter gae the ba' a chap,   gave; a stroke
        He ween'd he did a wark,   thought; did a good job
    While Sanny wi' a well-wyl'd wap,   well chosen blow
        Yowph'd her in o'er the park   Knocked her (the ball)
270   A space and mae.   A pace (yard) and more

31

Wi' that Rob Roy gae a rair,   gave a roar
    A rierfou' rowt rais'd he,   frantic roar
    Twas hard, they said, three mile and mair,   heard; more
        Wha likes may crydit gie: may credit give (believe)
275 His paughty heart was fou' o cair,   proud; distress
    And knell'd fell sair to see   throbbed very sorely
    The cleverest callant that was there,   young man
        Play himsell sic a slee   such a cunning
            Begeck that day.   trick

32

280 Jock Jalop shouted like a gun,
        As something had him ail'd,
    'Fy sirs,' quo' he, 'the bonspale's win,   match is won
        And we the ba' have hail'd.'   carried over the goal line
    Some grien'd for ae hawf hour's mair fun,   yearned; one half; more
285   'Cause fresh and nae sair fail'd,   Because; not sorely worn out
    Ithers did Sanny great thanks cunn,   Others; express
        And thro' their haffats trail'd   locks of hair
            Their nails that day.

33

    Syne a' consentit to be freins,   Then; friends
290   And lap like suckand fillies,   leaped; suckling (silly)
    Some redd their hair, some main'd their banes, tidied; moaned over; bones
        Some bann'd the bangsom billies: cursed; quarrelsome fellows
    The pensy lads dosst down on stanes,   sensible; flopped down; stones
        Whopt out their snishin-millies,   Whipped; snuff boxes
295 And a' were fain to tak' their einds   breaths
        And club a pint o' Lillie's   contribute (to buy)
            Best ale that day.

34

    In Monimuss was never seen
        Sae mony well beft skins,[n]   beaten
300 Of a' the ba'-men there was nane   football players; none
        But had twa bleedy shins: two bloody
    Wi' streinzeit shoulders mony ane   sprained
        Dree'd penance for their sins,   Suffered
    And what was warst, scowp'd hame, them lane,   worst; scurried home alone
305   Maybe to hungry inns   houses, dwellings
            And cauld that day.   cold

FINIS   THE END

Ad lectorem peroratio   A summary to the reader
    Now, cankart carl, wha-e'er ye be,   bad tempered fellow; whoever
        Of lay or haly calling,   holy
    Gin ye shou'd ever chance to see   If
310   This auld Scots way o' scrawling,   old
    Ye'd better steik your gab awee,   shut; mouth a little
        Nor plague me wi' your bawling,

In case ye find that I can gie   give
    Your censorship a mawling,
315   Some orra day.   other

11. Robert Fergusson, *Hallow-fair*, 1772

Robert Fergusson (1750–1774) was an obscure legal clerk in Edinburgh when he suddenly burst upon the literary scene in 1772. Both of his parents were from Aberdeenshire and had moved to Edinburgh where his father secured a low-paying clerical post. Robert, after four years at the University of St Andrews, ended up in a similar dismal position as a copyist of endless legal documents.

Since his St Andrews days (1764–1768), however, Fergusson had been experimenting with poetry, and he became a regular contributor to Ruddiman's *Weekly Magazine, or Edinburgh Amusement* in 1771, producing insipid poems in sentimental English before abruptly shifting to Scots in January 1772 with 'The Daft Days', the first of many brilliant satires on the follies of city life in Edinburgh. In all, during his two brief but prolific years of creative power (1772–1773) Fergusson published over thirty Scots poems, both comic and serious, of generally high artistic merit. These pieces constitute the finest body of poetry in Scots of the eighteenth century before Burns.

As a social satirist of Edinburgh life Fergusson was almost inevitably drawn to the *Christis Kirk* genre, a medium in which he produced three major poems: 'Hallow-fair', 'Leith Races', and 'The Election'. In the first two of these Fergusson was working in a more or less traditional vein, describing annual festivities in Auld Reekie. But in 'The Election' Fergusson was breaking new ground in extending the subject matter of the genre into political satire. In all three he raised the *Christis Kirk* form to a new level of artistic excellence for the eighteenth century.

In 'Hallow-fair', his first attempt in this genre, Fergusson introduced an important modification in the traditional stanza by loosening the rime scheme of the octave with four instead of two rimes (A B A B / C D C D / F), a change that Burns was to adopt in 'Halloween' and 'The Holy Fair'. Furthermore, Fergusson showed that this kind of poetry was an ideal vehicle for him, since it called for the lively, swift-paced method of description at which he was already adept. From the tradtional point of view of a detached, amused observer, we get in this poem a series of vivid vignettes of various kinds of folk at this annual fair in the first week of November – maidens seeking boy friends, brewers, beggars, tinkers, horse traders, fortune tellers, Aberdeen peddlers, recruiting sergeants, and the notorious City Guard of Edinburgh – a rich

panorama, full of life, colour, noise, and general confusion. This is
Fergusson in his spriteliest style.

1

At Hallowmas,[n] whan nights grow lang,
    And starnies shine fu' clear,   *stars*
Whan fock, the nippin cald to bang,   *folk; cold; overcome*
    Their winter hap-warms wear,   *warm clothes*
5 Near Edinbrough a fair there hads,   *holds, is held*
    I wat there's nane whase name is,   *know*
For strappin dames and sturdy lads,
    And cap and stoup, mair famous   *wooden cup; flagon*
        Than it that day.

2

10 Upo' the tap o' ilka lum   *top; every chimney*
    The sun began to keek,   *peep*
And bad the trig made maidens come   *neat*
    A sightly joe to seek   *good-looking sweetheart*
At Hallow-fair, whare browsters rare   *brewers, ale-wives*
15   Keep gude ale on the gantries,   *barrel stands*
And dinna scrimp ye o' a skair   *stint; share*
    O' kebbucks frae their pantries,   *cheeses*
        Fu' saut that day.   *Very salty*

3

Here country John in bonnet blue,
20   An' eke his Sunday's claise on,   *also; clothes*
Rins after Meg wi' rokelay new,   *Runs; mantle*
    An' sappy kisses lays on;   *juicy*
She'll tauntin say, 'Ye silly coof!   *fool*
    Be o' your gab mair spairin;'   *mouth*
25 He'll tak the hint, and criesh her loof   *grease; palm*
    Wi' what will buy her fairin,   *treat from the fair*
        To chow that day.   *chew*

4

Here chapmen billies[n] tak their stand,   *peddlers*
    An' shaw their bonny wallies;   *show; trinkets*
30 Wow, but they lie fu' gleg aff hand   *very cleverly off hand*
    To trick the silly fallows: *fellows*

Heh, Sirs! what cairds and tinklers come,   *vagabonds; tinsmiths*
    An' ne'er-do-weel horse-coupers,   *horse-traders*
An' spae-wives fenying to be dumb,   *fortune tellers; pretending*
35   Wi' a' siclike landloupers,   *such vagabonds*
      To thrive that day.

5

Here Sawny[n] cries, frae Aberdeen;
    'Come ye to me fa need: *who*
The brawest shanks that e'er were seen
40   I'll sell ye cheap an' guid.   *good*
I wyt they are as protty hose   *know; pretty*
    As come frae weyr or leem: *knitting needle; loom*
Here tak a rug, and shaw's your pose: *bargain; shows us; hoarded cash*
    Forseeth, my ain's but teem   *In truth; own's; empty*
45   An' light this day.'

6

Ye wives, as ye gang thro' the fair,   *go*
    O mak your bargains hooly!   *carefully*
O' a' thir wylie lowns beware,   *those wily rascals*
    Or fegs they will ye spulyie.   *faith!; rob*
50 For fairn-year Meg Thamson got,   *last year*
    Frae thir mischievous villains,   *those*
A scaw'd bit o' a penny note,   *faded*
    That lost a score o' shillins   *shillings*
      To her that day.

7

55 The dinlin drums alarm our ears,   *rattling*
    The serjeant[n] screechs fu' loud,   *full, very*
'A' gentlemen and volunteers
    That wish your country gude,
Come here to me, and I shall gie   *give*
60   Twa guineas and a crown,
A bowl o' punch, that like the sea
    Will soum a lang dragoon   *swim, float; tall*
      Wi' ease this day.'

8

Without the cuissers prance and nicker,   *stallions; whinny*

65   An' our the ley-rig scud;   over; grass field race
      In tents the carles bend the bicker,   men; drink heartily
        An' rant an' roar like wud.   mad
      Then there's sic yellowchin and din,   such yelling
        Wi' wives and wee-anes gablin,   little ones
70 That ane might true they were a-kin   one; believe
        To a' the tongues at Babylon,
           Confus'd that day.

9

      Whan Phoebus ligs in Thetis lap,[n]   lies
        Auld Reikie gies them shelter,   Old Smokey (Edinburgh)
75 Whare cadgily they kiss the cap,   happily; kiss the cup
        An' ca't round helter-skelter.   send it
      Jock Bell gaed furth to play his freaks,   went; tricks
        Great cause he had to rue it,
      For frae a stark Lochaber aix[n]   axe
80   He gat a clamihewit,   heavy blow
           Fu' sair that night.   sore

10

      'Ohon!' quo' he, 'I'd rather be   Alas!
        By sword or bagnet stickit,   bayonet
      Than hae my crown or body wi'
85 Sic deadly weapons nicket.'   cut
      Wi' that he gat anither straik   another stroke
        Mair weighty than before,   more
      That gar'd his feckless body aik,   made; feeble; ache
        An' spew the reikin gore,   steaming
90   Fu' red that night.

11

      He peching on the cawsey lay,   gasping; street
        O' kicks and cuffs weel sair'd;   well served
      A highland aith[n] the serjeant gae,   oath; gave
        'She maun pe see our guard.'   He must; seen by
95 Out spak the weirlike corporal,   warlike
        'Pring in ta drunken sot.'   Bring; the
      They trail'd him ben, an' by my saul,   inside; soul
        He paid his drunken groat[n]
           For that neist day.   next

12

100	Good fock, as ye come frae the fair,	folk
	Bide yont frae this black squad;	stay away
	There's nae sic savages elsewhere	no such
	Allow'd to wear cockade.	
	Than the strong lion's hungry maw,	
105	Or tusk o' Russian bear,	
	Frae their wanruly fellin paw	unruly killing
	Mair cause ye hae to fear	more
	Your death that day.	

13

	A wee soup drink dis unco weel	little drop; does very
110	To had the heart aboon;	hold; up
	It's good as lang's a canny chiel	careful fellow
	Can stand steeve in his shoon.	steadily; shoes
	But gin a birkie's owr weel sair'd,	if; lad's too well served
	It gars him aften stammer	makes; often blunder into
115	To pleys that bring him to the guard,	schemes, sports
	An' eke the council-chawmir,	also; chamber
	Wi' shame that day.	

12. Robert Fergusson, *Leith Races,* 1773

Containing 180 lines, 'Leith Races' is Fergusson's longest effort in the
Christis Kirk genre and an even finer achievement than 'Hallow-fair'.
The poem begins with the narrator meeting 'Mirth' who offers to take
him to the 'Races' on Leith Sands to see the amusing sights there – a
device that inspired Burns's use of 'Fun' as the tour guide in 'The Holy
Fair'. Here again Fergusson employs his modified stanza with four
rimes in the octave. Here again we have a series of sparkling vignettes –
of Edinburgh dames, gamblers, the City Guard (once more), tinkers,
brewers, fishmongers, crooked tricksters – all executed with superb
craftsmanship. In terms of sustained brilliance this is Fergusson's
masterwork in the *Christis Kirk* form.

Leith Races

1

In July month,[n] ae bonny morn,	one
Whan Nature's rokelay green	mantle
Was spread o'er ilka rigg o' corn	every strip of land
To charm our roving een;	eyes
5 Glouring about I saw a quean,	Gazing; young woman
The fairest 'neath the lift;	sky
Her een ware o' the siller sheen,	eyes were; silver
Her skin like snawy drift,	snowy
Sae white that day.	

2

10 Quod she, 'I ferly unco sair,	Said; wonder very sorely
That ye sud musand[n] gae,	should musing go
Ye wha hae sung o' Hallow-fair,	who have
Her winter's pranks and play:	
Whan on Leith-Sands the racers rare,	When
15 Wi' Jocky louns are met,	fellows
Their orro pennies there to ware,	spare; spend
And drown themsel's in debt	
Fu' deep that day.'	

3

'An' wha are ye, my winsome dear,
20   That takes the gate sae early?   road
Whare do ye win, gin ane may spier,   live; if one; ask
For I right meikle ferly,   greatly wonder
That sic braw buskit laughing lass   such well dressed
Thir bonny blinks shou'd gi'e,   Those; glances
25 An' loup like Hebe[n] o'er the grass,   leap
As wanton and as free
Frae dule this day.'   sorrow

4

'I dwall amang the caller springs   dwell; fresh
That weet the Land o' Cakes,[n]   wet, moisten, irrigate
30 And aften tune my canty strings   happy
At bridals and late-wakes:[n]   funeral parties
They ca' me Mirth; I ne'er was kend   call; known
To grumble or look sour,
But blyth wad be a lift to lend,   happy; boost
35   Gif ye wad sey my pow'r   If; would try
An' pith this day.'   strength

5

'A bargain be't, and, by my feggs,   by my faith (truly)
Gif ye will be my mate,   If
Wi' you I'll screw the cheery pegs,   (tune the fiddle)
40   Ye shanna find me blate;   shall not; shy
We'll reel an' ramble thro' the sands,
And jeer wi' a' we meet;   with all
Nor hip the daft and gleesome bands   miss; giddy
That fill Edina's street   Edinburgh's
45   Sae thrang this day.'   crowded

6

Ere servant maids had wont to rise
To seeth the breakfast kettle,   boil
Ilk dame her brawest ribbons tries,   Each; prettiest
To put her on her mettle,
50 Wi' wiles some silly chiel to trap,   fellow
(And troth he's fain to get her,)   truly; eager
But she'll craw kniefly in his crap,[n]   crow; vigorously; stomach

Whan, wow! he canna flit her   get her to move
    Frae hame that day.   From home

7

55 Now, mony a scaw'd and bare-ars'd lown   worthless, scruffy; lad
    Rise early to their wark,   work
Enough to fley a muckle town,   frighten; large
    Wi' dinsome squeel and bark.   noisy
'Here is the true an' faithfu' list
60   O' noblemen and horses;
Their eild, their weight, their height, their grist,   age; size
    That rin for plates or purses   run
    Fu' fleet this day.'

8

To whisky plooks that brunt for wooks   pimples; burned; weeks
65   On town-guard soldiers' faces,
Their barber bauld his whittle crooks,   bold; razor
    An' scrapes them for the races:
Their stumps erst us'd to filipegs,   legs once; the kilt
    Are dight in spaterdashes,   dressed; gaiters
70 Whase barkent hides scarce fend their legs   tanned
    Frae weet, and weary plashes   wet; splashes
    O' dirt that day.

9

'Come, hafe a care[n] (the captain cries),   have
    On guns your bagnets thraw;   bayonets twist
75 Now mind your manual exercise,
    An' marsh down raw by raw.'   march; row
And as they march he'll glowr about,   glare
    'Tent a' their cuts and scars: Notice all
'Mang them fell mony a gausy snout   very many a handsome nose
80   Has gusht in birth-day wars,[n]
    Wi' blude that day.   blood

10

Her nanesel maun be carefu' now,   Herself (=we) must
    Nor maun she pe misleard,   must; be ill-bred
Sin baxter lads[n] hae seal'd a vow   Since baker lads
85   To skelp and clout the guard: beat; hit

I'm sure Auld Reikie kens o' nane — Old Smokey (Edinburgh) knows
    That wou'd be sorry at it,
Tho' they should dearly pay the kane, — penalty
    An' get their tails weel sautit — salted, punished
90   And sair thir days. — sore those

11

The tinkler billies i' the Bow[n] — tinsmith fellows
    Are now less eidant clinking, — busy
As lang's their pith or siller dow, — strength; cash allow
    They're daffin', and they're drinking. — carousing
95 Bedown Leith-walk[n] what burrochs reel — Down; crowds, clusters
    Of ilka trade and station, — every
That gar their wives an' childer feel — make; children
    Toom weyms for their libation — Empty bellies
        O' drink thir days. — those

12

100 The browster wives thegither harl — ale-wives together drag
    A' trash that they can fa' on; — obtain
They rake the grounds o' ilka barrel, — dregs; every
    To profit by the lawen: — tavern bill
For weel wat they a skin leal het — know; very hot
105   For drinking needs nae hire; — no inducement
At drumbly gear they take nae pet; — impure stuff; no offence
    Foul water slockens fire — quenches
        And drouth thir days. — thirst those

13

They say, ill ale has been the deid — bad; death
110   O' mony a beirdly lown; — sturdy lad
Then dinna gape like gleds wi' greed — do not; kites
    To sweel hail bickers down; — swill whole wooden cups
Gin Lord send mony ane the morn,[n] — If; many a one
    They'll ban fu' sair the time — curse very sorely
115 That e'er they toutit aff the horn — drank off the cup
    Which wambles thro' their weym — rumbles queasily; belly
        Wi' pain that day.

14

The Buchan bodies[n] thro' the beech — beach, seashore

Their bunch of Findrums cry,[n] — smoked haddocks
120 An' skirl out baul', in Norland speech, — shriek; boldly; northern
'Gueed speldings, fa will buy.' — Good haddocks; who
An', by my saul, they're nae wrang gear — soul; not bad stuff
To gust a stirrah's mow; — please; fellow's mouth
Weel staw'd wi' them, he'll never spear — Well stuffed; ask
125 The price o' being fu' — drunk
Wi' drink that day.

15

Now wyly wights at rowly powl,[n] — cunning men; (a game of skill)
An' flingin' o' the dice,
Here brake the banes o' mony a soul[n] — broke; bones
130 Wi' fa's upo' the ice: — falls
At first the gate seems fair an' straught, — road; straight
So they had fairly till her; — hold; to
But wow! in spite o' a' their maught, — might, skill
They're rookit o' their siller — robbed; silver
135 An' goud that day. — gold

16

Around whare'er ye fling your een, — eyes
The haiks like wind are scourin'; — hacks (hired coaches); racing
Some chaises honest folk contain, — carriages
An' some hae mony a whore in; — have
140 Wi' rose and lilly, red and white,
They gie themselves sic fit airs, — give; such pretentious
Like Dian,[n] they will seem perfite; — perfect
But its nae goud that glitters — not gold
Wi' them thir days. — those

17

145 The Lyon[n] here, wi' open paw,
May cleek in mony hunder, — seize; hundreds
Wha geck at Scotland and her law, — mock
His wyly talons under; — clever claws
For ken, tho' Jamie's laws[n] are auld, — know; James VI's; old
150 (Thanks to the wise recorder),
His Lyon yet roars loud and bawld, — bold
To had the Whigs[n] in order — hold; (upstarts)
Sae prime this day. — So drunk

18

To town-guard drum of clangor clear,
155   Baith men and steeds are raingit;   *Both; lined up*
Some liveries red or yellow wear,
    And some are tartan spraingit;   *striped*
And now the red, the blue e'en-now
    Bids fairest for the market;
160 But, 'ere the sport be done, I trow   *believe*
    Their skins are gayly yarkit   *badly bruised*
    And peel'd thir days.   *those*

19

Siclike in Robinhood[n] debates,   *Just as*
    Whan twa chiels hae a pingle;   *two fellows; quarrel*
165 E'en-now some couli gets his aits,   *low fellow; deserts*
    An' dirt wi' words they mingle,
Till up loups he, wi' diction fu',   *jumps; words full*
    There's lang and dreech contesting;   *long; dull*
For now they're near the point in view;
170   Now ten miles frae the question
    In hand that night.

20

The races o'er, they hale the dools,[n]   *celebrate wildly*
    Wi' drink o' a' kin-kind;   *every kind*
Great feck gae hirpling hame like fools,   *numbers go hobbling home*
175   The cripple lead the blind.
May ne'er the canker o' the drink   *affliction*
    E'er make our spirits thrawart,   *ill-humoured*
'Case we git wharewitha' to wink   *In case; get wherewithal*
    Wi' een as blue's a blawart   *eyes; bluebell*
180   Wi' straiks thir days!   *blows those*

13. Robert Fergusson, *The Election*, 1773

This is the first instance of the *Christis Kirk* genre used as a vehicle for political satire, and it works very well. Fergusson here is exposing the deep corruption in Edinburgh municipal politics, with fantastically complicated procedures which are guaranteed to keep the same councillors in power in a self-perpetuating oligarchy. He concentrates, however, on the election of the lower class representatives – the 'deacons' of the various 'trades' in the Town Council – and on the luxurious drunken party given by the victorious candidates. In so doing Fergusson is able to make fun of the pretentious strutting of the tradesmen on this occasion, of their coarseness and greed, as well as their good-natured reconciliations when sober the next morning. The result is a satire that is both devastating and hilarious.

In this poem Fergusson makes yet another modification of the verse form, this time compromising with three rimes in the octave (A B A B / A C A C / D), in search of a perfect balance.

Nunc est bibendum, et bendere BICKERUM *magnum;*
Cavete TOWN-GUARDUM, *Dougal Geddum atque Campbellum.*[n]

1

Rejoice, ye Burghers, ane an' a',	Citizens; one and all
Lang look's for's come at last;	Long looked for has
Sair war your backs held to the wa'	Sorely were; wall
Wi' poortith an' wi' fast:	poverty
5 Now ye may clap your wings an' craw,	crow
And gayly busk ilk' feather,	dress each
For Deacon Cocks hae pass'd a law[n]	
To rax an' weet your leather	stretch; wet
Wi' drink thir days.	these

2

10 'Haste, Epps,' quo' John, 'an' bring my gez,	Elizabeth; wig
Take tent ye dinna't spulyie:	care; spoil
Last night the barber ga't a friz,	gave it a curl
An' straikit it wi' ulzie.	stroked; oil

91

Hae done your paritch lassie Liz,   Have; porridge
15 Gi'e me my sark an' gravat;   Give; shirt; scarf
I'se be as braw's the Deacon is   I'll; handsome as
    Whan he taks affidavit   takes the oath
        O' faith[n] the day.'

3

'Whar's Johnny gaun,' cries neebor Bess,   going; neighbour
20 'That he's sae gayly bodin   arrayed
Wi' new kam'd wig, weel syndet face,   combed; washed
    Silk hose, for hamely hodin?'   instead of homely homespun
'Our Johny's nae sma' drink you'll guess,   no small beer (unimportant)
    He's trig as ony muir-cock,   smart; male grouse
25 An' forth to mak a Deacon, lass:
    He downa speak to poor fock   will not
        Like us the day.'

4

The coat ben-by i' the kist-nook,   in inner room; chest corner
    That's been this towmonth swarmin,   twelvemonth
30 Is brought yence mair thereout to look,   once more
    To fleg awa the vermin: scare away
Menyies o' moths an' flaes are shook,   crowds; fleas
    An' i' the floor they howder,   swarm
Till in a birn beneath the crook   heap; hook hung over fire
35   They're singit wi' a scowder   singed; scorching
        To death that day.

5

The canty cobler quats his sta',   happy; quits; stall
    His rozet an' his lingans;   resin; threads
His buik has dree'd a sair, sair fa'   body; suffered; sore decline
40 Frae meals o' bread an' ingans: From; onions
Now he's a pow o' wit an' law,   head
    An' taunts at soals an' heels;   soles
To Walker's[n] he can rin awa,   run away
    There whang his creams an' jeels   slice; jellies
45   Wi' life that day.   vigour

6

The lads in order tak their seat,

(The de'il may claw the clungest)	devil; grab; hungriest
They stegh an' connach sae the meat,	stuff; devour so
Their teeth mak mair than tongue haste:	make more
50 Their claes sae cleanly dight an' feat,	clothes; brushed; smart
An' eke their craw-black beavers,	also; crow-black beaver hats
Like masters' mows hae found the gate	mouths; way
To tassels teugh wi' slavers	struggles tough; spittle
Fu' lang that day.	Very long

7

55 The dinner done, for brandy strang	strong
They cry, to weet their thrapple.	wet; throat
To gar the stamack bide the bang,	make; stomach cope with; blow
Nor wi' its laden grapple.	load struggle
The grace is said – its no o'er lang;	not overly long
60 The claret reams in bells;	red wine foams; bubbles
Quod Deacon, 'Let the toast round gang,[n]	Said; go
Come, here's our noble sel's	selves
Weel met the day.'	

8

'Weels me o' drink,' quo' cooper Will,	Blessings on
65 'My barrel has been geyz'd ay,	warped from dryness
An' has na gotten sic a fill	such
Sin fu' on handsel-Teysday:[n]	Since full; New Year's Tuesday
But makes-na, now it's got a sweel,	no matter; swill
Ae gird I shanna cast lad,	barrel hoop; shall not
70 Or else I wish the horned de'el	devil
May Will wi' kittle cast dad	clever throw dash
To hell the day.'	today

9

The Magistrates fu' wyly are,	full cunning
Their lamps[n] are gayly blinking,	
75 But they might as leive burn elsewhere,	as well
Whan fock's blind fu' wi' drinking.	folk's; drunk
Our Deacon wadna ca' a chair,	would not call; sedan chair
The foul ane durst him na-say;	devil a one (none); contradict
He took shanks-naig, but fient may care,	walked; the devil
80 He arselins kiss'd the cawsey	on his backside; street
Wi' bir that night.[n]	With force

10

Weel loes me o' you, souter Jock[n]   My blessings on you, cobbler
    For tricks ye buit be trying,   must
Whan greapin for his ain bed-stock,   groping; footboard of bed
85   He fa's whare Will's wife's lying,   falls
Will coming hame wi' ither fock,   other folk
    He saw Jock there before him;
Wi' master laiglen, like a brock   chamber pot; badger
    He did wi' stink maist smore him   almost smother
90   Fu' strang that night.   Very strong

11

Then wi' a souple leathern whang   supple; strap
    He gart them fidge and girn ay,   made; jump; grimace
'Faith, chiel, ye's no for naething gang   fellow; ye'll; go, get away
    Gin ye man reel my pirny.'[n]   If; must; bobbin
95 Syne wi' a muckle alshin lang   Then; big long awl
    He brodit Maggie's hurdies;   jabbed; buttocks
An' 'cause he thought her i' the wrang,   wrong
    There pass'd nae bonny wordies
        'Mang them that night.   Among

12

100 Now, had some laird his lady fand   lord; found
    In sic unseemly courses,   such
It might hae loos'd the haly band,   holy bond
    Wi' law-suits an' divorces:
But the niest day they a' shook hands,
105   And ilka crack did sowder,   every; solder (mend)
While Megg for drink her apron pawns,
    For a' the gude-man cow'd her   husband
        Whan fu' last night.   drunk

13

Glowr round the cawsey, up an' down,   Stare; street
110   What mobbing and what plotting!
Here politicians bribe a loun[n]   fellow
    Against his saul for voting.   soul
The gowd that inlakes half a crown   gold; is lacking
    Thir blades lug out to try them,   Those fellows
115 They pouch the gowd, nor fash the town   pocket; gold; bother

For weights an' scales to weigh them
    Exact that day.

14

Then Deacons at the counsel stent   strain
    To get themsel's presentit: presented
120 For towmonths twa their saul is lent[n]   twelvemonths two; soul
    For the town's gude indentit: good, benefit; obligated
Lang's their debating thereanent;   Long is; about it
    About protests[n] they're bauthrin,   fussing
While Sandy Fife,[n] to mak content,
125   On bells plays *Clout* the *caudron*[n]
    To them that day.

15

Ye lowns that troke in doctor's stuff,   fellows; deal
    You'll now hae unco slaisters;   have amazing concoctions
Whan windy blaws their stamacks puff,   drinks; stomachs
130   They'll need baith pills an' plaisters;   both; plasters
For tho' ev'now they look right bluff,   healthy
    Sic drinks, 'ere hillocks meet,   Such; before (soon)
Will hap some Deacons in a truff,   cover; turf
    Inrow'd in the lang leet[n]   enrolled; long list.
135   O' death yon night.

14. John Mayne, *Hallowe'en*, 1780

John Mayne (1759–1836) was a talented poet and songwriter from Dumfries who spent most of his adult life in London as part owner of the *Star* newspaper. His best-known song is 'Logan Braes', written to the tune of 'Logan Water', both of which inspired Burns's lyric beginning 'O, Logan, sweetly didst thou glide'. Burns, in fact, incorporated in his version Mayne's two refrain lines verbatim, while wholly rewriting the rest of the song. As a descriptive poet Mayne's two best works are in the *Christis Kirk* tradition: 'Hallowe'en' and 'The Siller Gun'.

'Hallowe'en', first published in Ruddiman's *Weekly Magazine or Edinburgh Amusement* for November 1780, was inspired by the youthful Mayne's admiration for Robert Fergusson whom he had met during Fergusson's visit to Dumfries in 1773. In turn, Mayne passed on the idea to Burns, who certainly knew this poem since he echoes some of Mayne's imagery in stanzas 11 and 12 of his own 'Halloween'. For his verse form, however, Mayne employs instead of the *Christis Kirk* stanza the six-line *Habbie* stanza made famous in the comic elegy of 'The Life and Death of Habbie Simson, the Piper of Kilbarchan' (*c.* 1640) by Robert Sempill of Beltrees, a form which became the favourite metre of Ramsay and Fergusson, and, later, of Burns himself. In all other respects the poem is in the pure tradition of *Christis Kirk*, describing rustic behaviour from a detached and semi-satirical point of view.

1

Of a' the festivals we hear,
Frae Handsel-Monday till New-Year[n]   First Monday of year
There's few in Scotland held mair dear[n]   more
    For mirth, I ween,   guess
5 Or yet can boast o' better cheer,
    Than Hallowe'en.

2

Langsyne indeed, as now in climes[n]   Long ago
Where priests for siller pardon crimes,   silver, money
The kintry 'round in Popish rhymes   country
10   Did pray and graen;   groan
  But customs vary wi' the times

At Hallowe'en.

3

Ranged round a bleezing ingleside,   *blazing fireside*
Where nowther cauld nor hunger bide,   *neither cold*
15 The farmer's house, wi' secret pride,
     Will a' convene;   *all*
For that day's wark is thrawn aside   *work; thrown*
     At Hallowe'en.

4

Placed at their head the gudewife sits,   *farmer's wife*
20 And deals round apples, pears, and nits;   *nuts*
Syne tells her guests, how, at sic bits   *Then; such places*
     Where she has been,
Bogle's ha'e gart folk tyne their wits   *Ghosts have made; lose*
     At Hallowe'en.

5

25 Grieved, she recounts how, by mischance,
Puir pussy's forced a' night to prance   *The poor cat is; all*
Wi' fairies, wha in thousands dance[n]   *who*
     Upon the green,
Or sail wi' witches ower to France   *over*
30   At Hallowe'en.

6

Syne, issued frae the gardy-chair,   *Then; armchair*
For that's the seat of empire there,
To co'er the table wi' what's rare,   *cover*
     Commands are gi'en;   *given*
35 That a' fu' daintily may fare   *all full (very)*
     At Hallowe'en.

7

And when they've toomed ilk heapit plate,   *emptied each heaped*
And a' things are laid out o' gate,   *out of the way*
To ken their matrimonial mate,   *know*
40   The youngsters keen
Search a' the dark decrees o' fate
     At Hallowe'en.

8

A' things prepared in order due,
Gosh guide's! what fearfu' pranks ensue!   God guide us! (mild oath)
45 Some i' the kiln-pat thraw a clew[n]   kiln chamber throw; yarn ball
        At whilk, bedene,   which, quickly
    The sweethearts by the far end pu'   pull
        At Hallowe'en.

9

Ithers, wi' some uncanny gift,   Others; weird
50 In an auld barn a riddle lift,   coarse-meshed sieve
    Where, thrice pretending corn to sift,
        Wi' charms between,
    Their joe appears, as white as drift,   sweetheart; snow
        At Hallowe'en.

10

55 But 'twere a langsome tale to tell   lengthy
    The gates o' ilka charm and spell.   ways; every
    Ance, gaen to saw hempseed himsel,[n]   Once; going; sow
        Puir Jock Maclean,   Poor
    Plump in a filthy peat-pot fell   peat hole
60   At Hallowe'en.

11

Half filled wi' fear, and droukit weel,   drenched well
He frae the mire dught hardly speel;   could hardly climb
But frae that time the silly chiel   fellow
    Did never grien   yearn
65 To cast his cantrips wi' the Deil   magic spells; Devil
        At Hallowe'en.

12

O Scotland! famed for scenes like this,
That thy sons walk where wisdom is,
Till death in everlasting bliss
70   Shall steek their e'en,[n]   close; eyes
    Will ever be the constant wish
            of
                Jockie Mein.[n]

15. John Mayne, *The Siller Gun*, 1808

Mayne (1759–1836) worked on this poem off and on during most of his long lifetime, producing at least six versions. Beginning with a very brief text (twelve stanzas) in 1777, he steadily expanded the scope of his work over the years – from two 'cantos' in 1779, to three in 1780 and 1783, to four in 1808, and finally to five cantos in 1836, the year of his death.

As in 'Hallowe'en' Mayne here uses the six-line *Habbie* stanza, but his subject matter and methods in all other ways are strictly in the *Christis Kirk* genre. The general scene is that of a traditional shooting competition, or 'Wapenshaw', held in the town of Dumfries on the King's Birthday (4 June). Here the seven incorporated 'trades' of Dumfries vied for the coveted trophy of a silver tube or 'siller gun', presented to the town by King James VI in 1617 to encourage good marksmanship with the rifle. The makeshift weapons of the tradesmen and their bungling performances, the widespread drunkennesss and resulting hangovers, the amusing pictures of military ineptness, the touching pride of the participants and onlookers, the general confusion and uproar – all of these are perfectly characteristic of our genre. Again, as in 'Hallowe'en', Mayne's satire is gentle and good-natured, but in this case far richer, more detailed, with a strong cumulative impact.

Only the first canto (of the four-canto version) is reprinted here.

> *A sight so* rare,
> Makes *Wisdom* smile, *and Folly* staré.
>
> Anon.

CANTO FIRST

1

For loyal feats, and trophies won,
Dumfries[n] shall live till time be done!
Ae simmer's morning, wi' the sun,   One summer's
    The sev'n trades there,[n]
5 Forgather'd, for their siller gun[n]   silver
    To shoot ance mair.   once more

99

2

To shoot ance mair in grand array,
And celebrate the King's birth-day,[n]
Crouds, happy in the gentle sway   crowds
10   Of ane sae dear,
Were proud their fealty to display,
And marshal here.

3

O, George! the best o' kings and men!
For thee our daily pray'rs ascend!
15 Of ilka blessing Heav'n can send,   every
May'st thou ha'e store;   have
And may thy royal race extend
'Till time be o'er!

4

For weeks before this fête sae clever,
20 The fowk were in a perfect fever,   folk
Scouring gun-barrels i' the river –
At marks practizing –   targets
Marching wi' drums and fifes forever –
A' sodgerizing!   All soldiering

5

25 And turning coats, and mending breeks,   breeches, trousers
New-seating where the sark-tail keeks;   shirt-tale peeks out
(Nae matter tho' the cloot that eeks   patch that joins together
Is black or blue);
And darning, with a thousand steeks,   stitches
30   The stockings too.

6

Between the last and this occasion,
Lang, unco lang, seem'd the vacation,   strangely long
To him wha wooes sweet recreation   who
In nature's prime;
35 And him wha likes a day's potation
At ony time.   any

7

The lift was clear, the morn serene,   sky
The sun just glinting owr the scene,   over
When James M'Noe[n] began again
40   To beat to arms,
Rouzing the heart o' man and wean   child (wee one)
    Wi' war's alarms.

8

Frae far and near, the country lads
(Their joes ahint them on their yads),   sweethearts behind; old mares
45 Flock'd in to see the show in squads;   groups
    And, what was dafter,   more foolish
Their pawky mithers and their dads   crafty mothers
    Came trotting after.

9

And mony a beau and belle were there,
50 Doited wi' dozing on a chair;   Stupified
For, lest they'd, sleeping, spoil their hair,
    Or miss the sight,
The gowks, like bairns before a fair,   fools; children
    Sat up a' night!

10

55 Wi' hats as black as ony raven,   any
Fresh as the rose, their beards new-shaven,
And a' their Sunday's cleeding having   all; clothing
    Sae trim and gay,
Forth came our trades, some ora saving   tradesmen; surplus
60   To wair that day.   spend

11

Fair fa' ilk canny caidgy carl!   befall each wise cheerful man
Weel may he bruik his new apparel!   Well; enjoy
And never dree the bitter snarl   suffer
    O' scowling wife;
65 But, blest in pantry, barn, and barrel,
    Be blithe thro' life!

12

Heh, Sirs! what crouds were gather'd round,   Lord!
To see them marching up and down!
Lasses and lads, sun-burnt and brown –
70   Women and weans,   children
Gentle and semple, mingling, crown   Upper and lower (classes)
       The gladsome scenes!

13

Meanwhile, before ilk deacon's dwalling,   each; dwelling
His ain brigade was made to fall in;   own
75 And, while the muster-roll was calling,
       Mull'd ale and wine
Were dealt about in mony a gallon,
       And gardevine: two-quart bottle

14

And cheese-and-bread, and bits o' ham,
80 Laid the foundation for a dram
O' whisky, gin frae Amsterdam,
       Or cherry-brandy;
Whilk after, a' was fish that cam   Which; came
       To Jock or Sandy.

15

85   For well ken they wha loo their chappin,   know; love; drink (quart)
Drink makes the auldest swack and strappen;   oldest supple; strapping
Gars Care forget the ills that happen –   Makes
       The blate, look spruce –   bashful; lively
And e'en the thowless cock their tappin,   listless; head
90   And craw fu' croose!   crow very boldly

16

The muster owr, the diff'rent bands   over
File aff in parties to the Sands,[n]
Where, midst loud laughs and clapping hands,
       Gleed Geordy Smith   squint-eyed
95 Reviews them, and their line expands
       Alang the Nith.   Along

17

And ne'er, for uniform or air,
Was sic a groupe review'd elsewhere!   such
The short, the tall; fat fowk, and spare;   folk; thin
100   Side coats, and dockit;[n]   long coats and shortened ones
Wigs, queus, and clubs, and curly hair;   pigtails; hair worn in a knot
Round hats, and cockit!   cocked, pointed

18

As to their guns – thae fell engines,   those dangerous
Borrow'd or begg'd, were of a' kinds
105 For bloody war, or bad designs,
Or shooting cushies –   wild pigeons
Lang fowling-pieces, carabines,   Long; short rifles
And blunder-busses!

19

Maist feck, tho' oil'd to make them glimmer, Most of their number
110 Hadna been shot for mony a simmer;   summer
And Fame, the story-telling limmer,   bold hussy
Jocosely hints,
That some o' them had bits o' timmer,   wood
Instead o' flints.

20

115 Some guns, she threeps, within her ken,   insists; knowledge
Were spik'd, to let nae priming ben;   no priming inside
And, as in twenty there were ten
Worm-eaten stocks,   wooden parts of rifles
Sae, here and there, a rozit-end   So; piece of resined thread
120   Held on their locks!

21

And then, to show what diff'rence stands
'Tween him that gets, and gi'es commands,   gives
Claymores that, erst, at Prestonpans,[n]   Highlanders' swords; once
Gart faes stand yon',   Made foes; back
125 Were quiv'ring i' the feckless hands   feeble
O' mony a drone!

22

'Ohon!' quo' George, and ga'e a graen,   gave a groan
'The age o' chivalry is gane!'   gone
Syne, having owr and owr again   Then; over
130   The hale survey'd,   whole
Their route, and a' things else, made plain,
He snuff'd, and said:

23

'Now, Gentlemen! now mind the motion,
And dinna, this time, make a botion: do not; botch
135 Shouther your arms! – O! had them tosh on,   Shoulder; hold; straight
And not athraw!   awry
Wheel wi' your right-hands to the ocean,
And march awa!'   away

24

Wi' that, the dinlin drums rebound,   vibrating
140 Fifes, clarionets, and hautboys sound!   oboes
Thro' crouds on crouds, collected round,
The corporations   companies of tradesmen
Trudge aff, whilst Echo's self was drown'd
With acclamations!

25

145 Their steps to martial airs agreeing,
And a' the Sev'n-Trades' colours fleeing,   flying
Bent for the Craigs,[n] O! weel worth seeing!   well
They hy'd awa';   hurried away
Their bauld Convener proud o' being   bold
150   The chief owr a'.   over all

26

Attended by his body-guard,
He stepp'd in gracefu'ness unpair'd!   alone
Straight as the poplar on the swaird,   meadow
And strong as Sampson,
155 Nae eie cou'd look without regard   No eye
On Robin Tamson.

27

His craft, the blacksmith's, first ava,   of all
Led the procession, twa and twa;   two
The squaremen follow'd i' the raw,   carpenters; in the row
160   And syne the weavers,   then
The taylors, souters, skinners a',   shoemakers; all
And marrow-cleavers.   butchers

28

Their journeymen were a' sae gaucy,   so cheerful
Th' apprentices sae kir and saucy,   so lively
165 That, as they gaed alang the causey,   went along; street
Sae tight and braw,   shapely; fine
Th' applauding heart o' mony a lassie
Was stown awa.   stolen away

29

Brisk as a bridegroom gawn to wed,   going
170 Ilk deacon march'd before his trade: Each
Foggies the zig-zag followers led,   Old soldiers
But scarce had pow'r
To keep some, fitter for their bed,
Frae stoit'ring owr.   From keeling over

30

175 For blithesome Sir John Barleycorn   (whisky)
Had sae allur'd them i' the morn,
That, what wi' drams, and mony a horn,
And reaming bicker,   foaming cup
The ferly is, withouten scorn,   wonder
180   They wauk'd sae sicker!   wakened so steady

31

As thro' the town their banners fly,
Frae windows low, frae windows high,
A' that cou'd find a nook to spy,
Were leaning o'er;
185 The street, stair-heads, and carts, forbye,   as well
Were a' uproar!

32

To see his face whom she loo'd best,   loved
Hab's wife was there amang the rest;
And, while wi' joy her sides she prest,
190   Like mony mae,   more
Her exultation was exprest
        In words like thae: these

33

'Wow! but it makes ane's heart lowp light   one's; leap
To see auld fowk sae cleanly dight!   old folk; dressed
195 E'en now our Habby seems as tight   well put together
        As when, lang syne,   long ago
His looks were first the young delight
        And pride o' mine!'

34

But on the meeker maiden's part,
200 Deep sighs alane her love impart!   alone
Deep sighs, the language o' the heart,
        Will aft reveal
A flame which a' the pow'rs of art
        In vain conceal!

35

205 Frae rank to rank while thousands bustle,
In front, like waving corn, they hustle;
Where, deck'd wi' ribbons round its muzzle,
        The Siller Gun,
A trinket like a penny whustle,   whistle
210   Gleam'd i' the sun!

36

Suspended frae a painted pole,
A glimpse o't sae inspir'd the whole,
That auld and young, wi' heart and soul,
        Their heads were cocking,
215 Keen as ye've seen, at bridals droll,
        Maids catch the stocking![n]

37

In honour o' this gaudy thing,
And eke in honour o' the King,   also
A fouth o' flow'rs the gard'ners bring,   plenty
220   And frame sweet posies
Of a' the relics o' the spring,
And simmer's roses!   summer's

38

Amang the flow'ry forms they weave,
There's Adam, to the life, and Eve:
225 She, wi' the apple in her neeve,   fist
Enticing Adam;
While Satan's laughing in his sleeve,
At him and madam!

39

The lily white, the vi'let blue,
230 The heather-bells of azure hue;
And birken chaplets not a few,   of birch
And yellow broom –
Athwart the scented welkin threw   Across; air
A rich perfume!

40

235 Perfume, congenial to the clime,
The sweetest, i' the sweetest time!
The merry bells, in jocund chime,
Rang thro' the air,
And minstrels play'd, in strains sublime,
240   To charm the fair!

41

And fairer than our Nithsdale Fair,
Or handsomer, there's nane elsewhere!
Pure as the streams that murmur there,
In them ye'll find
245 That Virtue and the Graces rare
Are a' enshrin'd!

42

Lang may the bonny bairns recline   Long; children
On Plenty's bosom, saft and kind!
And, O! may I, ere life shall dwine   waste away
250   To its last scene,
Return, and a' my sorrows tine   lose
         At hame again!   home

16. Robert Burns, *A Mauchline Wedding*, 1785

Robert Burns (1759–1796) was, and is, the great national poet of Scotland. He was born in the tiny village of Alloway in Ayrshire, the son of a struggling tenant farmer who never quite 'made it' financially in the bitterly depressed agricultural economy of that time and place. Mainly self-educated, Burns began writing poems and songs at an early age, at first vainly imitating fashionable English poets in the sentimental vein of Gray, Young, and Shenstone. Finally, however, in 1784 Burns began to find his real strength in the Scots poetic heritage, especially as embodied in Fergusson, and turned to native genres like the verse epistle, comic elegy, Scots pastoralism, and the *Christis Kirk* tradition, producing a remarkable series of brilliant poems that made up his volume published obscurely at Kilmarnock in July 1786. This constituted perhaps the most astonishingly good first volume of poetry in all British literary history, and it made Burns instantly famous.

The poet moved to Edinburgh in November 1786 to arrange for a second edition of his poems, larger and far more expensive that the first. This, too, was a huge success. Burns, however, was forced to linger in the city, waiting for his money from the publisher William Creech who was unconscionably slow in paying. At last, in 1788, Burns settled for a new rented farm near Dumfries and the promise of a modest government position in the Excise there. The last four years of the poet's life (1792–1796) were spent as an able Excise officer in Dumfries until his premature death of heart disease at the age of thirty-seven. During the final phase of his creative career (1788–1796) Burns devoted his poetic powers mainly to the writing of songs – new words to traditional tunes – including many of the most beautiful in our culture.

The *Christis Kirk* genre was an ideal medium for Burns, as it had been for Fergusson, and he began his experiments in this form with the fragmentary 'A Mauchline Wedding' in the early autumn of 1785. This piece was never published by Burns, but was embedded in a letter to his middle-aged friend Mrs. Frances Dunlop, dated 21 August 1788. In fact, the fragment was not included in the multitudes of collected editions of Burns's poems until 1896, over a century later. Nevertheless, 'A Mauchline Wedding' is important and fascinating as a first attempt.

This poem, as Burns explained to Mrs. Dunlop, was based on a real wedding in the village of Mauchline, Ayrshire, where Burns was living at the time, and was intended to make fun of the pretensions of a local family. It was probably never meant for publication and was broken off when the poet became reconciled with the girl whose family was involved. The five stanzas that Burns completed are generally lively and skilful in style. For his verse form Burns here adopted Fergusson's modification of the *Christis Kirk* stanza with four rimes in the octave. On his own he introduced for the first time in this genre internal rimes in the tetrameter lines of stanzas 2, 3, and 4, a device that he carried over sporadically into 'Halloween', stanzas 1, 3, and 6. In phrasing the last lines owe a good deal to Fergusson's 'The Election' (Stanza 2), but otherwise this piece is notably original, a breezy and promising experiment.

Burns's informal introduction of the poem to Mrs. Dunlop: 'You would know an Ayr-shire lad, Sandy Bell, who made a Jamaica fortune, & died some time ago. – A William Miller, formerly a Mason, now a merchant in this place, married a sister german of Bell's for the sake of a 500£ her brother had left her. – A Sister of Miller's who was then Tenant of my heart for a time being, huffed my Bardship in the pride of her new Connection; & I, in the heat of my resentment resolved to burlesque the whole business, & began as follows – [n]

1

WHEN Eighty-five was seven months auld	old
And wearing thro' the aught,	eighth
When rolling[n] rains and Boreas bauld	north wind bold
Gied farmer-folks a faught;	Gave; struggle, fight
5 Ae morning quondam Mason W . . .,	One, former
Now Merchant Master Miller,	
Gaed down to meet wi' Nansie B . . .,	Went
And her Jamaica siller	silver, money
To wed, that day.	

2

10 The rising sun o'er Blacksideen[n]	
Was just appearing fairly,	
When Nell and Bess got up to dress[n]	
Seven lang half hours o'er early!	long, over, too
Now presses clink and drawers jink,	clank; jerk open
15 For linens and for laces:	
But modest Muses only *think*	
What ladies' underdress is	
On sic a day!	such

3

But we'll suppose the stays are lac'd,   corsets
20   And bonie bosoms steekit,   pretty; confined, laced up
Tho' thro' the lawn – but guess the rest!   sheer linen
        An angel scarce durst keek it.   dare steal a glance at it
Then stockins fine, o' silken twine
        Wi' cannie care are drawn up;   prudent
25 An' garten'd tight whare mortal wight—   gartered; where

....
....

As I never wrote it down my recollection does not entirely serve me[n]

4

But now the gown wi' rustling sound
        Its silken[n] pomp displays;
30 Sure there's nae sin in being vain
        O' siccan bony claes!   such pretty clothes
Sae jimp the waist, the tail sae vast—   So slender
        Trouth, they were bonie birdies!   In truth; girls
O Mither Eve, ye wad been grieve[n]   Mother; would have; grieved
35   To see their ample hurdies   buttocks
            Sae large that day!   So

5

Then Sandy,[n] wi's red jacket braw,   with his; splendid
        Comes, whip-jee-woa! about,   like a shot, in a jiffy
And in he gets the bony twa—   pretty two
40   Lord, send them safely out!
And auld John[n] Trot wi' sober phiz,[n]   face
        As braid and braw's a Bailie,   broad, fine as a magistrate
His shouthers and his Sunday's jiz   shoulders; wig
        Wi' powther and wi' ulzie   powder; oil
            Weel smear'd that day....[n]   Well

17. Robert Burns, *Halloween*, 1785

This poem of 252 lines is a major effort, Burn's longest work in the genre except for 'Love and Liberty'. It was written shortly after 'A Mauchline Wedding' and the poet here follows the verse form of that experimental fragment, with the four-rime octave, and occasional internal rimes in stanza 1, 3, and 6.

'Halloween', like Ramsay's 'Christ's Kirk' cantos and Skinner's 'Christmass Bawing', is heavy with folklore, describing superstitious rites so specialized that Burns felt he had to provide notes that are actually longer than the poem's text. Despite this self-conscious antiquarianism, however, 'Halloween' is an impressive piece of work. Most of the individual vignettes are skilfully realized (there are just too many of them for comfort), and the style throughout is vigorous, often brilliant. Here again we have the pure pattern of the *Christis Kirk* tradition, with spritely rustic follies as seen by a superior and amused spectator. As Burns's first formal attempt at this genre the poem is a work of admirable craftsmanship.

Burns's headnote: 'The following poem will, by many readers, be well enough understood; but, for the sake of those who are unacquainted with the manners and traditions of the country where the scene is cast, notes are added, to give some account of the principal charms and spells of that night, so big with prophecy to the peasantry in the west of Scotland. The passion of prying into futurity makes a striking part of the history of human-nature, in its rude state, in all ages and nations; and it may be some entertainment to a philosophic mind, if any such should honor the author with a perusal, to see the remains of it, among the more unenlightened in our own.'

> *Yes! let the rich deride, the proud disdain,*
> *The simple pleasures of the lowly train;*
> *To me more dear, congenial to my heart,*
> *One native charm, than all the gloss of art.*

Goldsmith[n]

1

Upon that night, when fairies light,[n]
    On Cassilis Downans[n] dance,
Or owre the lays, in splendid blaze,   over untilled fields
    On sprightly coursers prance;
5 Or for Colean,[n] the rout is taen,   way is taken
    Beneath the moon's pale beams;
There, up the Cove,[n] to stray an' rove,
    Amang the rocks an' streams
        To sport that night.

2

10 Amang the bonie, winding banks,
    Where Doon[n] rins, wimplin', clear,   runs; winding
Where Bruce[n] ance rul'd the martial ranks,   once
    An' shook his Carrick spear,
Some merry, friendly, countra folks,   country
15   Together did convene,
To burn their nits, an' pou their stocks,   nuts; pull; stems
    An' haud their halloween   hold
        Fu' blythe that night.   Full, very

3

The lasses feat, an' cleanly neat,   spruce
20   Mair braw than when they're fine;   More handsome; finely dressed
Their faces blythe, fu' sweetly kythe,   show
    Hearts leal, an' warm, an' kin':   loyal; kind
The lads sae trig, wi' wooer-babs,[n]   neat; two-loop knots
    Weel knotted on their garten,   garters
25 Some unco blate, an' some wi' gabs,   very shy; bold chatter
    Gar lasses' hearts gang startin   Make; start beating
        Whyles fast at night.   At times

4

Then, first an' foremost, thro' the kail,   borecole (curly cabbage)
    Their stocks[n] maun a' be sought ance'   plants must all; once
30 They steek their een, an' grape an' wale, close; eyes; grope; choose
    For muckle anes, an' straught anes.   big ones; straight
Poor hav'rel Will fell aff the drift,   simpleton; fell behind
    An' wander'd thro' the bow-kail,   ordinary cabbage
    An' pow't, for want o' better shift,   pulled

35   A runt was like a sow-tail   *stock, stem; pig's tail*
         Sae bow't that night.   *So bent*

5

     Then, straught or crooked, yird or nane,   *straight; with earth; none*
       They roar an' cry a' throw'ther;   *through each other (in disorder)*
     The vera wee-things, toddlan, rin,   *very little ones, toddling, run*
40   Wi' stocks out owre their shouther: *over; shoulder*
     An' gif the custock's sweet or sour,   *if; stalk of kale*
       Wi' joctelegs they taste them;   *clasp knives*
     Syne coziely, aboon the door,   *Then; above*
       Wi' cannie care, they've plac'd them   *knowing, cautious*
45   To lye that night.   *lie*

6

     The lasses staw frae 'mang tham a',   *steal away from among*
       To pou their stalks o' corn;[n]   *pull; oats*
     But Rab slips out, an' jinks about,   *dodges*
       Behint the muckle thorn: *behind; big thorn tree*
50   He grippet Nelly hard an' fast;   *grabbed*
       Loud skirl'd a' the lasses;   *shouted all*
     But her tap-pickle maist was lost,   *maidenhead almost*
       When kiutlan in the fause-house[n]   *cuddling; frame inside stack*
        Wi' him that night.

7

55 The auld guidwife's weel-hoordet nits[n]   *old; well-hoarded nuts*
       Are round an' round divided,
     An' monie lads' an lasses' fates
       Are there that night decided:
     Some kindle, couthie, side by side,   *sociably*
60   An' burn thegither trimly;   *together*
     Some start awa, wi' saucy pride,   *leap away*
       An' jump out owre the chimlie   *over; fireplace*
        Fu' high that night.   *Full, very*

8

     Jean slips in twa, wi' tentie e'e;   *two; watchful eye*
65   Wha 'twas, she wadna tell;   *would not*
     But this is Jock, an' this is me,
       She says in to hersel: *herself*

He bleez'd owre her, an' she owre him,   blazed over
   As they wad never mair part,   would; more
70 Till fuff! he started up the lum,   chimney
   An' Jean had e'en a sair heart   sore
      To see't that night.

9

Poor Willie, wi' his bow-kail runt,   common cabbage stalk
   Was brunt wi' primsie Mallie;   burned; demure
75 An' Mary, nae doubt, took the drunt,   sulks
   To be compar'd to Willie:
Mall's nit lap out, wi' pridefu' fling,   nut leaped; fit of ill-humour
   An' her ain fit, it brunt it;   own foot; burned
While Willie lap, an' swoor by jing,   jumped up; swore
80   'Twas just the way he wanted
      To be that night.

10

Nell had the fause-house in her min',   mind
   She pits hersel an' Rob in;   puts
In loving bleeze they sweetly join   blaze
85   Till white in ase they're sobbin: ash
Nell's heart was dancin at the view;
   She whisper'd Rob to leuk for't: look
Rob, stownlins, prie'd her bonie mou,   secretly tasted; mouth
   Fu' cozie in the neuk for't,   Full, very; corner
90   Unseen that night.

11

But Merran sat behint their backs,
   Her thoughts on Andrew Bell;
She lea'es them gashan at their cracks,   leaves; chatting; talk
   An' slips out by hersel:
95 She thro' the yard the nearest taks,   the shortest way takes
   An' for the kiln she goes then,   grain-drying oven
An' darklins grapet for the bauks,   in dark groped; cross beams
   And in the blue-clue[n] throws then,   ball of blue woollen yarn
      Right fear't that night.   frightened

12

100 An' ay she win't, an' ay she swat,   continually; wound it; sweated

I wat she made nae jaukin;   I'm sure; no dallying
Till something held within the pat,   pot (drying chamber)
    Guid Lord! but she was quaukin!   quaking, shivering
But whether 'twas the deil himsel,   devil
105   Or whether 'twas a bauk-en',   beam end
Or whether it was Andrew Bell,
    She did na wait on talkin   not delay
        To spier that night.   ask

13

Wee Jenny to her graunie says,   grandmother
110   'Will ye go wi' me, graunie?
I'll eat the apple[n] at the glass,   mirror
    I gat frae uncle Johnie':   got from
She fuff't her pipe wi' sic a lunt,   puffed; such a puff
    In wrath she was sae vap'rin,   so fuming
115 She notic't na, an aizle brunt   not; ember burned
    Her braw, new, worset apron   fine; worsted (cloth)
        Out thro' that night.

14

'Ye little skelpie-limmer's face!   hussy's face
    I daur you try sic sportin,   dare; such sporting
120 As seek the foul thief onie place,   devil any
    For him to spae your fortune: foretell
Nae doubt but ye may get a sight!
    Great cause ye hae to fear it;[n]
For monie a ane has gotten a fright,
125   An' liv'd an' di'd deleeret,   died delirious
        On sic a night.   such

15

'Ae hairst afore the Sherra-moor,[n]   One harvest before; (battle)
    I mind't as weel's yestreen,   recall it; yesterday
I was a gilpey then, I'm sure,   lively girl
130   I was na past fyfteen:
The simmer had been cauld an' wat,   summer; cold; wet
    An stuff was unco green;   grain unusually
An' ay a rantan kirn we gat,   always; jolly harvest party
    An' just on Halloween
135   It fell that night.

16

'Our stibble-rig was Rab M'Graen,   leader of reapers
   A clever, sturdy fallow;
His sin gat Eppie Sim wi' wean,   got; with child
   That liv'd in Achmacalla:ⁿ
140 He gat hemp-seed,ⁿ I mind it weel,   remember it well
   An' he made unco light o't;   very
But monie a day was by himsel,   beside himself, demented
   He was sae sairly frighted   so sorely
     That vera night.'   very

17

145 Then up gat fechtan Jamie Fleck,   fighting, belligerent
   An' he swoor by his conscience,   swore
That he could saw hemp-seed a peck;   sow
   For it was a' but nonsense: all nothing but
The auld guidman raught down the pock,   old farmer reached; bag
150   An' out a handfu' gied him;   handful gave
Syne bad him slip frae 'mang the folk,   Then; from among
   Sometime when nae ane see'd him,   no one saw
     An' try't that night.

18

He marches thro' amang the stacks,
155   Tho' he was something sturtan;   frightened
The graip he for a harrow taks,   iron fork
   An' haurls at his curpan: rakes; rump
And ev'ry now an' then, he says,
   'Hemp-seed I saw thee,   sow
160 An' her that is to be my lass,
   Come after me an' draw thee
     As fast this night.'

19

He whistled up lord Lenox' march,   (a tune)
   To keep his courage cheary;
165 Altho' his hair began to arch,   curl
   He was sae fley'd an' eerie: scared; frightened
Till presently he hears a squeak,
   An' then a grane an' gruntle;   groan; grunt
He by his showther gae a keek,   shoulder gave a glance

170   An' tumbl'd wi' a wintle   staggering motion
              Out owre that night.   over

                        20
        He roar'd a horrid murder-shout,
            In dreadfu' desperation!
        An' young an' auld come rinnan out,   old; running
175   An' hear the sad narration;
        He swoor 'twas hilchan Jean M'Craw,   swore; limping
            Or crouchie Merran Humphie,   hump-backed
        Till stop! she trotted thro' them a';
            An' wha was it but Grumphie   who; the sow
180   Asteer that night?   A-stirring

                        21
        Meg fain wad to the barn gaen,   gladly would; go
            To winn three wechts o' naething;[n]   winnow; sievefuls; nothing
        But for to meet the deil her lane,   devil by herself
            She pat but little faith in: put
185   She gies the herd a pickle nits,   gives; herder; few nuts
            An' twa red cheeket apples,   two; cheeked
        To watch, while for the barn she sets,
            In hopes to see Tam Kipples
                That vera night.   very

                        22
190   She turns the key, wi' cannie thraw,   with careful twist
            An' owre the threshold ventures;   over
        But first on Sawnie gies a ca',   Alexander (devil) gives; call
            Syne bauldly in she enters: Then boldly
        A ratton rattl'd up the wa',   rat; wall
195   An' she cry'd, 'Lord preserve her!'
        An' ran thro' midden-hole an' a',   foundation of dunghill; all
            An' pray'd wi' zeal and fervour,
                Fu' fast that night.   Full, very

                        23
        They hoy't out Will, wi' sair advice;   summoned; stern
200   They hecht him some fine braw ane;   promised; good-looking one
        It chanc'd the stack he faddom't thrice,[n] measured with arms
            Was timmer-propt for thrawin: timber-propped against warping

He taks a swirlie, auld moss-oak, knotty, gnarled
 For some black, grousome carlin; horrible old woman (witch)
205 An' loot a winze, an' drew a stroke, let out a curse
 Till skin in blypes cam haurlin shreds came peeling
  Aff's nieves that night. Off his fists

24

A wanton widow Leezie was,
 As cantie as a kittlen; lively; kitten
210 But och! that night, amang the shaws, among; small woods
 She gat a fearfu' settlin!
She thro' the whins, an' by the cairn,[n] gorse; pile of stones
 An' owre the hill gaed scrievin, over; went speeding swiftly
Where three lairds' lan's met at a burn,[n] landlords' lands; brook
215 To dip her left sark-sleeve in, shirt-sleeve
  Was bent that night.

25

Whyles owre a linn the burnie plays,[n] Sometimes; waterfall; brook
 As thro' the glen it wimpl't; twisted
Whyles round a rocky scar it strays; cliff, crag
220 Whyles in a wiel it dimpl't; eddy
Whyles glitter'd to the nightly rays,
 Wi' bickerin, dancin dazzle; scurrying
Whyles cooket underneath the braes, appeared and disappeared; hills
 Below the spreading hazle hazel tree
225   Unseen that night.

26

Amang the brachens, on the brae, bracken; hill
 Between her an' the moon,
The deil, or else an outler quey, young cow lying out
 Gat up an' gae a croon: gave a moo
230 Poor Leezie's heart maist lap the hool; almost leaped out of skin
 Near lav'rock-height she jumpet, high as a lark; jumped
But mist a fit, an' in the pool, misplaced a foot
 Out owre the lugs she plumpet, over the ears; plunged
  Wi' a plunge that night.

27

235 In order, on the clean hearth-stane,

The luggies[n] three are ranged;   wooden bowls
And ev'ry time great care is taen,   taken
    To see them duely changed;
Auld uncle John, wha wedlock's joys,   Old; who
240   Sin' Mar's-year[n] did desire,   Since (the year 1715)
Because he gat the toom dish thrice,   empty
    He heav'd them on the fire,
        In wrath that night.

28
Wi' merry sangs, an' friendly cracks,   songs; conversation
245   I wat they did na weary;   know
And unco tales, an' funnie jokes,   strange
    Their sports were cheap and cheary:
Till butter'd so'ns,[n] wi' fragrant lunt,   porridge; steam
    Set a' their gabs a steerin;   all; mouths in motion
250 Syne, wi' a social glass o' strunt,   Then; strong spirits (whisky)
    They parted aff careerin
        Fu' blythe that night.

18. Robert Burns, *The Holy Fair*, 1785

This satiric masterpiece was largely based on Burns's observations of the actual 'holy fair' held in the kirkyard of the church in Mauchline in August of 1785. In Burns's Ayrshire a holy fair was an annual communion service and religious 'revival' meeting at which the folk of several parishes would get together to receive communion and to hear their various ministers preach in turn. In this superb extravaganza Burns extends the subject matter of the *Christis Kirk* genre to include religious satire for the first time. Still, the traditional satiric presentation of the folk in holiday mood is retained, as the poem flashes back and forth from the crowd to the outdoor pulpit and back again, to illuminate both the hypocrisy of the hysterical hell-fire preachers and the earthy and sexual concerns of the congregation. What is new here is the poet's hilarious depiction of the fanatical 'Auld Licht' ministers – Moodie, Peebles, Miller, and Russel – the favourites of a mindless mob who detest the cold rationality of the 'New Licht' Smith.

In this great poem Burns raised the art of the *Christis Kirk* tradition to a new level of excellence and power. In the introductory section he took over Fergusson's 'Mirth', the guide in 'Leith Races', and transformed her into his own, more delightful, 'Fun'. He again used Fergusson's four-rime octave throughout, but retained the device of internal rime from 'A Mauchline Wedding' and 'Halloween' only in part of the final stanza (lines 235, 237), where these rimes help to create a ceremonial effect, building to a triumphant conclusion.

> *A robe of seeming truth and trust*
> *   Hid crafty observation;*
> *And secret hung, with poison'd crust,*
> *   The dirk of defamation:*
> *A mask that like the gorget show'd,*
> *   Dye-varying, on the pigeon;*
> *And for a mantle large and broad,*
> *   He wrapt him in religion.*

HYPOCRISY A-LA-MODE[N]

1

Upon a simmer Sunday morn,   summer
    When nature's face is fair,
I walked forth to view the corn,
    An' snuff the callor air.   fresh
5 The rising sun, ower Galston muirs,[n]   over; moors
    Wi' glorious light was glintan;   glinting
The hares were hirplan down the furrs,   hopping; furrows
    The lav'rocks they were chantan   larks, chanting
        Fu' sweet that day.

2

10 As lightsomely I glowr'd abroad,
    To see a scene sae gay,
Three hizzies, early at the road,   young women
    Cam skelpan up the way.   Came hurrying
Twa had manteeles o' dolefu' black,   Two; mantles, cloaks
15   But ane wi' lyart lining;[n]   one; grey
The third, that gaed a wee aback,   went a bit behind
    Was in the fashion shining
        Fu' gay that day.

3

The twa appear'd like sisters twin,
20   In feature, form an' claes;   clothes
Their visage wither'd, lang an' thin,   long
    An' sour as ony slaes: sloes
The third cam up, hap-step-an'-loup,   hop, step, and jump
    As light as ony lambie,   lamb
25 An' wi' a curchie low did stoop,   curtsy
    As soon as e'er she saw me,
        Fu' kind that day.

4

Wi' bonnet aff, quoth I, 'Sweet lass,
    I think ye seem to ken me;   know
30 I'm sure I've seen that bonie face,   pretty
    But yet I canna name ye.'
Quo' she, an' laughan as she spak,   laughing; spoke
    An' taks me by the han's,   takes; hands
'Ye, for my sake, hae gien the feck   given; majority

35   Of a' the ten comman's   commandments
          A screed some day.   tear, rent

                    5
'My name is Fun[n] – your cronie dear,   close friend
      The nearest friend ye hae;   have
An' this is *Superstition* here,
40   An' that's *Hypocrisy*.
I'm gaun to Mauchline[n] holy fair,   going
      To spend an hour in daffin: fun
Gin ye'll go there, yon runkl'd pair,   If; wrinkled
      We will get famous laughin
45   At them this day.'

                    6
Quoth I, 'Wi' a' my heart, I'll do't;
      I'll get my sunday's sark on,   shirt
An' meet you on the holy spot;
      Faith, we'se hae fine remarkin!'   we'll have; things to see
50 Then I gaed hame at crowdie-time,   went; porridge (breakfast)
      An' soon I made me ready;
For roads were clad, frae side to side,
      Wi' monie a wearie bodie,   many; person
            In droves that day.

                    7
55 Here, farmers gash, in ridin graith,   smart; dress
      Gaed hoddan by their cotters;   jogging on horseback
There, swankies young, in braw braid-claith,   agile lads; fine broad cloth
      Are springan owre the gutters.   jumping over
The lasses, skelpan barefit, thrang,   scampering barefoot, crowded
60   In silks an' scarlets[n] glitter;
Wi' sweet-milk cheese, in monie a whang,   thick slice
      An' farls, bak'd wi' butter,   quarters of large oatcakes
            Fu' crump that day.   Fully crisp

                    8
When by the plate we set our nose,   collection plate
65   Weel heaped up wi' ha'pence,   halfpennies
A greedy glowr black-bonnet throws,   the elder (with black bonnet)
      An' we maun draw our tippence.   must; twopence

Then in we go to see the show,
   On ev'ry side they're gath'ran;   *gathering*
70 Some carryan dails, some chairs an' stools,   *wooden planks*
   An' some are busy bleth'ran   *talking foolishly*
      Right loud that day.

9

Here, stands a shed to fend the show'rs,
   An' screen our countra gentry;   *country, rural*
75 There, racer Jess,[n] an' twathree whores,   *two or three*
   Are blinkan at the entry.   *leering*
Here sits a raw o' tittlan jads,   *row; chattering hussies*
   Wi' heaving breasts an' bare neck;
An' there, a batch o' wabster lads,   *weaver*
80   Blackguarding frae Kilmarnock   *Behaving riotously from*
      For *fun* this day.

10

Here, some are thinkan on their sins,
   An' some upo' their claes;   *clothes*
Ane curses feet that fyl'd his shins,   *soiled*
85   Anither sighs an' prays:
On this hand sits a chosen[n] swatch,   *sample*
   Wi' screw'd-up, grace-proud faces;[n]
On that, a set o' chaps, at watch,
   Thrang winkan on the lasses   *Busy winking*
90   To chairs that day.

11

O happy is that man, an' blest![n]
   Nae wonder that it pride him!
Whase ain dear lass, that he likes best,
   Comes clinkan down beside him!   *flopping down suddenly*
95 Wi' arm repos'd on the chair-back,
   He sweetly does compose him;
Which, by degrees, slips round her neck,
   An's loof upon her bosom   *And his palm*
      Unkend that day.   *Unnoticed*

12

100 Now a' the congregation o'er

Is silent expectation;
For Moodie[n] speels the holy door,   climbs; pulpit door
    Wi' tidings o' damnation.[n]
Should Hornie, as in ancient days,   the Devil
105   'Mang sons o' God present him,   Among
The vera sight o' Moodie's face,   very
    To's ain het hame had sent him   own hot home
        Wi' fright that day.

13

Hear how he clears the points o' faith
110   Wi' rattlin an' thumpin!
Now meekly calm, now wild in wrath,
    He's stampan, an he's jumpan!
His lengthen'd chin, his turn'd up snout,
    His eldritch squeel an' gestures,   hideous
115 O how they fire the heart devout,
    Like cantharidian plaisters[n]   Spanish fly plasters
        On sic a day!   such

14

But hark! the tent has chang'd its voice;   field pulpit
    There's peace an' rest nae langer;   no longer
120 For a' the *real judges* rise,
    They canna sit for anger.   cannot
Smith[n] opens out his cauld harangues,   cold
    On practice and on morals;
An' aff the godly pour in thrangs,   off; crowds
125   To gie the jars an' barrels   give
        A lift that day.

15

What signifies his barren shine,
    Of moral pow'rs an' reason?
His English style, and gesture fine,
130   Are a' clean out o' season,
Like Socrates or Antonine,[n]
    Or some auld pagan heathen,
The moral man he does define,
    But ne'er a word o' faith in
135   That's right that day.

16

In guid time comes an antidote
    Against sic poison'd nostrum;   *such; quack medicine*
For Peebles, frae the water-fit,[n]   *rivermouth*
    Ascends the holy rostrum:
140 See, up he's got the word o' God,
    An' meek an' mim has view'd it,   *prudishly*
While common-sense has taen the road,[n]   *taken*
    An' aff, an' up the Cowgate[n]   *off*
        Fast, fast that day.

17

145 Wee Miller[n] neist, the guard relieves,   *next*
    An' orthodoxy raibles,   *gabbles*
Tho' in his heart he weel believes,
    An' thinks it auld wives' fables:
But faith! the birkie wants a manse,   *fellow; minister's house*
150   So, cannilie he hums them;   *shrewdly; deceives*
Altho' his carnal wit an' sense[n]
    Like hafflins-wise o'ercomes him   *halfways overcomes*
        At times that day.

18

Now, butt an' ben, the change-house fills,   *outer and inner (rooms); tavern*
155   Wi' yill-caup commentators: *ale cup*
Here's crying out for bakes an' gills,   *biscuits; drinks*
    An' there the pint-stowp clatters;   *pint flagon*
While thick an' thrang, an' loud an' lang,   *crowded*
    Wi' Logic, an' wi' Scripture,
160 They raise a din, that, in the end,
    Is like to breed a rupture
        O' wrath that day.

19

Leeze me on drink! it gies us mair[n]   *Dear is to me; more*
    Than either school or colledge:
165 It kindles wit, it waukens lear,   *wakens learning*
    It pangs us fou o' knowledge.   *crams us full*
Be't whisky-gill or penny-wheep,   *small beer*
    Or ony stronger potion,
It never fails, on drinkin deep,

170   To kittle up our notion,   *stimulate; understanding*
            By night or day.

20

The lads an' lasses, blythely bent
    To mind baith saul an' body,   *both soul*
Sit round the table, weel content,
175   An' steer about the toddy.   *pass around; hot whisky drink*
On this ane's dress, an' that ane's leuk,   *look*
    They're makin observations;
While some are cozie i' the neuk,   *corner*
    An' forming assignations
180   To meet some day.

21

But now the Lord's ain trumpet[n] touts,
    Till a' the hills are rairan,   *roaring*
An' echos back return the shouts;
    Black Russel[n] is na spairan: *not sparing*
185 His piercin words,[n] like highlan swords,
    Divide the joints an' marrow;
His talk o' hell, whare devils dwell,
    Our vera 'Sauls does harrow'[n]   *very souls*
        Wi' fright that day!

22

190 A vast, unbottom'd boundless pit,
    Fill'd fou o' lowan brunstane,   *full; flaming brimstone*
Whase raging flame, an' scorching heat,   *Whose*
    Wad melt the hardest whun-stane!   *Would; whinstone*
The half asleep start up wi' fear,
195   An' think they hear it roaran,
When presently it does appear,
    'Twas but some neebor snoran   *neighbour snoring*
        Asleep that day.

23

'Twad be owre lang a tale to tell,   *overly long*
200   How monie stories past,
An' how they crouded to the yill,   *crowded; ale*
    When they were a' dismist: *all dismissed*

How drink gaed round, in cogs an' caups,   went; wooden mugs and bowls
    Amang the furms an' benches;   Among; forms, benches
205 An' cheese an' bread, frae women's laps,
    Was dealt about in lunches,   large slices
        An' dawds that day.   chunks

24

In comes a gawsie, gash guidwife,   plump, well-dressed farm wife
    An' sits down by the fire,
210 Syne draws her kebbuck an' her knife;   Then; cheese
    The lasses they are shyer.
    The auld guidmen, about the grace,   old husbands
    Frae side to side they bother,
    Till some ane by his bonnet lays,   one
215   An' gies them't, like a tether,   gives them it
        Fu' lang that day.   Very long

25

Waesucks! for him that gets nae lass,[n]   Alas! no
    Or lasses that hae naething!   have nothing
    Sma' need has he to say a grace,   Small
220   Or melvie his braw claithing!   soil with meal; fine clothes
    O wives be mindfu', ance yoursel,   once yourself
    How bonie lads ye wanted,
    An' dinna, for a kebbuck-heel,   do not; heel of cheese
    Let lasses be affronted
225   On sic a day!   such

26

Now clinkumbell, wi' rattlan tow,   the town bell; banging rope
    Begins to jow an' croon;   ring; sing (resonate)
    Some swagger hame, the best they dow,   home; can
    Some wait the afternoon.
230 At slaps the billies halt a blink,   gaps in fences; lads; moment
    Till lasses strip their shoon: shoes
    Wi' *faith* an' *hope,* an' *love*[n] an' *drink,*
    They're a' in famous tune
        For crack that day.   conversation

27

235 How monie hearts this day converts,

O' sinners and o' lasses!
Their hearts o' stane, gin night, are gane   stone; by night; gone
    As saft as ony flesh is.[n]   soft
There's some are fou o' love divine;   drunk, intoxicated
240   There's some are fou o' brandy;
An' monie jobs that day begin,
    May end in houghmagandie   fornication
        Some ither day.   other

19. Robert Burns, *The Ordination*, 1786

In this incisive satire Burns breaks new ground in the *Christis Kirk* tradition once again – this time by using a narrator who is not detached, but is a member of the 'Auld Licht' faction in Ayrshire church politics that the poet is attacking. For this purpose he creates a speaker who is vulgarly gloating over the ordination of William Mackinlay, a staunch Auld Licht who succeeds a series of New Licht ministers in Kilmarnock. There is clear evidence that this piece was written sometime during the first six weeks of 1786. Since Mackinlay was not actually ordained until 6 April, the poem must have been composed in anticipation of the event. Burns makes his narrator here as loathsome and ridiculous as possible in order to discredit the whole system of belief for which he stands. This ironic method derives most probably from Allan Ramsay's 'Elegy on John Cowper', and Burns had used it before with devastating effect in 'Holy Willie's Prayer'. At any rate, in 'The Ordination' it works extremely well; it would be difficult to think of a better way than this to make fun of the gross and mean-spirited victory of the Auld Licht or Evangelical party on this occasion – a party consisting mainly of the flea-bitten weavers and grubby leather workers of Kilmarnock.

In other respects Burns follows the pattern of the genre quite closely, including the use of the strict two-rime octave of the original 'Christis Kirk'. The subject, too, is a lower class celebration, treated in such a way as to bring out the irrationality and vulgarity of the participants. In this poem, however, the tone of the satire is less genial, more sharp edged than is usual in the *Christis Kirk* tradition.

> *For sense they little owe to frugal Heav'n –*
> *To please the mob they hide the little giv'n.*[n]

1

Kilmarnock wabsters, fidge an' claw,[n]	weavers; fidget; scratch
An' pour your creeshie nations;	greasy
An' ye wha leather rax an' draw,	who; stretch
Of a' denominations;	all
5 Swith to the Laigh Kirk,[n] ane an' a',	Quickly; Low Church; one
An' there tak up your stations;	take

Then aff to Begbie's[n] in a raw,   off; row (single file)
    An' pour divine libations
        For joy this day.

2

10 Curst Common-sense, that imp o' hell,[n]
        Cam in wi' *Maggie Lauder;*[n]   Came in with
    But Oliphant[n] aft made her yell,   often
        An' Russell[n] sair misca'd her: sorely miscalled
    This day Mackinlay[n] taks the flail,   thresher's stick
15   An' he's the boy will blaud her!   slap, strike
    He'll clap a shangan on her tail,[n]   cleft stick
        An' set the bairns to daud her   children; pelt
            Wi' dirt this day.   With

3

    Mak haste an' turn King David owre,[n]   Make; over
20   An' lilt wi' holy clangor;
    O' double verse[n] come gie us four,   give
        An' skirl up the *Bangor:*[n]   sing shrilly
    This day the Kirk kicks up a stoure,   Church makes a disturbance
        Nae mair the knaves shall wrang her,   No more; wrong
25 For Heresy is in her pow'r,
        And gloriously she'll whang her   flog
            Wi' pith this day.   strength

4

    Come, let a proper text[n] be read,
        An' touch it aff wi' vigour,   off with
30 How graceless Ham leugh at his dad,[n]   laughed
        Which made Canaan a nigger;[n]   slave
    Or Phineas[n] drove the murdering blade,
        Wi' whore-abhorring rigour;
    Or Zipporah,[n] the scauldin jad,   scolding hussy
35   Was like a bluidy tiger   bloody
            I' th' inn that day.

5

    There, try his mettle on the Creed,
        And bind him down wi' caution,
    That stipend is a carnal weed[n]

40 He taks but for the fashion;   takes
      And gie him o'er the flock, to feed,   give
         And punish each transgression;
      Especial, rams that cross the breed,   (fornicators)
         Gie them sufficient threshin,   Give; beating
45   Spare them nae day.   no

                          6

      Now auld Kilmarnock, cock thy tail,[n]
         An' toss thy horns fu' canty;   full joyful
      Nae mair thou'lt rowte out-owre the dale,   No more; bellow out over
         Because thy pasture's scanty;
50 For lapfu's large o' gospel kail   lapfuls; cabbage
         Shall fill thy crib in plenty,   bowl
      An' runts o' grace, the pick an' wale,   stalks; choice
         No gien by way o' dainty,   given; special treat
               But ilka day.   every

                          7

55 Nae mair by Babel's streams we'll weep[n]   No more
         To think upon our Zion;
      And hing our fiddles up to sleep,   hang
         Like baby-clouts a-dryin: baby napkins
      Come, screw the pegs wi' tunefu' cheep,   (tune the fiddle)
60   And o'er the thairms be tryin;   strings of gut
      O, rare! to see our elbucks wheep,   elbows swoop, jerk
         And a' like lamb-tails flyin   all
               Fu' fast this day!   Very

                          8

      Lang, Patronage, wi' rod o' airn,[n]   iron
65   Has shor'd the Kirk's undoin,   threatened
      As lately Fenwick, sair forfairn,   sorely undone
         Has proven to its ruin:
      Our patron, honest man! Glencairn,
         He saw mischief was brewin;
70 An' like a godly, elect bairn,   chosen son
         He's waled us out a true ane,   picked us out; one
               And sound this day.

9

Now Robertson[n] harangue nae mair,   no more
    But steek your gab for ever;   shut; mouth
75 Or try the wicked town of Ayr,[n]
    For there they'll think you clever;
Or, nae reflection on your lear,   no; learning
    Ye may commence a shaver;   barber
Or to the Netherton[n] repair,
80   An' turn a carpet-weaver
        Aff-hand this day.   Without delay

10

Mu'trie[n] and you were just a match,
    We never had sic twa drones;   such two
Auld Hornie did the Laigh Kirk watch,   The Devil
85   Just like a winkin baudrons;   cat
And ay he catch'd the tither wretch,   always; other
    To fry them in his caudrons;   caldrons
But now his Honor maun detach,   must
    Wi' a' his brimstone squadrons,   With all
90   Fast, fast this day.

11

See, see auld Orthodoxy's faes   old; foes
    She's swingein thro' the city!   flogging
Hark, how the nine-tail'd cat she plays!
    I vow it's unco pretty: very
95 There, Learning, with his Greekish face,
    Grunts out some Latin ditty;
And Common Sense is gaun, she says,   going
    To mak to Jamie Beattie[n]   make
        Her plaint this day.

12

100 But there's Morality himsel,
    Embracing all opinions;
Hear, how he gies the tither yell   gives; other
    Between his twa companions!
See, how she peels the skin an' fell,   underskin
105   As ane were peelin onions!   As though one
Now there, they're packed aff to hell,

An' banish'd our dominions,
    Henceforth this day.

13
O happy day! rejoice, rejoice!
110   Come bouse about the porter!   drink; dark, bitter ale
Morality's demure decoys
    Shall here nae mair find quarter: no more
Mackinlay, Russell, are the boys
    That Heresy can torture;
115 They'll gie her on a rape a hoyse,   give; rope; hoist
    And cowe her measure shorter   cut short
        By th' head some day.

14
Come, bring the tither mutchkin in,   other pint
    And here's, for a conclusion,
120 To ev'ry New Light[n] mother's son,
    From this time forth, confusion:
If mair they deave us wi' their din,   more; deafen
    Or patronage intrusion,
We'll light a spunk, and, ev'ry skin,   match
125   We'll rin them aff in fusion   off; melting (to nothing)
        Like oil, some day.

20. Robert Burns, *Love And Liberty – A Cantata* (also known as *The Jolly Beggars*), 1785–1786

This great 'cantata' was inspired by Burns's looking in on a wild drinking party of beggars in 'Poosie-Nansie's', a disreputable tavern in Mauchline. The actual event took place in the autumn of 1785, at which time Burns composed a first draft that he later revised with many changes sometime in 1786. The poet probably intended to publish this major work in his first Edinburgh edition of 1787, but was dissuaded by conservative friends. In the end the cantata was never printed during his lifetime.

In 'Love and Liberty' Burns combined the ancient tradition of beggar songs with the conventions and techniques of the *Christis Kirk* tradition. The beggar 'philosophy', celebrating the idea that beggars (with nothing to lose) were the only really 'free' people in our society, was accessible to Burns through the innumerable beggar songs in Scots and English and also through John Gay's *The Beggar's Opera* (1728). But 'Love and Liberty' is predominantly a *Christis Kirk* poem with the dramatic songs functioning in lieu of the extensive dialogue that is typical of the genre.

There are many different verse forms used in the cantata, but in the recitativo sections the *Christis Kirk* stanza is most common – in its strict form in Recitativo 6, and in modified form (without the tag-line) in Recitativos 2 and 5. In substance Burns here uses precisely the *Christis Kirk* kind of brief characterization, rapid transition, rollicking tempos, and broad humour, together with the typical drunkenness, horseplay, tolerant satire, and the point of view of a superior and detached spectator. The whole is brilliantly organized in a tight dramatic structure. With the tension that is built up between the radical attitudes of the beggars and the conservative views of the narrator 'Love and Liberty' is an artistic triumph – the climax of the entire *Christis Kirk* tradition.

RECITATIVO 1

When lyart leaves bestrow the yird,[n]	grey, withered; earth
Or wavering like the bauckie-bird,	bat
Bedim cauld Boreas' blast;	cold north wind's
When hailstanes drive wi' bitter skyte,	hailstones; glancing blow

135

5   And infant frosts begin to bite,
        In hoary cranreuch drest;   white frost
    Ae night at e'en a merry core   One; company
        O' randie, gangrel bodies,   Of riotous, vagabond
    In Poosie-Nansie'sⁿ held the splore,   drinking party
10   To drink their orra dudies: spare rags
        Wi' quaffing, and laughing,
            They ranted an' they sang;   roistered
        Wi' jumping, an' thumping,
            The vera girdle rang.   very griddle (baking plate)

15 First, niest the fire, in auld, red rags,   next to
    Ane sat; weel brac'd wi' mealy bags,   One; well; with
        And knapsack a' in order;   all
    His doxy lay within his arm;   harlot
    Wi' usquebae an' blankets warm,   whisky
20   She blinket on her sodger: leered at; soldier
    An' ay he gies the tozie drab   always; gives; tipsy slut
        The tither skelpan kiss,   another smacking
    While she held up her greedy gab,   mouth
        Just like an aumous dish: alms dish for food scraps
25   Ilk smack still, did crack still,
            Just like a cadger's whip;   pedlar's
        Then staggering, an' swaggering,
            He roar'd this ditty up –

SONG 1

AIR

Tune: *Soldier's joy.*   [McGlashan's *Scots Measures*, 1781, p. 32.]

Boldly

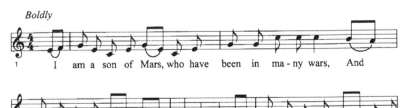

1   I   am a   son of Mars, who have been in ma-ny wars, And
4   show my cuts and scars wher-ever I come; This here was for a wench, and that

I am a son of Mars who have been in many wars,[n]
30   And show my cuts and scars wherever I come;
        This here was for a wench, and that other in a trench,
            When welcoming the French at the sound of the drum.
                    Lal de daudle, &c.

        My prenticeship I past where my leader breath'd his last,
            When the bloody die was cast on the heights of Abram;[n]
35   And I served out my trade when the gallant game was play'd,
            And the Moro[n] low was laid at the sound of the drum.

        I lastly was with Curtis[n] among the floating batt'ries,
            And there I left for witness, an arm and a limb;
        Yet let my country need me, with Elliot[n] to head me,
40   I'd clatter on my stumps at the sound of a drum.

        And now tho' I must beg, with a wooden arm and leg,
            And many a tatter'd rag hanging over my bum,
        I'm as happy with my wallet, my bottle and my callet,   wench
            As when I us'd in scarlet to follow a drum.

45 What tho', with hoary locks, I must stand the winter shocks,
    Beneath the woods and rocks oftentimes for a home,
When the tother bag I sell and the tother bottle tell,
    I could meet a troop of hell at the sound of the drum.

RECITATIVO 2

He ended; and the kebars sheuk,[n]   rafters
50   Aboon the chorus roar;   Above
While frighted rattons backward leuk,   rats; look
    An' seek the benmost bore;   innermost hole
A fairy fiddler frae the neuk,   tiny; corner
    He skirl'd out, ENCORE.   yelled, squealed
55 But up arose the martial chuck,   military whore
    An' laid the loud uproar –

SONG 2

AIR

Tune: *Sodger laddie.*   [*Orpheus Caledonius*, 1733, No. 27.]

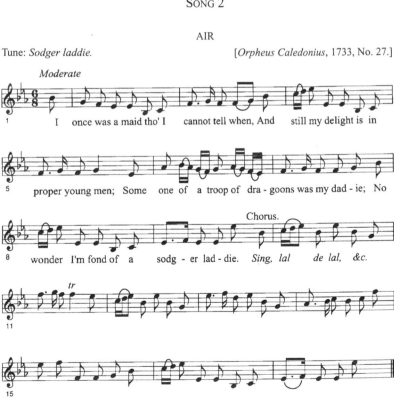

I once was a maid tho' I cannot tell when,
And still my delight is in proper young men: handsome (also 'polite')
Some one of a troop of dragoons was my dadie,
60   No wonder I'm fond of a sodger laddie.   soldier
               Sing lal de lal, &c.

The first of my loves was a swaggering blade,
To rattle the thundering drum was his trade;
His leg was so tight and his cheek was so ruddy,
Transported I was with my sodger laddie.

65   But the godly, old chaplain left him in the lurch,
The sword I forsook for the sake of the church;
He ventur'd the soul, and I risked the body,
'Twas then I prov'd false to my sodger laddie.

Full soon I grew sick of my sanctified sot,
70   The regiment at large for a husband I got;
From the gilded spontoon to the fife I was ready;   officer's short pike; flute
I asked no more but a sodger laddie.

But the Peace[n] it reduc'd me to beg in despair,
Till I met my old boy in a Cunningham fair;[n]
75   His rags regimental they flutter'd so gaudy,
My heart it rejoic'd at a sodger laddie.

And now I have lived – I know not how long,
And still I can join in a cup and a song;
But whilst with both hands I can hold the glass steady,
80   Here's to thee, my hero, my sodger laddie.[n]

Recitativo 3

Then niest outspak a raucle carlin,[n]   next; tough old woman
Wha kent fu' weel to cleek the sterlin;   knew; hook (steal) cash
For mony a pursie she had hooked,   purse
An' had in mony a well been douked: ducked, immersed
85   Her love had been a Highland laddie,
But weary fa' the waefu' woodie![n]   devil take; woeful noose

Wi' sighs an' sobs she thus began
To wail her braw John Highlandman –   handsome

SONG 3

AIR

Tune: *O, an ye were dead, Guidman.*   [*Cal. Pocket Companion*, 1752, iv. p. 24.]

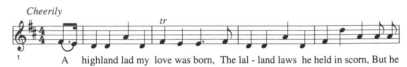

A highland lad my love was born, The lal - land laws he held in scorn, But he

still was faith - fu' to his clan, My gal - lant, braw John Highlandman.   *Sing*

hey my braw John Highlandman! Sing ho my braw John Highlandman! There's

not a lad in a' the lan' Was match for my John High - land - man!

A highland lad my love was born,
90   The lalland laws he held in scorn;   lowland (opposed to Highland)
But he still was faithfu' to his clan,
My gallant, braw John Highlandman.

Chorus
Sing hey my braw John Highlandman!
Sing ho my braw John Highlandman!
95   There's not a lad in a' the lan'   all the land
Was match for my John Highlandman.

With his philibeg, an' tartan plaid,   kilt; mantle, blanket
An' guid claymore down by his side,   good Highland sword
The ladies' hearts he did trepan,[n]   ensnare
100 My gallant, braw John Highlandman.
Sing hey &c.

We ranged a' from Tweed to Spey,[n]
An' liv'd like lords an' ladies gay:
For a lalland face he feared none,   lowland
My gallant, braw John Highlandman.
   Sing hey &c.

105 They banish'd him beyond the sea,
But ere the bud was on the tree,
Adown my cheeks the pearls ran,
Embracing my John Highlandman.
   Sing hey &c.

But och! they catch'd him at the last,   alas!
110 And bound him in a dungeon fast,
My curse upon them every one,
They've hang'd my braw John Highlandman.
   Sing hey &c.

And now a widow I must mourn
The pleasures that will ne'er return;
115 No comfort but a hearty can,   drinking vessel
When I think on John Highlandman.
   Sing hey &c.

   RECITATIVO 4

A pigmy scraper wi' his fiddle,[n]
Wha us'd to trystes an' fairs to driddle,   Who; markets; saunter
Her strappan limb an' gausy middle,   robust; portly waist
120 (He reach'd nae higher)
Had hol'd his heartie like a riddle,   pierced; heart; sieve
  An' blawn't on fire.   blown it

Wi' hand on hainch, and upward e'e.   hip; eye
He croon'd his gamut, one, two, three,   hummed; musical scale
125 Then in an arioso key,[n]   melodious
  The wee Apollo   little
Set off wi' allegretto glee   moderately fast
  His giga solo.   jig

SONG 4

AIR

Tune: *Whistle owre the lave o't.*   [Bremner's *Scots Reels*, 1759, p. 56.]

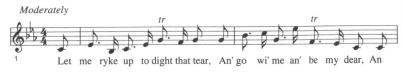

Let me ryke up to dight that tear, An' go wi' me an' be my dear, An

then your every care an' fear May whistle owre the lave o't. I

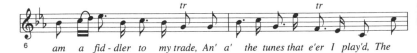

am a fid - dler to my trade, An' a' the tunes that e'er I play'd, The

sweet - est still to wife or maid Was — Whistle owre the lave o't.

	Let me ryke up to dight that tear,	reach; wipe
130	An' go wi' me an' be my dear;[n]	
	An' then your every care an' fear	
	May whistle owre the lave o't.[n]	over the rest of it

Chorus

	I am a fiddler to my trade,	
	An' a' the tunes that e'er I play'd,	And all
135	The sweetest still to wife or maid,	
	Was whistle owre the lave o't.	

	At kirns an' weddins we'se be there,	harvest parties; we'll
	An' O sae nicely's we will fare!	so nicely
	We'll bowse about till Dadie Care	drink
140	Sing whistle owre the lave o't.	
	I am &c.	

	Sae merrily's the banes we'll pyke,	So; bones; pick
	An' sun oursells about the dyke;	ourselves; dry-stone wall
	An' at our leisure when ye like	

We'll whistle owre the lave o't.
   I am &c.

145 But bless me wi' your heav'n o' charms,[n]
   An' while I kittle hair on thairms[n]   tickle; guts (play fiddle)
   Hunger, cauld, an' a' sic harms   cold; all such
     May whistle owre the lave o't.
     I am &c.

Recitativo 5

   Her charms had struck a sturdy caird,[n]   tinker
150   As weel as poor gutscraper;   well; fiddler
   He taks the fiddler by the beard,   take
    An' draws a roosty rapier –   rusty
   He swoor by a' was swearing worth
    To speet him like a pliver,   spit (pierce); plover
155 Unless he would from that time forth
    Relinquish her for ever:

   Wi' ghastly e'e poor tweedledee   eye; (fiddler)
    Upon his hunkers bended,   squatted down
   An' pray'd for grace wi ruefu' face,   with rueful
160   An' so the quarrel ended;
   But tho' his little heart did grieve,
    When round the tinkler prest her,
   He feign'd to snirtle in his sleeve   snigger
    When thus the caird address'd her –

Song 5

AIR

Tune: *Clout the caudron.*   [*Scots Musical Museum*, 1787, No. 23.]

Lively

1   My bon - ie lass, I   work   in brass,   A tink - ler is   my sta - tion;   I've

4   travell'd round all Christian   ground   In   this my oc - cu - pa - tion;   . I've

7 ta'en the gold, an' been en - roll'd   In   many a   no - ble squadron: But

9 vain they search'd, when off I march'd   To   go an' clout the   caudron.

165 My bonie lass I work in brass,[n]
      A tinkler is my station;
    I've travell'd round all Christian ground
      In this my occupation;
    I've ta'en the gold an' been enroll'd[n]   taken
170   In many a noble squadron;
    But vain they search'd when off I march'd
      To go an' clout the caudron.   mend the pot
            I've ta'en the gold &c.

    Despise that shrimp, that wither'd imp,
      With a' his noise an' cap'rin;   capering
175 An' take a share, with those that bear
      The budget and the apron!   bag (of tools)
    And *by* that stowp! my faith an' houpe,   drinking mug; hope
      And *by* that dear keilbaigie,[n]   (kind of whisky)
    If e'er ye want, or meet with scant,
180   May I ne'er weet my craigie!   wet my gullet
            And by that stowp &c.

                RECITATIVO 6

    The caird prevail'd – th' unblushing fair[n]
      In his embraces sunk;
    Partly wi' love o'ercome sae sair,[n]
      An' partly she was drunk:
185 Sir Violino with an air,
      That show'd a man o' spunk,
    Wish'd unison between the pair,
      An' made the bottle clunk   gurgle
    To their health that night.

190 But hurchin Cupid shot a shaft,   urchin
        That play'd a dame a shavie –   trick
    The fiddler rak'd her, fore and aft,[n]   swept her with shot
        Behint the chicken cavie: Behind; coop
    Her lord, a wight of Homer's craft,   man
195   Tho' limpan wi' the spavie,[n]   spavin (horse disease)
    He hirpl'd up an' lap like daft,   hobbled; leaped
        An' shor'd them Dainty Davie[n]   offered them (a song)
            O' boot that night.   To boot (in addition)

    He was a care-defying blade,
200   As ever Bacchus listed!   enlisted
    Tho' Fortune sair upon him laid,   sorely
        His heart she ever miss'd it.
    He had no wish but – to be glad,
        Nor want but – when he thristed;   thirsted
205   He hated nought but – to be sad,
    An' thus the Muse suggested
            His sang that night.   song

Song 6

AIR

Tune: *For a' that, an' a' that.*   [Bremner's *Scots Reels*, 1759, p. 52.]

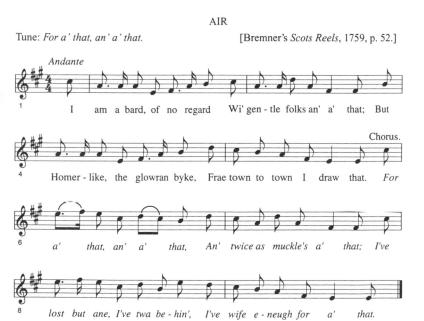

I am a bard of no regard,
   Wi' gentle folks an' a' that;[n]   *and all*
210 But Homer like the glowran byke,   *staring crowd*
   Frae town to town I draw that.   *From*

Chorus
For a' that an' a' that,[n]   *In spite of all that*
   An' twice as muckle's a' that,   *as much as*
I've lost but ane, I've twa behin',   *two behind*
215   I've wife eneugh for a' that.   *enough*

I never drank the Muses' stank,[n]   *pool*
   Castalia's burn an' a' that,   *stream, brook*
But there it streams an' richly reams,   *foams*
   My Helicon I ca' that.   *call*
     For a' that &c.

220 Great love I bear to all the fair,
   Their humble slave an' a' that;
But lordly will, I hold it still
   A mortal sin to thraw that.   *thwart, go against*
     For a' that &c.

In raptures sweet this hour we meet,
225   Wi' mutual love an' a' that;
But for how lang the flie[n] may stang,   *long; fly; sting*
   Let inclination law that.   *control that*
     For a' that &c.

Their tricks an' craft hae put me daft,[n]   *have made me crazy*
   They've ta'en me in, an' a' that,   *taken me in (sexually)*
230 But clear the decks an' here's the sex!
   I like the jads for a' that.   *hussies*

For a' that an' a' that
   An' twice as muckle's a' that,
My dearest bluid to do them guid,[n]   *blood (semen); good*
235   They're welcome till't for a' that.   *to it*

RECITATIVO 7

So sung the bard – and Nansie's waws   walls
Shook with a thunder of applause
 Re-echo'd from each mouth!
They toom'd their pocks, they pawn'd their duds; emptied; bags; clothes
240 They scarcely left to coor their fuds cover; backsides
 To quench their lowan drouth; burning thirst
Then owre again the jovial thrang over; throng
 The poet did request
To lowse his pack an' wale a sang, loosen; choose a song
245 A ballad o' the best.
  He, rising, rejoicing,
   Between his twa Deborahs,[n] two
  Looks round him an' found them
  Impatient for the chorus.

SONG 7

AIR

Tune: *Jolly Mortals, fill your glasses.*   [Ritson's *English Songs*, 1783.]

1 See the smok-ing bowl be-fore us,   Mark our jo-vial, rag-ged ring!

5 Round and round take up the chor-us,   And in rap-tures let us sing, —

250 See the smoking bowl before us,
 Mark our jovial, ragged ring!
Round and round take up the chorus,
 And in raptures let us sing –

Chorus

A fig for those by law protected!
255 Liberty's a glorious feast!
Courts for cowards were erected,
 Churches built to please the priest.

What is title, what is treasure,
    What is reputation's care?
260 If we lead a life of pleasure,
    'Tis no matter how or where.
      A fig &c.

With the ready trick and fable
    Round we wander all the day;
And at night, in barn or stable,
265   Hug our doxies on the hay.   wenches
      A fig &c.

Does the train-attended carriage
    Thro' the country lighter rove?
Does the sober bed of marriage
    Witness brighter scenes of love?
      A fig &c.

270 Life is all a variorum,   changing scene
    We regard not how it goes;
Let them cant about decorum,   preach
    Who have character to lose.
      A fig &c.

Here's to budgets, bags and wallets!   tool bags
275   Here's to all the wandering train!
Here's our ragged brats and callets!   wenches
    One and all cry out, Amen!
      A fig for those by law protected,
      Liberty's a glorious feast!
280   Courts for cowards were erected,
      Churches built to please the priest.

Notes

The editor wishes to express his gratitude for the great dictionaries that we all rely on in working with Scottish texts; these indispensable authorities are abbreviated in these notes as follows:

DOST – *The Dictionary of the Older Scottish Tongue* (in progress)
SND – *The Scottish National Dictionary*
OED – *The Oxford English Dictionary,* 2nd ed.
MED – *The Middle English Dictionary* (in progress)
EDSL – *An Etymological Dictionary of the Scottish Language* by
     John Jamieson
EDD – *The English Dialect Dictionary* by Joseph Wright

In addition, I am obviously deeply indebted to the notes and glosses in various scholarly editions of the poems included here, where such editions exist, especially to *Longer Scottish Poems*, I, edited by Bawcutt and Riddy, and II, edited by Crawford, Hewitt, and Law; to Kinsley's edition of Dunbar, Hamer's of Lindsay, Cranstoun's of Alexander Scott, Kastner's of Drummond, Martin and Oliver's and Kinghorn and Law's of Ramsay, McDiarmid's of Fergusson, and Kinsley's of Burns.

1. Anon., *Peblis To The Play, c.* 1430–1450

TEXT: Based on the Maitland Folio Manuscript in the Pepys Library in Magdalene College, Cambridge, the only known source for this poem, as printed in *The Maitland Folio Manuscript*, ed. William A. Craigie, Scottish Text Society, 2nd Ser., 7 (Edinburgh and London, 1919), I, 176–183. This transcript, abbreviated in the notes as 'M', has been carefully checked against the original MS at Cambridge, and a few discrepancies have been detected and explained in the notes to individual lines. The present editor has slightly modernised the text according to the principles spelled out in 'A Note on the Texts', and is responsible for the punctuation (non-existent in the MS). A few obvious scribal errors have also been corrected, but all such changes are duly recorded in the notes that follow. As for the layout of the stanza, in the actual manuscript the short 'bob' line (line 9) is added to the end of line 8 after a space, and raised slightly above the level of line 8. John Pinkerton, in the first printing of this poem in *Select Scottish Ballads* (London, 1783), II, 1–14, adopted the arrangement of the stanza that he found in William Tytler's edition of 'Christis Kirk on the Grene' in *The Works of James the First, King of Scotland* (Perth,

1783) and in some of the earlier printings of the same poem. This standard layout has been followed in all later editions of 'Peblis' and 'Christis Kirk', including this one.

The language of this text suggests a fifteenth-century date of composition. The vocabulary is solidly of the fifteenth century, and there is a total lack of vocalised 'l's before other consonants – a change that occurred in the pronunciation of Middle Scots about 1450, according to Professor A.J. Aitken, retired chief editor of *DOST*. On the whole, a date of about 1430–1450 would be the best guess, with the authorship left anonymous.

Since this poem remained in MS until 1783, unlike 'Christis Kirk' which was extremely popular and was printed and reprinted many times through the 17th and 18th centuries, it has generally been assumed that 'Peblis' had 'disappeared' for centuries until 'discovered' in the Maitland Folio MS by Thomas Percy in the 1780s. One scrap of evidence, however, tends to modify this view. Sir David Lindsay refers to something called 'Peblis on the greine' in his great morality play *Ane Satyre of the Thrie Estaitis*, 1552 and 1554 (see *The Works of Sir David Lindsay*, ed. Douglas Hamer (Edinburgh and London, 1931–1936), II, 45). The passage (lines 154–57) reads as follows:

> Thocht [Though] I ane seruand lang haif bene,
> My purchase [gain] is nocht worth ane preine [pin]:
> I may sing Peblis on the greine
>   For ocht [anything] that I may tursse [carry away].

Hamer, IV, 171, quotes a note on this point by George Chalmers, ed., *The Works of Sir David Lindsay*, (London, 1806), I, 368: 'The allusion is to some popular song, quite different from the ludicrous poem of *Peblis at the Play*.' Chalmers, however, may have been wrong, may have dismissed this too easily as a reference to our poem. Perhaps Lindsay's allusion is a humorous conflation of two titles that would be known to his audience – 'Peblis to the Play' and 'Christis Kirk on the Grene'. Such an interpretation is supported by the context, where the speaker, Solace, is complaining that even a performance by him of a long poem of this kind would gain him nothing in the way of a solid reward. If this is, in fact, a reference to 'Peblis', then we have proof that the poem had not 'disappeared' but was well known in Lindsay's time (the 1550s), and perhaps circulated widely in manuscripts that have been lost.

1 *Beltane:* an ancient Druid holy day on the first of May, for many centuries celebrated at Peebles with a cattle market, general fair, and festival.

2 *Peblis:* modern Peebles, an ancient town on the River Tweed, about 20 miles south of Edinburgh, where the Beltane Fair was held annually on 1 May.

6 *graythit:* M reads 'graythhit', the first 'h' being the expansion of the abbreviation for 'th'; the second 'h' is unnecessary, added by the scribe by mistake.

7 *that:* M reads 'thai', clearly a slip of the pen for 'that'.

8 *For:* M reads 'ffor', the 'ff' being simply a sign for capital 'F' when it occurs at the beginning of a line, here and elsewhere.

15 *Ane:* M reads 'And', which makes no sense and must be a scribal error for

'Ane' – meaning one of the wenches. *nocht:* M has 'gude' deleted here after 'nocht'.

21. *tippet:* the precise meaning here is problematic. The more likely of the two definitions of this noun in *OED* reads as follows: 'a long narrow strip of cloth or hanging part of dress, formerly worn, either attached to and forming part of the hood, head-dress, or sleeve, or loose, as a scarf or the like'. In this context, in view of the *hude* specified in line 17 and the business of allowing the tippet to *hing* in line 22, it is most probable that the tippet here is a strip of cloth attached to the hood and hanging down a girl's back.

23 *bend:* this word can mean 'blow' or 'ribbon' (band). In light of line 24, however, 'blow' seems the preferable interpretation – perhaps a bawdy suggestion that her back (and tippet) will take some punishment when he gets her laid on her back.

24 *We meit nocht:* apparently this curious expression means that 'you can chase me but you won't catch me' – we will never meet together in a love tryst. See *DOST* under *mete*, to meet together, 'said of a pursuer and the pursued, when the former overtakes the latter'. This same usage occurs in 'Sym and his Bruder', line 94.

26 *That:* M has 'Thay', but this is a misreading by Craigie; the actual MS reads 'That'.

27 *Than:* M reads 'That', a slip of the pen.

31 *'Ever,'* etc: M at first had a wholly different line here, as follows – 'Allace,' quod scho, 'what sall I do?' This was crossed out and replaced by the line as given.

33 *yon mercat to:* M at first read 'amang na ging', but this phrase was crossed out and replaced with the one given, which makes more sense.

35 *Amang:* M had 'To mok' here, but this is deleted.

36 *Marie:* Presumably 'Mary', the name of the sunburnt wench's girl friend. *anis mynt,* etc: This expression signifies that on this one occasion (*anis*) she will venture (*mynt*) to stand off at a distance and peek at the merchants; she is too embarrassed by her sunburn to approach them any closer.

41 *Hopcalye and Cardronow:* two small villages on the south bank of the Tweed, about three and five miles east of Peebles respectively; modern Kailzie and Cardrona. George Eyre-Todd, ed. *Scottish Poetry of the Sixteenth Century* (London and Edinburgh, 1892), p. 160, grossly misread these place-names as common nouns – hob, caile, and curdower – and glossed them as 'man, woman, and apprentice-lad'.

43 *rohumbelow:* M has 'rolumbelow', but this is likely to be a slip of the pen for 'rohumbelow' – a common song refrain formula. Pinkerton in *Select Scotish Ballads* (London, 1783), II, 3, was the first to make this emendation.

44 *folkis:* M reads 'foltis', a slip of the pen.

45 *bagpipe:* M reads 'byg pyk', another scribal blunder.

49 *Thair west:* this means that the folk were heading westward toward Peebles from the villages named in line 41.

61 *gane:* M reads 'gang', then corrected to 'gane'.

67 *lat me be:* M reads 'me lat be', but this is almost certainly a scribal error.

68 *Tweddell syd:* 'Tweddell' seems to be an affectionate diminutive for Tweed;

the whole phrase refers to inhabitants of the Tweed valley around Peebles, men of Tweedside.

81   *townis:* town's – i.e., town of Peebles.

85–6 Townspeople laughing at the behaviour and dress of country bumpkins is a widespread folk motif.

92   *oly prance:* M gives a hyphen between these words, but careful scrutiny of the actual MS shows only a space.

100 This line in M reads, 'Of Peblis etc.'

104 *we:* the actual MS has 'he' crossed out and replaced by 'we', a correction unnoted in M.

115 *uther:* M reads 'vthe'.

117 *tak:* M reads 'stak'.

118 *service:* M reads 'sseruice', which may be a scribal error for 'servite', meaning 'deserved', or, more probably, for 'service', meaning 'deserves'.

141–150 Two lines are apparently missing here in M; no doubt the copyist simply skipped over them by accident. Craigie (ed. M) placed the hiatus at lines 143 and 144; Eyre-Todd, *Scottish Poetry of the Sixteenth Century*, p. 164, more plausibly, suggested 145 and 146. The latter arrangement seems preferable in the context, since line 144 ('Scantlie scho micht owr hy him') means his wife could scarcely catch up to her husband who was running to get into the fight. The missing lines (145–146) probably described how the 'cadgear' actually got mixed up in the confused struggle in the rubbish heap, followed by his wife's effort to extricate him ('He held, scho drew').

153 *Hald one:* this is the reading in M and it is confirmed by a scrutiny of the MS itself. Eyre-Todd and others have emended 'one' to 'our', so that the whole phrase means 'Hold our gudeman', that is, 'Restrain my husband'. A more likely reading, however, would go back to the MS version and interpret 'Hald one gud man!' as 'Hold on, husband', in the sense of 'Wait!' This view is corroborated by the parallel pattern two lines later in '"Abyd," quod scho'.

173 *fell:* M reads 'feill', which could be interpreted as 'feel', but makes far better sense as 'fell' since the wife is inquiring as to how the cadger fell off his horse. He explains in the following lines.

175 *nocht:* this word is missing in M, but is wholly necessary to the sense: the cadger knows *not* what it was.

184 *grufling:* M reads 'gruflingis'; the 'is' ending could possibly indicate a plural form ('grovelling ones'), but is more probably a scribal error by contamination from 'stokkis' and should be omitted.

186 *ox:* in the actual MS this word is written with what looks like a hook at the end, the normal abbreviation for 'is', similar to the 'is' abbreviations for 'nokkis', 'stokkis', and 'cockkis' in the same stanza – suggesting that the author intended a comic distortion of the pronunciation of 'ox' as 'ockis'.

187 *cum:* M reads 'cuming', which makes no sense and must be another slip of the pen.

188 *be Goddis cokkis:* this is a more or less meaningless oath; more often 'cokkis' is used as a euphemism for 'Godis', as in 'By cokkis woundis', meaning 'by God's wounds' (wounds of Christ on cross). Swearing 'by God's cocks' makes no rational sense in itself.

195 *schamous dance:* this is a phrase that has baffled editors of the poem from

John Pinkerton (*Select Scotish Ballads*, London 1783) who guessed at 'salmon' and James Sibbald (*Chronicle of Scottish Poetry*, Edinburgh, 1802) who suggested more plausibly 'show-man' or 'shaw-man', to recent times. John Jamieson in *EDSL*(1882) was amusingly vague also, calling it, 'Some particular kind of dance anciently used in Scotland'. Part of the problem is simply a matter of spelling: John Pinkerton, in the Preface to his *Ancient Scotish Poems, Never Before in Print*, 2 vols. (London and Edinburgh, 1786), tells us that this piece was 'discovered' by Bishop Thomas Percy in the Maitland Folio MS in the Pepys Library at Magdalene College, Cambridge, and that Percy had 'communicated' to him a complete transcript of the poem. Pinkerton used Percy's transcript as the copy-text for the first printing of the poem in *Select Scotish Ballads* (London, 1783), II, 1–14, in which the unfortunate misspelling of *schamous* as *schamons* first appears. The error may have originated in Percy's transcript (which has not survived), or Pinkerton may have misread Percy's handwriting. At any rate, Pinkerton, intrigued by Percy's account of the Maitland Folio, went to Cambridge himself in December 1782 and made his own hurried transcript of the entire MS, completing the task in a few days. Pinkerton misread this word as *schamons* and repeated the error in his important printing of most of the Maitland Folio in *Ancient Scotish Poems*. This error has been perpetuated in almost all subsequent editions of the poem, including the authoritative Scottish Text Society edition by William A. Craigie (M). Craigie, of course, went back to the original MS for his text; but, no doubt biased by Pinkerton's reading, his eye must have passed over the mistake. The present editor in examining the MS itself has determined that *schamous* is the correct reading – the letters 'ou' here are identical in form to the 'ou' in 'about' two lines later (197). It is, of course, easy to confuse 'u' with 'n', and that is what has happened here. Pinkerton's mistake has been repeated over and over, and this misspelling has hopelessly confused efforts to make sense of the entire phrase. To my knowledge, only one editor – George Eyre-Todd in *Scottish Poetry of the 16th Century* (London, [1892]), p. 165 – has suspected a mistake here and has emended the spelling to 'schamou's'. This seems to have been a guess, however, since Eyre-Todd did not consult the MS and glossed the phrase in the usual vague way as 'a dance now unknown'; his apostrophe is purely apocryphal. The correct form, 'schamous', is a variant spelling for 'shalmuse', meaning a medieval wind instrument with a double reed, the 'shawm', a forerunner of the oboe, or 'hautboy' (i.e., French 'hautbois' or 'high-pitched wood'). The term *shawm* in its various spelling was also used more generally for a pipe or flute of any kind. The specific form 'shalmuse' is derived from the Old French word for shawm, namely *chalemiaus* or *chalemeaux* (plurals of *chalemel* – from Latin *calamus*, a reed). The singular *shalmuse*, according to *MED*, was 'perhaps formed under the influence of OF *muse*, a wind instrument, as in the second element of ME *cornemuse* = hornpipe, an early form of bagpipe'. See also *OED* under *shawm*, where several quotations are given for the word in this form (*shalmuse*) for the years 1430, 1440, 1480, 1483, etc., including some from Middle Scots texts. The *schalmuse dance*, then, literally means a dance to the music of the shawm; but in view of the reference to *bagpyp* in line 194 it may in this context be simply a dance to bagpipe music. Clearly, this was a dance named after the accompanying instrument, as in the case of the dance called 'the hornpipe'. The only previous scholar who has suggested the connection with 'shawm' seems to have been Francisque Xavier Michel (also known as Francisque-Michel) who in an obscure note in his book *A Critical Inquiry into the Scottish Language with the view of illustrating the Rise and Progress of Civilization in Scotland* (Edinburgh and London, 1882), p. 236, says: '*Schamon's dance* seems to be so named from the musical instrument named *schawme* (O. Fr. *chalemie*)'.

207 *your:* M reads 'yon', but this is very likely a scribal error; to go (or come) 'your gaitis' is a common Scots idiom.

217 This line apparently means that 'she went away with him as her tail was burning with lust'.

221 *The:* M reads 'Thy'.

222 *Too:* M reads 'to'.

231 *Be that:* M reads 'Bayth', almost certainly a scribal error – see lines 181 and 251 which also begin with 'Be that'.

235 *Wat:* M reads 'Quhat' (i.e., 'What'), but the proper name makes more sense here.

238 *sweit of swair:* this is a common romance formula for a lady with a sweet neck; *OED* gives several examples from the 15th and early 16th centuries (1440–1513), including two from Middle Scots writers (Holland and Douglas).

251 *settand schaftis:* John Pinkerton in *Ancient Scotish Poems* (London and Edinburgh, 1786), I, 452, says '"Schaftes" is certainly a false reading taken from the close of this line by some weary transcriber. Lines 1 and 3 never rime towards the end of the poem. Read "settand *reid*."' Pinkerton's substitution of 'reid' for 'schaftis' here is pure guesswork, based on a shaky statement concerning rimes; but it is, of course, possible that the copyist's eye picked up 'schaftis' from the end of line 253 and inserted it here for some other word by mistake. However, 'schaftis', meaning rays or beams of the sun, makes good sense here.

251–58 The final stanza is foreshortened through the omission of the two 'bobwheel' lines at the end, and the incorporation of the refrain as the last line of the octave. It will be noted that the final two lines (257, 258) echo the opening two lines of the poem, rounding it off rather neatly.

253 *schukin of chaftis:* this is an obscure phrase. The first word appears as *schukin* in M, but Craigie marks it *Sic*, implying an error in spelling. Pinkerton (1783) renders the phrase as *schriken of chaftis*, whatever that means. Eyre-Todd accepts Pinkerton's revision and interprets it as 'shock of lips' (kissing). The MS 'schaftis' is probably a scribal slip for 'chaftis', by contamination from the last word of line 251, but 'chaftis' never seems to mean 'lips'. The best guess here, and it is only a guess, would be that *schukin of chaftis* means shaking of jaws, i.e., a lot of talking, tongue wagging.

2. Anon., *Christis Kirk on the Grene, c.* 1490–1510

TEXT: This poem has come down to us in at least seven manuscript versions as well as several early printed texts. The three most important manuscript texts are referred to in these notes by the following abbreviations:

B: *The Bannatyne Manuscript, 1568*, by George Bannatyne, ed. W. Tod Ritchie, 4 vols., STS, 2nd Ser., 22, 23, 26, 3rd Ser. 5 (Edinburgh, 1928–1932), II, 262–268.

M: *The Maitland Folio Manuscript, c.* 1570–1586, ed. William A. Craigie, 2 vols., STS, 2nd Ser., 7, 20 (Edinburgh 1919, 1926), I, 149–155.

L: The Laing Manuscripts, *c.* 1640, in Edinburgh University Library, as printed in 'Seventeenth-century Versions of *Christis Kirk on the Grene* and *The Wyf of Awchtirmwchty*', by Janet M. Templeton, in *Studies in Scottish Literature*, 4 (1966–67), 127–137. The title of the poem in this MS is given as 'A merry ballad Compyled (as is Propposed) by King James the fifth Called kettes kirkle on the grein'.

Of these three manuscript sources B and M are almost equally good, careful transcripts in the ten-line 'bobwheel' stanza form. Together they represent the earliest and most authoritative textual tradition for this poem – the basic source for all modern editions, with relatively few scribal errors. In M, however, two pairs of stanzas (3–4, 5–6) are reversed out of the logical order they follow in B. On the other hand, stanza 12, which seems to be an authentic part of the poem, is missing in B and is inserted here from M, in square brackets. On the whole, the text in B seems slightly superior and is followed here as the copy-text, except for a few readings (in lines 62, 67, 75, 144, 154 and 225) where the M version is clearly preferable. All departures from the B text are carefully recorded in these notes.

L, in contrast, seems to be the parent of a much later (*c.* 1640) and more corrupt textual tradition, with the truncated nine-line stanza form that was perpetuated in all the 17th-century printed texts of the poem. The gross corruption of L is shown in the garbled title of 'kettes kirkle', which seems to be a curious conflation of 'Christis Kirk' and 'kitteis... kirtillis' (see lines 7, 8). This error, like scores of others throughout the text, is so gross as to suggest that the copyist often had no understanding at all of what he was reading. Nevertheless, in a very few instances L is useful in confirming interpretations of B or M. L is of interest also as the earliest known example of the simplified bobwheel, shortened to a single dimeter tag line ending in 'that day'.

Apart from these manuscripts, the text of 'Christis Kirk' has been preserved in an impressive number of early printed versions of the seventeenth century, attesting to the immense popularity of this poem in Scotland. Printed texts have survived, for example, from the earliest in 1643, followed by others in 1660, 1663, and 1684, to the influential edition of Bishop Edmund Gibson in 1691. All of these early printings, unfortunately, belong to the flawed textual tradition of L, and are marred by errors and inaccuracies so that no single one of them is as clean and authoritative as either B or M. Thorough descriptions and collations of all seven manuscripts and of five of the early printed texts can be found in Christine Marie Harker's unpublished M.A. thesis, 'Chrystis Kirk of the Grene: A Critical Edition' (University of Victoria, Victoria, B.C., Canada, 1990), to which I am indebted.

The date of composition of this poem remains problematic. George Bannatyne in his great manuscript of 1568 attributed it to King James I (died 1437), but the linguistic evidence points to a considerably later date. However, language alone is an uncertain guide to dating in the case of a poem such as 'Christis Kirk', a poem that undoubtedly circulated in manuscript texts for generations before being fixed in print. Such texts were subject to constant scribal revision, most commonly in response to the natural human tendency toward modernisation. Nevertheless, the language tells us something; at least it suggests some probabilities, if not certainties. For one thing, stanza 18 (see note on line 171) shows clear evidence of the vocalisation of 'l' before another consonant, a development that did not take place in Middle Scots until 1450, according to Professor A.J. Aitken, the retired chief editor of the *DOST*. Equally suggestive of a date after 1450 is the evidence given by Earl F. Guy in his unpublished Ph.D. thesis, 'Some Comic and Burlesque Poems in the Sixteenth Century Scottish Manuscript Anthologies' (Edinburgh University, 1952), pp. 24–25. He points out that the poem contains 'a high percentage of words not recorded until 1500 or later', though he admits that most of these are colloquialisms which may have been in the spoken Scots for many years before finding their way into written literature. Guy's list of these 'late' words is as follows: *barrow trammis, baty bummill, bobbit, bougaris, chat, clokkis, dirdum, dulis, gympt, gobbis, gammis, hensour, jummill, kensy, lynkome, murionit, mudlet, nevell, paikis,* and *yunkeris.* Altogether, the linguistic evidence, inconclusive as it is, points to a date of about 1500 – and that is the best we can do. Such a dating would rule out both James I and James V (who has also been credited with the poem on much shakier external evidence than Bannatyne's); and, unless and until new facts turn up, we must continue to regard 'Christis Kirk' as an anonymous masterpiece.

3 *Falkland on the grene:* Falkland is a village in central Fife, the site of a royal palace that was once a favourite residence of the Scottish kings. The parallel phrasing of 'Falkland on the grene', 'Peblis at the play', and 'Christis Kirk on the grene' strongly suggests that these were the titles of well-known poems all of the same genre. The later two, of course, we have; but the poem of 'Falkland on the grene' has perished. Its mention here, however, suggests that there may have existed a considerable number of similar pieces that have since been lost.

4 *Peblis at the play:* this is beyond doubt a reference to the companion poem of 'Peblis to the Play'. M reads 'Peblis to the play' for this phrase. The reference also proves that the poems on 'Peblis' and on 'Falkland' were composed, in circulation, and popularly known *before* the composition of 'Christis Kirk'.

6 *Christ Kirk:* of several churches in Scotland with this name only two have been suggested as the locale of this poem: near Dunnideer in the parish of Leslie, Aberdeenshire, and Leslie in Fife. The former church, near the small village of Dunnideer, is about a mile and a half west south west of the town of Insch, about a mile and a half north of Leslie, and about ten miles

west north west of Inverurie, off highway B9002. On Ordinance Survey maps the building is specifically identified as 'Christ's Kirk on the Green', a fact that indicates a local tradition connecting this place with the poem. The identification of this site in central Aberdeenshire was first made in 1783 by William Tytler in his edition of *The Works of James the First, King of Scotland* (Perth). Tytler states that the green near this church was used for an annual fair on the first day of May for centuries, until as late as 1700. His opinion on the locale was accepted by John Pinkerton in 1786 in *Ancient Scotish Poems*, and has generally been concurred in by those modern editors who have considered the matter at all.

The idea that the church was in the small town of Leslie in central Fife is based on a groundless assumption by Allan Ramsay in his 'Canto II' continuation of 'Christis Kirk' in 1715. In his ninth stanza Ramsay gives a satiric portrait of a foppish young man ('a pensy blade') who is jeered by the local folk – 'they said that he was Falkland bred, / And danced by the book'. Since Leslie is only about seven miles south of Falkland and the royal palace, this was intended by Ramsay as a local joke. In all probability Ramsay simply confused the church in Leslie, Fife, with the one in Aberdeenshire; but there is no real evidence to connect it with the poem.

Equally fanciful is John Pinkerton's notion that James I in writing these three poems (he assumes that the king was also the author of 'Falkland on the grene') was attempting to illustrate three different Scots dialects: Northern Scots in 'Christis Kirk', Middle Scots in 'Falkland', and Southern Scots in 'Peblis'. Of 'Christis Kirk' he says (*Ancient Scotish Poems*, London and Edinburgh, 1786, I, 449–450) that it 'refers to the rural manners of the North of Scotland; and is composed in the Scandinavian alliteration, and with many Norse words. The other, or *Peblis*, to those of the South of Scotland; and is full of the southern Scotish, or north English, words of old metrical romances. *Falkland* is unfortunately lost; but we may well suppose it described the sports of Fifeshire, or the middle of Scotland in words adapted to that part'. This is pure fantasy, wholly unfounded linguistically – a preposterous theory!

7 *our kitteis:* M reads 'our kittie', and this has been interpreted by some editors as a reference to a particular girl called 'Kitty'; but the version in B seems to make more sense, especially in view of the plural forms in lines 8, 10 and 11, clearly indicating a group of girls.

9 This 'bob' line here and throughout the poem is presented in the MSS as a tag at the end of line 8, separated from it by small spaces and a slash in B (generally) and by a large space in M. In L, of course, the 'bobwheel' is eliminated altogether and replaced by a single dimeter tag line ending in 'that day'.

10 *of the grene:* B has this phrase for stanzas 1–8, shifts to 'on the grene' for stanzas 9–12, then back to 'of the grene' for stanzas 13–22. M has 'on' for stanzas 1–10, 'of' for stanzas 11–20, 'on' for stanzas 21–23. Traditionally, the phrase 'on the grene' has been used for the poem's title.

15 *lynkome licht:* this phrase has commonly been glossed as 'Lincoln green', but as long ago as 1802 Sibbald argued rather cogently that 'lynkome' simply means 'linen'. He gave evidence of the manufacture of linen in Scotland in 1426 in the reign of James I. See James Sibbald, *Chronicle of*

Scottish Poetry, II, 368.

20 *that day:* in B this tag is added to the normal refrain here and in lines 200 and 230; it does not appear anywhere as part of the refrain in M. The same tag is used as the 'bob' line in one other stanza (6 in B, 5 in M). In Alexander Scott's 'Justing and Debait' (*c.* 1560) this phrase became part of the refrain throughout ('Up at the Drum that day') and in the Laing MS version of 'Christis Kirk' (*ca.* 1640) the 'bobwheel' is shortened to one dimeter line ending always in 'that day'. This last arrangement became the standard for the 18th century, but the first hint of it goes back, as we see here, all the way to the original 'Christis Kirk'.

21–40 In M these two stanzas are reversed, but the order in B is surely correct here.

32 *murionit:* for this verb form both M and L have 'morgeound'.

41–60 These two stanzas are reversed in M, but the order in B (and L) makes more sense.

45 *Auld lychtfute:* M has 'All auld licht futtis he', which may be the better reading here, since the context seems to mean that the fiddler turned away from native 'light-foot' dance tunes, and instead tried to imitate foreign French melodies. *thair:* in B the abbreviation for this word is inserted within the line, and the word *did* is inserted above the line – both in a different coloured ink (faded brown instead of black) and in a different hand from Bannatyne's. Both words are necessary to the sense of the line.

48 *moreiss danss:* the mention of this popular rural dance, often performed on May Day, fits in with Tytler's statement that the annual fair at Christ's Kirk near Dunnideer, Aberdeenshire, was also held on 1 May.

49 *Full lowd:* M has 'scho tuik' for this line, presumably referring back to 'Towsy' in line 44; but this makes little sense in the context. In this instance L confirms the reading in B.

62 *Dowie:* B renders the girl's name as 'Dwny', but this seems to be a scribal error. M gives the name as 'dowie', L as 'tusie'. On the whole, 'Dowie' would appear to be the best choice.

65 *javell:* M has 'gavell', but this seems to be simply an alternative spelling for the same word.

65 *kensy:* an obscure 'term of abuse applied to men' (*DOST*); the gloss 'scoundrel' is a guess or rather a rough approximation of what this word signifies.

67 This line is defective in B, reading 'They pairtit hir manly with a nevell', which makes no sense. In this instance the wording in M has been substituted.

71–130 These stanzas (8–13) contain an extended satire on peasant archery, a ludicrous picture of repeated bungling with bow and arrow. William Tytler in *The Works of James the First, King of Scotland* (Perth, 1783), pp. 49–53, 225–226, makes a strong argument in favour of the authorship of this poem by James I, based on the fact that this king was deeply concerned over the decline of archery in Scotland and passed legislation to revive traditional military skills with bow and arrow. In the succeeding reign of James II, however, gunpowder and artillery came into use in Scotland, making archery obsolete in warfare. Tytler maintains that this burlesque of peasant archery would have been pointless after the reign of James I.

74 *'Dirdum Dardum':* the first word of this phrase clearly means 'a loud noise or uproar'; the two words together suggest a term of contempt or derision – 'Big Noise!' – spoken sarcastically and implying that the other's words are an empty threat, 'hot air', all noise but no real substance.

75 *Throw:* B reads 'Throwt', a copying error – see *throw* in the next line; M has 'Throw'.

78 This line, in the context, is probably an arch suggestion that the rustic threatened by the bungling archer was 'marred' only by fear causing a spontaneous bowel evacuation – a common motif in folklore. The narrator cannot, or chooses not to, explain exactly what happened to him.

91 *hensure:* this term is of uncertain meaning and etymology. *DOST* cites one other use of the word (in Sir David Lindsay) and gives the conjectural definition of an 'idle young fellow'.

104 *weddir:* George Chalmers in his edition of the poem in *The Poetic Remains of Some of the Scottish Kings* (London, 1824), p. 155, says that this was 'a legal forfeiture for not practising archery' – according to a parliamentary act in the reign of James I. In a sheep-raising country like Scotland a wether or neutered ram was a common unit of value. For northern Europe generally rams were often offered as prizes in village contests, as in Chaucer's description of the Miller in the General Prologue (line 550) of *The Canterbury Tales* ('At wrastling he wolde have alway the ram'). Christine Harker, who pointed out this legal usage to me, also thinks (in her edition of the poem cited above in the section on the Text) that there may be as well a sexual innuendo here – Lowry suggesting that Hary is as impotent as a *weddir*.

111–120 This stanza, missing in B, is included in M and (in corrupt form) in L. Since it follows logically from the last lines of the previous stanza it would seem to be a genuine part of the poem and is inserted here within square brackets. The text is that of M.

137 *The:* B reads 'Thy', an obvious error.

144 *eschewit:* B has 'mischevit' here, but this is most probably a scribal error since this verb is repeated as the rime in line 148; moreover, 'eschewit' fits the sense much better here as part of a proverbial phrase 'to eschew evil'. M has 'eschewit', clearly the preferable reading in this instance.

153 *down:* in B this word is inserted above the line in a different coloured ink and in a different hand – the same as in line 45 and as in the ascription of 'Peder Coffeis' to 'Linsday' (see also note in discussion of possible authorship of 'Sym and his Bruder'). Since the handwriting in all these places, and *passim* throughout the MS, is not Bannatyne's but is in the same general style and period, the probability is that Bannatyne had some knowledgeable person (a friend, perhaps) proofread the entire MS, making occasional insertions or corrections in a different ink.

154 *baty bummill:* this is the reading in M; B has 'barty bummill', but the M version makes better sense here. The 'barty' form seems to be a scribal error, probably by contamination from 'Barla' in line 158. The phrase 'baty bummill' was apparently a folk idiom for a clumsy oaf.

157 *his:* in the actual MS this word is repeated by mistake.

158 *Barla fummyll:* the first word of this phrase is clear – it is a corruption of the French 'Parlez!' meaning 'Talk!' and is a cry for a truce, still current in

some children's games in Scotland in the form 'Barley!' The second term is of uncertain etymology, but there is no doubt that the entire phrase, as *DOST* states, is 'an exclamation requesting a truce in fighting or play'. It occurs also in William Drummond of Hawthornden's 'Polemo-Middinia', in line 164. See the note on Drummond's line in Bishop Edmund Gibson's edition of 1691, as presented in the article by Beatrice White, 'Two Notes on Middle English', *Neophilologus*, 37 (1953), 114–115.

171 *bowdin:* this is an instance of the vocalisation of 'l' before another consonant in Middle Scots (*bowdin* < *boldin*), a development that did not occur until about 1450. In the opinion of Professor A.J. Aitken, as the retired editor of *DOST* to whom I am indebted here, this would suggest a date of composition after 1450, perhaps as late as the first decade of the sixteenth century. In this stanza the third and fourth rimes – *goldin, yoldin* – would presumably also be vocalised in actual pronunciation. An exactly parallel phenomenon of the vocalisation of 'l' before another consonant occurred in the evolution from Latin to Old French to Middle and Modern French. Examples of this can be seen in Latin 'alba' becoming French 'aube', and 'ultra' becoming 'oltra' and finally 'outre'.

193 *Than followit feymen:* this phrase in M reads 'thai forsey freikis' (those strong fellows), which makes good sense and fits the meter better; the version in B followed here, however, is equally sensible and has the added attraction of comic humour in the idea that these men were 'fated to die' in the fracas – an amusing exaggeration.

212 *branewod:* a difficult term in this context. The rest of the line ('brynt in bailis') certainly means 'burned in bonfires', so that 'branewod' probably is 'brain-mad', 'crazy ones', 'madmen', making lines 211 and 212 mean something like 'When they had roared like baited bulls, or like madmen burned in fires'. Another possible reading is John Pinkerton's guess (in *Ancient Scotish Poems*, London and Edinburgh, 1786, I, 450) that 'branewod' is 'a kind of matchwood', that is kindling wood that burns very quickly and in so doing makes a *roaring* sound. On the whole, however, the first explanation seems more plausible.

217 *held thair dulis:* in M this phrase is 'halit the dulis', which may be correct since this was a sporting cry in football – to 'hale the dule' was to 'salute the goal' or to cry 'Victory!' The wording in B given here, however, also makes sense: they 'held thair dulis' may simply mean that they held their stations (goals), held their ground against attack.

225 *gud glaikis!:* B has 'gub glaikis' for this phrase, which makes little or no sense, and is almost certainly an error. The correct reading, 'gud glaikis', is in M (also L) and is a colloquial expletive meaning 'You silly fool!' The same phrase occurs in Sir David Lindsay's *Ane Satyre of the Thrie Estaitis* (*c.* 1552), lines 4390, 4394: 'Cum heir gude Glaikis my dochter deir... Cum hidder stult [Stupid] my sone and air'. See *The Works of Sir David Lindsay*, ed. Douglas Hamer, 4 vols, STS, 3rd Ser. 1, 2, 6, 8 (Edinburgh and London, 1930–1934), II, 387; and Hamer's note, IV, 234; also Allan H. MacLaine, '*Christis Kirk on the Green* and Sir David Lindsay's *Satyre of the Thrie Estaitis*', *Journal of English and Germanic Philology*, 56 (1957), 596–601.

3. William Dunbar, *The Justis Betwix the Talyeour and the Soutar, c.* 1500

TEXT: This poem has survived in three manuscript texts as follows:

A: *The Asloan Manuscript, A Miscellany in Prose and Verse, Written by John Asloan in the Reign of James the Fifth,* ed. William A. Craigie, 2 vols., Scottish Text Soc., 2nd Ser., 14, 16, Edinburgh and London, 1923, 1925.
B: *The Bannatyne Manuscript,* ed. W. Tod Ritchie, II, 295–298.
M: *The Maitland Folio Manuscript,* ed. William A. Craigie, II, 184–187.

The most authoritative modern scholarly edition of the poem is that of James Kinsley in *The Poems of William Dunbar,* Oxford, 1979, pp. 154–157, 339–341. Of the three manuscript texts the earliest, A, seems to be the best on the whole, though Kinsley bases his edition on B. In the present edition A is used as the copy-text, with readings from B substituted in two or three lines where B is clearly superior. All such departures from A are carefully recorded in the notes that follow.

3 *Mahoun:* Mahomet, or Mohammed, or Muhammad, A.D. 570–632, the prophet of Islam and founder of the Moslem religion, was frequently identified with the Devil himself in Christian medieval literature; 'Mahoun' was the normal Middle Scots spelling of the name.
5 *pricklouss, coble cloutare:* these were popular contemptuous terms for tailors and shoemakers or cobblers. *pricklouss* was a humorous name for a tailor who with his needle would often prick a louse in sewing lice-infested cloth.
10 *best gnapparis:* Kinsley's gloss on 'best' as 'basting thread' seems mistaken; I can find no evidence of this usage in *DOST, MED,* or *OED;* however, all three include under 'beist', 'best', or 'beast' the 'skin of a fur-bearing animal', and this seems preferable since tailors stole not only fragments of cloth, but also hides with fur for trimming or lining clothes.
11 *stomok stelaris:* Kinsley's explanation of this phrase as 'those who work protective steel into horses' pectoral covers' is ludicrous; the definition of 'stomok' in *EDSL* as simply 'a fragment of cloth' is surely the meaning here. *cat knapparis:* tailors no doubt also killed cats to use their fur for trimmings; B has 'clayth takkaris' (cloth takers or stealers) for this phrase, but that seems redundant coming in the same line after 'stomok stelaris'.
17 *the se flude fillis:* M has 'the greit se fillis' here, but B reads 'the greik sie flowis', interpreted by Kinsley as 'the tideless Mediterranean'; this latter reading seems dubious in the context, since the poet is clearly saying that tailors will never be true as long as the tides come in and go out, endlessly.
19 *buthman:* B and M read 'tailyour' here, but Priscilla Bawcutt in 'The Text and Interpretation of Dunbar', *Medium Aevum,* 50 (1981), 92–93, points out that 'buthman' in A is 'metrically equivalent and alliteratively better', with the same contemptuous flavour as Dunbar's use of the same term in 'Ane Tretis', line 309.
22 *come furth:* A has 'him comfort' here, but this does not fit the metre, and I have substituted the superior reading from B in this case. M has 'to comfort

him', which is even worse than A.

27 *as mast:* as Kinsley points out, this phrase may mean 'as the greatest' or 'as a ship's mast'; on the whole the latter seems more likely.

44 *Sanct Girnyga:* a minor devil who in medieval satiric folk lore served as the god or patron saint of shoemakers. He appears in another poem in the Bannatyne MS, the anonymous 'Flyting betwix the Soutar and the Tailyour', as their 'girnand [snarling] god grit Garnega'. Kinsley's note on this character is helpful.

51 *Uneiss:* Priscilla Bawcutt, p. 93 (see note on 1. 19), argues convincingly that this is a better reading than B's 'He mycht nocht rycht upsitt'. See *OED* under *uneaths*; Dunbar used the word also in 'The Passion of Christ', line 45.

73 *His birnes brak:* Bawcutt, p. 93 (see above), sees this as a better reading than B's 'His Harnas brak' since 'birnes' has much stronger romantic connotations as an heroic term for armour, coat of mail, cuirass, and hence suits Dunbar's burlesque purposes far better than the neutral 'harnas'. She thinks 'harnas' is 'probably a modern gloss on "birnes"'.

74 *scarrit:* B has 'start' here, M 'stert', and these may be the better readings since, as Kinsley points out, in all other uses of 'scare' in Dunbar poems the word begins with 'sk'. In this context, however, 'was scared' makes slightly better sense than 'started'.

81 *stern ... in stele:* A has 'strenyt', but this seems to be an error; 'stern in steel', the reading in both B and M, is a commonplace in chivalric romance, and here as applied to the Soutar it is, as Kinsley says, 'ludicrous'.

99 *Belialis:* Satan's, the Devil's.

101 *socht:* B reads 'rocht' here, but 'socht' is equally appropriate in the context.

107 *heir:* B has 'air' here, presumably meaning 'heir', but this is an error; the correct reading is 'heir', meaning 'lord' or 'master'; see Priscilla Bawcutt (note on line 19), p. 93, also *DOST* under 'her(e)', and *MED* under 'herre'.

108 *Schirris,* etc: this direct address to male auditors is clear proof that this poem was intended for oral presentation to a listening audience, no doubt by Dunbar himself as court poet.

109 *Heir endis,* etc: A has the simple attribution 'Quod Dunbar' at this point, but I have preferred to insert the longer statement from B, which includes the delightful irony of crediting this scatological tour de force to the 'nobill poyet'. George Bannatyne surely had a robust sense of humour as well as sophisticated sensibilities.

4. Anon., *Sym and his Bruder,* c. 1530

TEXT: The Bannatyne Manuscript is the only source for the text of this poem, and in this instance it is very imperfect. See *The Bannatyne Manuscript, 1568,* ed. W. Tod Ritchie (Edinburgh and London, 1928), III, 39–43, hereafter abbreviated as 'B'. The complete text has been printed only three times: in B; in David Laing's edition of *Select Remains of the Ancient Popular and Romance Poetry of Scotland* (Edinburgh, 1825), re-edited by John Small (Edinburgh 1885), pp. 312–318; and in Laing's *Early Popular Poetry of Scotland and the Northern Border,* 2 vols. (London, 1822 and 1826), re-edited by W. Carew Hazlitt (London, 1895), II, 5–10. The first seven stanzas were also included in James Sibbald's *Chronicle of Scottish Poetry* (Edinburgh, 1802), I, 360–1. Both Sibbald and Laing provided punctuation (lacking in B) and capitalisation (sporadic in B), and a few silent emendations; both texts are marred by a few minor errors. Laing includes one general note quoted from Sir David Dalrymple, Lord Hailes, ed. *Ancient Scottish Poems* (Edinburgh 1770), p. 348, but no glossary; Sibbald quotes the same material from Hailes (unacknowledged), and his general cumulative glossary (Vol. IV) is of limited use since it covers only the first seven stanzas of the poem and tends to ignore the really difficult or obscure words. On the whole, then, the poem has never been properly edited, with detailed notes and glossary. The present edition is the first to attempt anything approaching a scholarly treatment. The present text is based, inevitably, upon B, but incorporates those emendations of Sibbald and Laing that seem to be valid, as well as a number of corrections of newly detected errors. All departures from the text of B are recorded and justified in the notes.

1–150 Since this entire poem has come down to us in a very corrupt form in the Bannatyne MS (its only source), a summary of the story, however conjectural, may be helpful to readers struggling with the text as we have it. The present editor, therefore, at the risk of grievous error, offers the following outline as an attempt to make sense of the work as a whole: Sym and his brother are two scoundrels in St Andrews who pretended to be 'palmers', itinerant pilgrims living on alms. When the begging wears thin in St Andrews, they decorate themselves with symbols of religious shrines and make forays into the countryside to prey upon simple folk; then they return to their home base to live well upon their gains until another sortie is called for. In a time of unusual prosperity Sym's brother marries a widow, presumably a well-to-do one, less than a month after the death of her husband. The men folk of the town gather for the wedding and the feast afterwards, at which, no doubt, everyone gets drunk. A group of the 'lads' invade the house to inspect the groom sexually; Sym takes offence at this rudeness to his brother. At this point, between stanzas 8 and 9, there seems to be at least one stanza missing from the text. We can guess that the poet here set up a farcical tournament between the boastful Sym and the ringleader of the lads who were harassing his brother. At any rate, Sym on horseback is chased by the townsfolk to the field of battle, where they knock him down and tie him up tightly, while his horse runs wildly away. The older men come to ask Sym his intentions; then the lads try to frighten him with an alarm bell. This was no joke to Brown Hill, an onlooker who got hurt in the struggle; he appealed to Squire John and was given a seat in the shelter (?), as were also Sym and his brother. Sym's 'second' in the tournament, Yob Symmer, the cattle herder for the town, now took up the challenge for Sym, but was promptly wounded – his mouth torn open. He nearly died from gasping. The doctor said he had lost a tooth; Sym and his brother hoped that Yob could keep from stuttering. But Yob's mouth was ruined; he ends with serious injury, while the cattle (his responsibility) begin to scatter and run away. Sym curses the time his brother married and caused all this mayhem.

The authorship of this piece is open to at least one intriguing possibility. George Bannatyne in 1568 made no attribution, but elsewhere in his manuscript we find the only known early reference to the poem 'Sym and his Bruder'. This occurs in a poem called 'Ane descriptioun of Peder Coffeis having na regaird till honestie in thair vocatioun', a satire on various kinds of racketeers (both clerical and secular), ascribed in the Bannatyne Manuscript in a different hand to Sir David Lindsay. The pertinent passage is in stanza 3, describing lewd parish priests who deceive country wives with subtle means such as fraudulent relics, sometimes speaking in snarling tones, or sometimes in pitiful groans 'Lyk fenyeit [charlatan] *Symmye* and his bruder'. It seems quite probable that 'Peder Coffeis' is the work of Lindsay, and it is possible that 'Sym' is also by him. One thing is certain: whoever wrote 'Sym' had an intimate knowledge of St Andrews, since he was familiar with at least three local places in the vicinity (see notes below on *Kinkell crags, Stratyrum,* and *Brown Hill* – lines 37, 102, 111). All of this fits in with what is known of Lindsay: he was probably born and brought up at the estate of the Mount, two and one half miles north west of Cupar, Fife, only a dozen miles from St Andrews; he was probably educated at the University of St Andrews; and he was certainly resident in the town off and on during the years 1538–1540 when King James V and his court were there. Lindsay wrote 'The Justing', his mock-tournament poem, there, probably in 1539, and we know that he was familiar with 'Christis Kirk' from several echoes of it in *Ane Satyre of the Thrie Estaitis* (ca. 1552–54). Since 'Sym' combines the stanza form and general satiric tone of the *Christis Kirk* genre with clear elements of the mock tournament, and shows as well a detailed mastery of St Andrews place-names, the authorship of this work by Sir David Lindsay appears a distinct possibility.

If 'Sym' is the work of Lindsay, then we can suggest a conjectural date of composition. Both 'Sym' and 'Peder Coffeis' contain themes of satire on the Church, but neither shows signs of the specific Reformation ideas that are prominent in Lindsay's work from about 1540 (*Ane Satyre*) onwards. Both poems, therefore, would seem to be early productions – certainly before 1540 – in Lindsay's career. A reasonable guess would be a date in the mid-1530s for 'Peder Coffeis' and sometimes around 1530 for 'Sym'; the casual reference to 'Sym' in 'Peder Coffeis' suggests that the earlier work was already well established in the popular mind. Such an approximate date for the poem would also fit in well with the probability that the author of 'Sym' was influenced by a passage in Dunbar's 'Flyting of Dunbar and Kennedie' (see note below on line 27).

2 *Johine nor Robene Hude:* a reference to two of the heroic figures in the Robin Hood ballads – the gigantic 'Little John' and Robin Hood himself.

3 *Wallace wicht but weir:* Sir William Wallace (1272?–1305), the 'Guardian of Scotland', hero of the Scottish War of Independence against England.

5 *palmaris:* Lord Hailes in *Ancient Scottish Poems* (Edinburgh, 1770), p. 348, gives the following note: 'In Lord Hyndford's MS [i.e., the Bannatyne Manuscript] there is a poem relative to *Symme and his Bruder*; it is obscure; but it seems to import that they were what is termed *quaestionarii* in the ancient Scottish canons, c. 48; that is, persons sent out by the church

upon a begging mission'. This identification by Lord Hailes may be correct, but it is open to considerable doubt. Hailes' notion seems to be supported by line 38, which could mean that the brothers decided to return to St Andrews with their loot 'as they were paid to do' – that is, paid by the church with a fee or a percentage of the winnings. In this context, however, *as thay war hyrit* more likely means 'as *if* they were paid to do so' – that is, with speed, quickly – as suggested by Earl F. Guy in his unpublished Ph.D. thesis 'Some Comic and Burlesque Poems in the Sixteenth Century Scottish Manuscript Anthologies' (Edinburgh University, 1952), p. 220. Moreover, other evidence in the text casts doubt upon the idea of the brothers as official *quaestionarii*. In lines 17–19 we are told that the brothers had not been inside a church since childhood; it would seem unlikely, though not impossible, that even a very corrupt church would employ complete frauds in an official capacity. How could such men be trusted at all? Even more telling against Hailes is the clear statement here in line 5 that the two are 'palmaris' – that is, begging pilgrims, a fact confirmed later in lines 25, 27, and 46. Such men would beg for support, supposedly to enable them to go on religious pilgrimages to sacred shrines. Sym and his brother carry the symbols of the three most famous shrines in Christendom in the Middle Ages, namely, Rome, Santiago de Compostella, and Jerusalem; but, in fact, they travel nowhere beyond St Andrews and its surrounding agricultural area. They are, in short, phoney palmers who beg only to avoid having to work for a living. In my earlier study of the 'Christis Kirk' genre (*Studies in Scottish Literature*, II, 15–16), I mistakenly identified these scoundrels as friars, a notion picked up, I think, too uncritically from Thomas F. Henderson (*Scottish Vernacular Literature*, Edinburgh, 1910, pp. 286–287); the actual text provides no support for this. Lord Hailes' theory of the brothers as the *quaestionarii* remains a possibility, though an unlikely one. Sym and his brother are totally fraudulent begging pilgrims.

8 *Sanct Andris:* modern St Andrews, a town that in the late Middle Ages was of very considerable importance, not only as the site of the oldest Scottish university, but also until the Reformation as the ecclesiastical capital of Scotland, with a magnificent cathedral, the seat of an archbishopric, and a frequent residence of the Scottish kings. The modern town remains notable for its ancient university and for the most famous golf course in the world.

17–20 These lines clearly mean that Sym and his brother have never seen the inside of a church since they had grown whiskers; as religious characters they were, in short, complete frauds, and therefore unlikely to have been official *quaestionarii* who would normally have preached and solicited gifts in churches.

21 *lowp owr leiss:* a problematic phrase that seems to mean 'leap over leas', that is, 'dash over meadows', or make a quick trip into the countryside to prey upon the gullible peasants.

25 *Sanct Peteris keiss:* St Peter's keys were and are a symbol of Rome, one of the three great shrines for pilgrimages in the Middle Ages. Sym and his brother wear on their sleeves cloth badges of the keys to indicate, falsely, that they have been on the pilgrimage to Rome.

27 *Sanct James schellis:* St James' shells (scallop shells) were and are symbols of the great shrine in northwest Spain of Santiago de Compostella, the burial place of St James the Greater. The connection may be seen in the modern scallop dish called 'Coquilles St Jacques'. Sym and his brother wear badges depicting these shells on their outer sleeves to show, falsely, that they have visited Santiago. There are some interesting parallels here with some lines in Walter Kennedy's part of 'The Flyting of Dunbar and Kennedie' (see *Poems of William Dunbar*, ed. James Kinsley, Oxford, 1979, pp. 76–95). Kennedy portrays Dunbar as a religious charlatan who 'beggit with a pardoun in all kirkis' (line 426), and says 'Thow has thy clamschellis and thy burdoun kelde [coloured staff]' (line 431). A little later (lines 509–510), he adds 'Thy cloutit cloke [patched cloak], thy skryp, and thy clamschellis, / Cleke [fasten] on thy cors [body]'. There are several details here which recur in 'Sym'; both brothers have 'burdouns', 'cloutit' overcoats decorated with clam shells, and 'pardouns'. It seems quite probable that the author of 'Sym' was influenced by his memories of the famous 'Flyting'.

28–9 This comparison ('As pretty as a crab's claw') must be understood ironically, since a crab's claw is not particularly pretty and is certainly very unlike a scallop shell. The implication is that the scallop shell badge is ugly and misshapen – a touch of comic irony.

32 *To rome:* this is the reading in B, and it is the infinitive of the verb to 'roam' or wander. David Laing amended this word incorrectly as 'Rome', and *DOST* has followed him in this. In this context the city of Rome makes no sense: Sym and his brother never go to Rome; they go only to wander around begging in the countryside near St Andrews.

34 *fyrit:* B reads 'hyrit', also Laing; but Sibbald corrected this to 'fyrit' in 1802, and that seems to be the accurate interpretation – 'fyrit' in the sense of 'inspired', 'fired up'. The reading of 'hyrit' is most probably a scribal error by contamination from 'hyrit' in line 38.

36 *Quhen:* B reads 'q^r', an abbreviation for 'quhair' (where), clearly a slip of the pen for 'q^n' (quhen); Sibbald (1802) made this correction, though he chose to expand the contraction as 'Quhan'; Laing changed the spelling to 'Quhen' in 1825.

37 *Kinkellis craggis:* the name of the cliffs plunging down to the sea just south of St Andrews (about one mile south of the Cathedral) from hills now known as 'Kinkell Braes', to the east of highway A917. For detailed information on this and two other place names in the poem – Strathtyrum (line 102) and Brown Hill (line 111) – the editor is indebted to one of his students, Mrs Lorraina Pinnell, a native of St Andrews. This line and the next apparently mean that Sym and his brother, towards the end of their foray into the countryside, stopped at Kinkell Crags and 'Tuk counsall', that is, they talked things over before deciding to end their excursion and return home to St Andrews.

43 *flew owr fellis:* a problematic phrase which seems to mean that they sped over the hills or upland pastures, that they made another quick foray into the countryside. There is a similar usage in Walter Kennedy's 'Flyting' with Dunbar (line 512) in the very same passage mentioning clam shells: 'The fend fare wyth the fortheward owr the fellis' (The devil go with you

forward over the hills). Perhaps 'flew owr fellis' was an alliterative formula comparable to 'lowp owr leiss' in line 21.

46 *pecis of palme treis:* these were symbols and souvenirs of the ultimate pilgrimage to the Holy Land, to Jerusalem. The brothers carry these together with emblems of St Peter's keys and St James' shells as parts of their imposture as professional pilgrims.

47 This line indicates that the brothers were involved in the spurious pardons business as part of their general begging technique. They compete with one another at 'spelling' or reading out the pardon to simple rustics, for a price.

64 *Syne:* B and Laing read 'Sym', but this is very likely a slip of the pen. Sibbald (1802) was the first to make this emendation.

65 This is an obscure line; we can only guess that it means that the townsmen were participants in some ceremony in which they removed Sym's brother's rags to clothe him in new garments for the wedding. This process lasted too long and delayed the feast. Such an interpretation would fit in with the reference to *widis* (clothes) in line 67.

70 *to his bruder:* B reads 'q sym etc.' Sibbald (1802) changed the 'and' implied by 'etc' to 'to', which makes more sense in this context. Sym is complaining *to* his brother about the delay. Laing (1825), mistakenly, I think, preferred 'and'.

71 *be lyne and levall:* a proverbial phrase derived from tools of the carpenter's trade – the plumb line and spirit level – but used in a general sense to mean doing anything with meticulous care and accuracy.

72 *to luk him:* this is the relatively uncommon use of *luke* as a transitive verb (see *DOST* under *luke*, sense 6), and it means 'to look him over', 'inspect him' or 'examine him' (sexually), in this context to see whether he is capable of his duties as a new husband. This same transitive usage occurs in Sir David Lindsay's *Ane Satyre of the Thrie Estaitis*, Version III (1554), 11. 3416–17, where 'persone' (parish priest) describes the new expensive hats worn by the clergy: 'Our round bonats we make them now four nuikit [four-cornered] / Of richt fyne stuiff gif yow list cum and luik it.' See Lindsay's *Works*, ed. Douglas Hamer (Edinburgh and London, 1931), Vol. II. The use of this unusual verb form in 'Sym' is further evidence that Lindsay may have been the author.

73 *To tak a justing of that javell:* in view of the clearly sexual context of this line, Professor A.J. Aitken suggests that it means 'To have a copulation with that penis' (of Sym's brother who has just been examined by the lads). For *justing* with this meaning there is support in a 1639 quotation in *OED* under sense 4 of the verb *just*, as a 'figurative application'. As for *javell* as a metaphor for penis, I can find no record of this usage in *DOST*, *OED*, *MED*, or elsewhere; I am therefore inclined towards the common meaning of *javell* as 'a low fellow', since this makes perfectly good sense here also, though it is entirely possible that Aitken is right on this point as well.

77 *I cleme to clergy:* Sym claims 'benefit of clergy', fraudulently pretending to be in some kind of holy office in order to enhance his credibility in confronting the lads. This may well be an echo of Dunbar's 'The Flyting of Dunbar and Kennedie', line 407: 'Clame not to clergy'.

81–90 In this stanza Sym accepts a challenge to a tournament with someone (possibly the leader of the lads who have been mistreating his brother).

Clearly, there is something missing here in the text between stanzas 8 and 9.

82 *glufe:* a rare spelling of Middle Scots 'gliff', meaning a startled glance or look.

84 *mouf:* this is the reading in B, which Laing mistakenly changed to 'moif'; 'mouf' or 'muffler' makes perfect sense here.

86 *Angus Dufe:* the second term here is very probably a corrupt form of the Gaelic adjective 'dubh' or 'black', so that the whole phrase means 'Black Angus'. This may refer to some well known local 'character' in St Andrews who was long in the back and generally rough hewn. Another possibility is that 'Black Angus' may have been a pejorative nickname for Archibald Douglas, 6th Earl of Angus, a political opponent of Sir David Lindsay and a very powerful nobleman who virtually ruled Scotland for four years (1524–28) during the minority of King James V. During his ascendancy, Lindsay was temporarily deprived of his official positions in the court. I have been unable, however, to find evidence for either of these identifications of *Angus Dufe.*

89 *Call to* is a difficult phrase here; it may signify 'Drive on' (to the field of battle), or it may be a form of summons for the combatants and spectators to prepare for the tournament.

98 *bind him:* B reads 'tird him'; Laing's correction here to 'tied him' seems invalid since it does not fit the rime scheme. The best guess, kindly suggested to me by Professor A.J. Aitken, is that the poet meant to repeat the 'bind him' rime from line 92, and 'tird' is simply a scribal error.

102 *Stratyrum:* this is not a spelling error for Strathtyrum, but rather a phonetic rendering of the local pronunciation, reflecting the common shortening in such place names of Strath- to Stra- (e.g., 'Strabogie' for 'Strathbogie'). Strathtyrum was a once extensive estate just to the east of St Andrews. Strathtyrum House and estate still exist on the southwest side of highway A91, across the road from the new golf course of the same name, on the main road to Dundee. Here it seems to be specified simply as a well known place in the vicinity at some distance from the town itself.

104 *'Ye meit nocht':* this curious idiom – 'you will not meet' in the sense of 'you won't catch him' (the horse) unless you drive him into the mire – also occurs in 'Peblis', line 24.

108 This is surely another line in which the text is corrupt. The best guess is that *flud* is a slip of the pen for 'fleid' (frightened), which in turn is an error in verb form for 'fley' (frighten). *Flyr* means 'mock', so that the whole line would translate: 'To frighten him and to mock him'.

110 *Bayth Symme:* the MS has 'Q Sym' here, which makes no sense in this context and is probably a slip of the pen for 'Bayth Sym'; the *Bayth* in the preceding line 109 is used in a different sense – 'Both to frighten and mock him', followed by 'Both Sym and his brother'.

111 *Brown Hill:* this is clearly a reference to a person, a man who is accidentally hurt in the scuffle; most likely it is a territorial name whereby the man is called by the name of the land that he owns or rents, rather than by his personal surname. Robert Burns, for example, was sometimes called 'Mossgiel' from the name of the farm he rented. Here the name almost certainly is that of a property (now including a 19th-century mansion like Strathtyrum) just to the south of St Andrews, now called 'Brown Hills',

located on the west side of highway A917 directly across from the 'Kinkell Braes' mentioned above in the note on line 37. In this context, 'Brown Hill' would simply be the farmer of that land.

112 *gatt betwene the browis:* a word or two may be missing here; Brown Hill got some kind of blow or injury between his eyebrows.

116 *Squyar Johine of Mowis:* this is a problematic name, open to at least two interpretations: (a) it may be a fictitious comic name, with 'Mowis' in the sense of 'jokes' or 'games' – 'Squire John of Jokes'; or, more probably, (b) it may be the actual name of a local estate or farm. If the latter is intended, there are several possibilities. It may be the name of an unidentified farm in the area; in Middle and Modern Scots the noun *mou* or *mow* means a large heap or stack of hay, unthreshed grain, peat, or dung – here the name of a farm meaning 'Stacks'. Or, it may be a gross miswriting (in the corrupt MS from which Bannatyne was presumably copying) of 'Magus' – the name of two farms, 'Upper Magus' and 'Nether Magus', about three miles west of St Andrews, on both sides of highway B939. Or, even more speculatively, it could be a badly skewed reference to the estate of Moonzie, a property that belonged to the Lindsay family, located about three miles northwest of Cupar and only one mile from the Mount, the home of Sir David Lindsay. In the 16th century Moonzie was sometimes spelled 'Monse', which could easily be misread as 'Mouse', hence 'Mowis'. Of all these possibilities, the most likely perhaps is an unidentified farm name meaning 'Stacks' – somewhere near St Andrews. For information on Moonzie I am indebted to Robert N. Smart, former keeper of the Muniments in the University of St Andrews Library, who reports that examples of the 'Monse' spelling can be found in the *Registrum Magni Sigilli Regum Scotorum*, in the Indices locorum for the years 1546–80 and 1593–1608.

117 *ane sit up in the schill:* an obscure image, possibly a seat in the hut for shepherds in the field where the tournament was held, a privilege allowed to Sym and his brother (and presumably also to Sym's challenger).

121 *Yob:* perhaps a scribal error for 'Job'? *stirrepman:* a stirrupman would be a servant who helps his master into the saddle, and who, in this instance, functions also as a kind of 'second' in the duel when the master is disabled.

127 *first rynk:* this would be the first charge on horseback, the first onset or 'round' of the tournament. *span:* the distance from the tip of the thumb to the tip of the little finger when the digits are spread out as far as possible, averaging about nine inches. There is no evidence in the text to support Douglas Hamer's fanciful notion that Sym's brother (rather than Yob Symmer) is ridden like a horse, and has his mouth torn by a bit between his teeth. See Hamer, ed., *Works of Sir David Lindsay* (Edinburgh and London, 1934), III, 488. The text, however, gives no clues as to how Yob suffered this unusual injury.

130 *By:* B reads *Bayth*, but this word makes no sense in the context of the entire sentence describing the fate of Yob Symmer; possibly it is a scribal error for 'By' in the sense of 'near', 'next to', or 'beside'.

131 *luggis:* for this word B has *leggis*, surely an error. Since Yob's injury is in the corners of his mouth, why would he need to be laced up or bandaged (laist) 'down from the legs'? 'Down from the ears' would be more logical in this context, with the *leich* or doctor mentioned in line

135 perhaps doing the bandaging. In a very sloppy transcript (from which Bannatyne was probably copying) *leggis* could easily be a miswriting of *luggis*. This emendation is guesswork, but makes sense of an otherwise baffling line.

135–140 B gives no punctuation at all for these lines, and that supplied by Laing seems faulty. There are clearly two sets of speakers here: the doctor (leich) for lines 135–136, and Sym and his brother for lines 137–139. Laing gives no quotation marks at all, and inserts a comma instead of a period at the end of line 136, as though the doctor were continuing to speak for the next three lines, rather than the two brothers. The reconstructed punctuation given here makes sense out of the whole stanza.

137 This line should be read as follows: 'God, and the Holy Ghost, save him…'

140 *Sym:* B reads 'suym', an obvious error.

146–7 With Yob Symmer out of action, the cattle begin to run wild; we should recall that he was the *nolthird* (line 122), the cattle herd in charge of keeping the animals properly confined to their pastures.

5. Sir David Lindsay, *The Justing betwix James Watsoun and Jhone Barbour, c.* 1539

TEXT: The best text of this poem, carefully followed here, is that edited by Douglas Hamer in *The Works of Sir David Lindsay of the Mount*, 4 vols., Scottish Text Soc., 3rd Ser., 1, 2, 6, 8 (Edinburgh, 1931–34), I, 114–116 (text); III, 140–142 (notes). Hamer's text itself is based on the earliest printing of the poem in 'The Second Series of Minor Poems' in *The Warkis of Sir David Lindsay*, Edinburgh, 1568, printed by John Scot for Henry Charteris. This text is remarkably clear and careful, except for some eccentric capitalisation of common nouns and adjectives in the first twenty lines and one confusing misprint in line 7 (noted below). In the present edition all unnecessary capitalisation is eliminated, and the few abbreviations (spelled out by Hamer but with the added letters italicised) are expanded in normal roman type.

1–68 The episode described here was most probably a real one, an actual *mock* tournament acted out with exaggerated clownishness by two servants in the royal household for the amusement of James V, his queen, and the court. James Watson was the king's barber and surgeon; John Barbour was of lower rank, a groom in the royal wardrobe, though Lindsay says (line 15) he was also a 'leche', or physician. For more information on these men, see Hamer's excellent notes on them. If the tournament actually took place in St Andrews on Whitmonday in the presence of both king and queen, then it can be dated in May of 1538, or 1539, or 1540. Hamer unaccountably rules out 1538 on the grounds that the queen (Marie de Lorraine) landed at Crail in Fife on Whitsunday and therefore 'could not have got to St Andrews in time for a joust on the next day'. One wonders why not. The distance, after all, is only about ten miles, and even allowing for the slowness of royal processions in the sixteenth century the queen could easily have arrived in St Andrews on the same day of her landing in Crail.

1 *Sanctandrois:* St Andrews, Fife, the ecclesiastical capital of Scotland until

the Reformation and a favourite residence of many of the Scottish kings. *Witsoun Monnunday:* Whitmonday, the day after Whitsunday, the seventh Sunday after Easter, probably so-called from the white baptismal robes worn that day.

3   *barres:* Dunbar, in his 'Justis' (line 6), had used the same term 'Thar barrass was maid boune' – but pronounced as two syllables whereas Lindsay's metre suggests one.

7   *banrent:* all editions read 'baurent' for this word, but this must be a misprint for 'banrent'. A *banrent* or *bannerent* according to *DOST* was 'a knight able to bring into the field a company of vassals under his own banner, and ranking next to a baron'. In this context, 'banrent' is clearly the word intended.

9–16 In identifying and describing his 'campionis' here Lindsay is not sharply satiric at all; in fact, he is respectful and mildly complimentary, especially to James Watson who seems to be the higher ranking of the two men – he later refers to Watson as 'gentil James' in two places (lines 23 and 55). The tone of lines 9–16 suggests that the men were not real buffoons or cowards, but were simply *acting* these parts to amuse the court.

20 *cadgeris rydand on thare creillis:* with this image compare the picture of the cadger with his horse and creels in 'Peblis', stanzas 15 and 16.

27 *my leggis lyke rokkis:* Lindsay here may be recalling line 38 of 'Christis Kirk' – 'His lymmis wes lyk twa rokkis'.

31 *goddes breid:* James Sibbald in *Chronicle of Scottish Poetry* (Edinburgh, 1802), II, 187, emends this phrase to 'Goddis Creid'; but there seems to be no justification for the change.

33–34 Here, as in line 27, Lindsay is echoing 'Christis Kirk', repeating this time the rimes in lines 192 and 194 of that poem: 'Ran upon utheris lyk rammis ... Bet on with barrow trammis'. That Lindsay was intimately familiar with 'Christis Kirk' is proven not only by these parallels but by several others in *Ane Satyre:* see Allan H. MacLaine, '*Christis Kirk on the Grene* and Sir David Lindsay's *Satyre of the Thrie Estaitis*', *Journal of English and Germanic Philology,* 56 (1957).

35–36 Three phrases in these lines – 'At that rude rink' ... 'strykin doun' ... 'fell in swoun' – are remarkably similar to phrases in the stanza on Yob Symmer in 'Sym', lines 124, 127, and 128 – 'strickin doun' ... 'The first rynk' ... 'fell in swoune'. These close parallels, occurring close together in similar passages of slapstick comedy, are strong evidence that Lindsay knew 'Sym' well, and may have been its author.

38 As Hamer points out, this line has six feet and is 'unmetrical'. A reasonable emendation would be to eliminate the 'is' ending on 'amangis', which is not required by the sense in any case, and to omit 'he'. The line would then read: 'Wer not amang his hors feit brak his speir'.

40 *thre market straikis:* Hamer was puzzled by this phrase, but it simply means three blows or strokes that are officially marked down, or tallied, or counted (see *DOST*). This was a common procedure in tournaments, when the combatants would agree between themselves to limit the fight to a fixed number of blows. Three, however, would be a ludicrously small number of blows, and this is part of the satire here on the cowardice of these ignoble champions.

41 This line seems to be misinterpreted by Hamer as 'I have had, quoth John, that which shall be revenged on thee', whatever that means. In the context, a better reading would be: 'I hold (believe), quoth John, that (idea of *thre market straikis*) shall be avenged on thee'.

47–50 Hamer plausibly explains line 47 as meaning that James attacked John not with his fists but with both hands on his sword (amateurish technique). In line 48 James's sword, missing John, hits the 'lystis' (wooden railings); there it is stuck fast (line 50) and James is never able to retrieve it.

56–58 As Hamer says, 'James tries to console John by blaming the swords, which they do not know how to use'. James's sword is stuck in the lists, John's has flown out of his hand, so they are reduced to bashing each other's faces with gloves of plate armour.

60 *Fy, red the men:* the verb 'red', to separate, had occurred earlier in 'Peblis' (lines 132, 149) in brawling contexts. Sibbald, II, 188, emended this to 'Fy redd for schame', but that seems to be an error. 'Red the men' was a standard order in tournaments. As Hamer points out, John's asking for an end to the fight and James's quick agreement are further comic touches of satire on their cowardice and ungentlemanly behaviour.

64–66 The motif of fear causing involuntary defecation, especially in untrained soldiers and lower class clownish characters, is widespread in folk literature and folklore. In the *Christis Kirk* poems it appears several times in the older specimens: here, in Dunbar's 'Justis' (lines 67–72, 97–99), in Drummond's 'Polemo-Middinia' (line 143), and, probably, in 'Christis Kirk' itself (line 78). The phenomenon, as Hamer says, is psychologically and physiologically real.

66 *dirt partis cumpany:* a proverb spoken when a boorish or undesirable person breaks into a congenial, well-mannered group, causing the group to break up.

68 This amusing close to the poem almost certainly suggested the final line of Drummond's 'Polemo-Middinia', which expresses the identical idea: 'Una nec intereaɩspillata est droppa cruoris' (Nevertheless, not one drop of blood was spilled).

6. Alexander Scott, *The Justing and Debait up at the Drum, c.* 1560

TEXT: With the kind permission of the editors, the text here reproduces that of *Longer Scottish Poems* (abbreviated below as *LSP*), Vol. I, edited by Priscilla Bawcutt and Felicity Riddy (Edinburgh: Scottish Academic Press, 1987), pp. 271–278, a slightly modernised version of the text in the Bannatyne Manuscript of 1568, the only source for this poem. The present editor owes much to this edition for the marginal gloss, and is heavily indebted to the excellent notes by Felicity Riddy (pp. 402–405). The layout of the stanza form I have modified slightly to make it consistent with the standard arrangement used throughout this volume. I have also normalised spellings of 'i' and 'y' and of 'v', 'u', and 'w' according to modern practice (see *A Note on the Texts*), and I have adopted two of the emendations suggested in Felicity Riddy's notes; otherwise I have followed the text in *LSP* faithfully. Earlier, and historically important, texts of the poem may be found in *The Bannatyne Manuscript*, 4 vols., ed. W. Tod

Ritchie, Scottish Text Soc. (Edinburgh and London, 1928), II, 343–349; *The Poems of Alexander Scott*, ed. James Cranstoun, Scottish Text Soc. (Edinburgh and London, 1896), pp. 9–15; and *Chronicle of Scottish Poetry*, ed. James Sibbald, 4 vols. (Edinburgh, 1802), III, 137–143.

2   *lusty lady gent:* this is a well worn formula from love romances, used here for burlesque effect in reference to an ordinary local girl. The entire poem (but especially the first half) is sprinkled with romantic or heroic clichés like this, absurdly misapplied to clownish characters and actions. Other notable examples of this technique are: *freikis fell* (line 4), *armipotent* (5), *duchty deidis* (11), *dousy peris* (12), *stoutly* and *stalwart* (15, 16), *Enarmit under scheild* (24), *men … of micht* (61), *vow … to the powin* (75), and *cursour* (168).

7–9   *Hercules, that aikkis uprent:* this appears to be an allusion to the dying Hercules, the legendary strongman of Greek mythology (called Heracles or Alcides in Greek), who tore up trees to make a funeral pyre for his own cremation. Lines 8–9 refer to Hercules' twelfth 'Labour', involving a descent into the underworld to abduct Cerberus, the three-headed dog monster who guarded the gates of hell. Scott here conflates the god of the underworld (Hades or Pluto) with the Scots folk image of the devil with horns ('Auld Hornie'). Cp. Burns's 'Address to the Deil'.

10   *the Drum:* the name of an estate in the open countryside about half way between Edinburgh and Dalkeith. In the sixteenth century it belonged to the family of the Somervilles of Cambusnethan who in 1584–85 built on this property the mansion house of the Drum which still exists, off highway A68 near the Edinburgh suburbs of Gilmerton and Ferniehill. When this poem was written (*c.* 1560) there was probably only a simple farmhouse at the Drum; at any rate, the location would be convenient for a tournament of this sort, easily reached from either Edinburgh or Dalkeith. *that day:* this tag phrase occurs thrice in the original 'Christis Kirk' (stanzas 2, 20, and 23) where it is tacked on to the usual refrain, 'At Christis Kirk on the grene'. Scott, no doubt taking this hint, made *that day* part of his refrains throughout – 'Up at the Drum that day' in stanzas 1–10, 'Up at Dalkeith that day' in stanzas 11–19, with a variation to 'Within the toun that night' in stanza 20.

12   *dousy peris:* the twelve (F. 'douze') peers or paladins of Charlemagne, here used in the general sense of noble knights.

14   *triumphand:* the standard '-and' ending for the present participle in Middle Scots, a form somewhat archaic in Scott's time but used here to give an old-fashioned heroic flavour to this mock-heroic stanza. See also *byand* in line 127.

29   *Or slane:* the absurd redundancy here suggests that Scott is making fun of the use of the 'bob' line as a meaningless filler, as Chaucer occasionally does in *Sir Thomas*.

45   *schalmis:* the shawn was a late medieval woodwind instrument with a double reed, the forerunner of the oboe and clarinet. It had, says Felicity Riddy, 'a particularly aggressive sound' (404). See note on *schamous dance* in 'Peblis' 195.

53   *with baith thair facis bair:* jousting knights would normally wear helmets

protecting the face.

58 *in secreit wyis:* the Bannatyne MS reads 'wayis' here, but this is almost
certainly a scribal error for 'wyis'. The phrase 'in secreit wyis', secretly,
occurs in Henryson's *Testament*, 381.

62 *sinder:* the Bannatyne MS has 'sidder' here, but Felicity Riddy is surely
right in proposing an emendation, at the suggestion of Prof. A.J. Aitken, to
'sinder', meaning to 'sunder' or 'separate'. This change results in an
approximate rime with 'togidder', 'hidder', and 'lidder', but it makes
excellent sense in the context.

71 *als fery as a fowne:* Cp. the common proverbial comparisons, 'as light as a
roe', 'as swift as a roe'; there is a similar comparison in line 155, also
referring to Sym.

75 *vow ... to the powin:* swearing oaths to the peacock, as centrepiece of a
feast, is a commonplace in heroic romance literature, used here for
purposes of burlesque, of course.

101 *Dalkeith:* a small town about four miles south-east of central Edinburgh,
two miles from the Drum.

108 *baikin loche:* a 'baked loach' was a small fish, delicious to eat.

127–8 *buyand hyddis / And wedder skynnis:* apparently both William Adamson
and John Sym are tanners or leather-workers by trade. A wether is a
castrated ram.

151 *haif and ga:* see *LSP*, I, 405, for the interpretation by Prof. A.J. Aitken,
whereby 'haif' means 'have at him' and 'ga' means 'go off', or 'go on'
(i.e., start the fight), or 'let go'.

177 *avairis:* this noun connotes common draught horses, broken down nags for
heavy farm work.

181 *gelly Johine:* this is apparently Will's brother 'Jok' who is challenged by
Sym in line 143. The adjective 'gelly' is cited as 'of unknown origin' in
OED and in *DOST*, but it may be a phonetic distortion of the French 'joli',
meaning good looking.

197 *Potter Raw:* the Potterrow was an ancient street (which still exists) on the
south side of Edinburgh that gave access to the town through a gate in the
town wall. People coming into Edinburgh from Dalkeith would normally
enter at the Potterrow.

201–10 This 'envoy' presents a conventional summary of the situation that gave
rise to the jousting. James Sibbald in *Chronicle of Scottish Poetry*
(Edinburgh, 1802), II, 143, saw this stanza as an 'absurd augmentation'
which was 'unconnected with any part of the poem'. There is no valid
reason, however, to doubt Scott's authorship of the envoy, and it is certainly
not 'unconnected'. It tells us that the girl was seduced by William
Adamson while engaged to John Sym. The cowardly Adamson had
promised to marry her if she would allow him sexual favours, but as soon
as she became pregnant he deserted her, slipped out of town, and went into
hiding. In view of the very specific particulars here and throughout the
poem it is quite possible, even probable, that the piece was based on a real-
life situation.

7. William Drummond of Hawthornden, *Polemo-Middinia, c.* 1645

TEXT: The best available text of this poem is that of L.E. Kastner, ed., *The Poetical Works of William Drummond of Hawthornden* (Manchester, 1913), II, 321–26, with notes in II, 418–24. Kastner's text is a reprinting of the earliest known edition, that of Edinburgh, 1684, collated with two later seventeenth-century printings of the poem. The present edition reproduces Kastner's text faithfully, and the editor is heavily indebted to his notes on the poem which are very good on the whole, though Professor Kastner leaves unexplained a few difficult Latinised Scots words, a few grammatical errors in the Latin (some or all of which may be misprints), and one serious printer's error. All of these problems are dealt with in the notes below.

In preparing the modern English translation for this entire poem the editor also owes much to his friend and colleague Professor Kenneth H. Rogers of the Department of Languages, University of Rhode Island, who was kind enough to cast his expert eye over the text, making several corrections and suggesting stylistic improvements. The translation itself is generally a very literal one, and for the most part I have tried, at the expense of some awkward sentence structure, to stick to the line-units of the original – that is to render in each line of the translation all of the words in the corresponding line of the Scoto-Latin text. This method, I hope, will make for faster and easier reading comprehension.

1 *Fifaea:* Fife-shire is the setting for the entire work, and specifically the adjacent properties of Thirdpart and Newbarns, belonging to two Fife lairds, Scot and Cunningham respectively. Sir John Scot of Scotstarvit, a personal friend and brother-in-law of Drummond of Hawthornden and a prominent political leader and judge, owned a large barony in Fife made up of several farms, beginning with Scotstarvit in the middle of Fife (about two miles south of Cupar) and extending to the coast of the East Neuk of Fife. His southernmost residence was the farm of Thirdpart in the parish of Kilrenny, perhaps his favourite country home. The adjacent estate to the east of Thirdpart was the farm of Barns or Newbarns, owned by the family of Cunningham, in the parish of Crail. The Cunninghams, too, were close friends of Drummond; he had, in fact, been engaged to marry the beautiful daughter of Cunningham of Barns prior to her untimely death in 1615. Drummond's very close relations with both families is strong evidence for his authorship of 'Polemo-Middinia'. The two farms still exist and can be located on the Ordnance Survey map of that part of Fife. They are on a small country road extending west from the town of Crail: Barns is about one mile west of Crail, and Thirdpart a half-mile farther out on the same road. In the title and the text of the poem the mistress of Thirdpart (Lady Scotstarvit) is personified as 'Vitarva', the mistress of Newbarns (Cunningham) as 'Neberna'.

2–3 *Pittenwema, Crelia,* and *Anstraea:* these are amusing Latinisations of the names of three towns and fishing ports on the southeast coast of Fife – modern 'Pittenweem', 'Crail', and 'Anstruther'.

7 *breddum:* Scots 'braid', that is 'broad'.

9 *scellatas:* this seems to mean 'shell-like', perhaps a misprint for 'shellatas';

compare the related form in line 12, *Cockelshelleatarum*.

10 *fechtam:* Scots 'fecht', fight.

13 *Maia* and *Bassa:* these are two famous islands in the Firth of Forth, easily visible (in clear weather) from the coast of Fife – modern 'Isle of May', and the 'Bass Rock'. *solgoosifera:* this is a contracted form of 'bearing the solan goose' or 'gannet', a large sea-fowl for which the Bass Rock is well known.

14–15 *Edenum:* Edinburgh – the joke here relates to the fact that the Scottish capital city, located across the Firth of Forth from Fife, then as now was notorious for its bad weather, especially for rain showers with high winds blowing in from the Firth.

18 *Bruntiliana:* Latinised name for the Fife coastal town of 'Burntisland'.

19 *Sea-sutor:* 'sea-souter' (cobbler) is the colloquial Scots name for the cormorant, a large, voracious sea bird, about three feet in length and having a membrane pouch on its neck front in which fish are stored for later eating. Perhaps this term derives from the similarity of the cormorant's pouch to the pouches in a cobbler's work apron in which he stores his shoemaking materials.

20 *Scartavit:* Scots 'scarted' or scratched.

22 *clig clag:* this is a remarkably accurate bit of onomatopoeia, as anyone will attest who has heard the sound of bird droppings hitting the surface of the sea.

24 *Muckrellium:* this seems to be a Latin form for a contraction of the Scots phrase 'muck-creels' (dung baskets), but in this context it means 'of dung basket carriers'.

24–25 *Vitarva ... Nebernae:* see note on line 1.

26 *armati greppis:* Scots 'armed with graips' or pitchforks (pronged forks); there are cognate nouns in northern Middle English ('grape'), Norwegian ('greip'), Swedish ('grep'), and Danish ('greb').

27 *Crofta:* Scots 'crofts' or small farms. *Nebernae:* of Newbarns mansion.

30–46 This is the first of two mock-epic rollcalls of rustic heroes, a burlesque device that became the overall satiric method of the later song of 'The Blythsome Wedding'. See the article by Allan H. MacLaine, 'Drummond of Hawthornden's "Polemo-Middinia" as a Source for "The Blythsome Bridal"', *Notes and Queries*, N.S. 1 (Sept., 1954), 384–86.

35 *Oldmoudus:* Scots 'auldmou'd', old-mouthed or sagacious in speech.

36 *pleugham:* Scots 'pleugh', plough. *gaddo:* Scots 'gaud', a pointed stick for driving cattle or horses.

38 *plouky-fac'd:* Scots for pimply-faced. *inkne'd:* Scots 'inkneed', knock-kneed. *Alshinder:* a Scots form of Alexander.

40 *Corn-greivus:* this almost certainly is Scots 'corn-grieve', that is, the man who is the overseer or bailiff in charge of the cultivation and harvesting of grain on a farm, a sort of foreman, or farm manager. The term recurs in line 159. The person referred to here seems to be Geordie Akinhead, the foreman of Scotstarvit, who is spoken to a little later in line 48, mentioned again in line 57 as foreman, and yet again as corngrieve in line 159. The foreman of Newbarns, in contrast, is called a 'jakman' or retainer in lines 72 and 151.

41 *Nout-headdum:* blockhead, from Scots 'nowt', cattle.

46 *dightabat:* Scots 'dight' or 'dicht', wiped. *assam:* Scots 'ass', or 'ase',

ashes. *jecerat* here seems to be an error in tense (pluperfect instead of imperfect).

47 *affatur:* this appears to be another error in Latin. This is a deponent verb (*affor*) with an active meaning – 'he speaks' – which makes no sense in this context. The intended meaning is that Geordie is spoken to by the lady of Scotstarvit.

49 *crooksaddeliis:* Scots 'crook-saddle', a special kind of saddle with hooks for supporting creels or panniers. *heghemis:* a curious distortion of Scots 'hems' or 'haims', equivalent to English 'hames', meaning the two curved pieces of wood or metal resting on the collar of a draught-horse, to which the traces are attached. Possibly Drummond used this spelling to suggest that the word was pronounced as two syllables in actual speech – something like 'hay-ems'.

50 *Brechimmis:* Scots 'brecham', a collar for a draught-horse.

51 *naiggam:* Scots 'naig', a nag or worn out horse.

52 *averos:* Scots 'avers', cart-horses, especially old ones of little value.

53 *yockato:* Scots 'yoke', to harness.

57 *flankavit:* this is a puzzling verb form – 'flanked', which in this context appears to mean 'harnessed'.

60 *swieros:* Scots 'sweir', lazy.

62 *mustrat:* this seems to mean 'is mustered' in the military sense of 'paraded', or 'displayed ostentatiously', or 'flaunted'.

63–64 This refers to the capture of Ostend on 20 September 1604 by the Spanish under Marquis Spinola, after a long siege of three years and seventy-seven days.

67 'The Battle of Harlaw' was a bagpipe tune inspired by a famous fight in 1411 when an army of Scots from the eastern Lowlands defeated the highlanders under Donald of the Isles at Harlaw in Aberdeenshire.

72 *Jackmannum:* Scots 'jakman', a retainer; this character seems to be the foreman of Newbarns, the opposite number to Geordie Akinhead, foreman on the Scotstarvit side. The Newbarns 'jakman' reappears in line 151.

73 *ricoso:* Scots 'reekie', smoky; full of 'reek' or smoke.

76 *saltpannifumos:* smoky salt-panners, men who make salt by heating sea water in shallow metal pans by means of coal fires. Drummond's Latin seems to have failed him here, since the proper form of the accusative plural here would be *saltpannifumosos*, though the shortened form used here may simply be a misprint. *widebricatos:* Kastner passes over this word in silence; it is based on Scots 'breeks', meaning trousers, so that the whole phrase can be translated as 'fishermen wearing wide trousers'.

77 *Hellaeos:* a difficult noun, the first two syllables of which probably represent Scots 'hellis', of hell or infernal, so that in this context *Hellaeos* would mean 'those from hell' or 'hellions'.

84 *longo bardo Anapellam:* there is a problem here with the meaning of *bardo*, a masculine ablative form that is probably a misprint for *beardo*, so that the whole phrase should mean 'Anabell with the long beard'. This interpretation is supported by the presence in this text of two other examples of 'beard' with Latin endings – *slaveri-beardus* (line 45) and *gash-beardum* (line 133). Even more conclusive is a variant reading for the Anabell phrase in Kastner's textual footnotes: *lango-berdamque*

Anapellam, where *berdam* certainly means 'bearded'. Giving Anabell whiskers here, an unattractive feature in a girl, is fully in line with the broad satiric tone of this whole catalogue of rustic heroines.

85 *gliedamque:* Scots 'gleid', squint-eyed.

86 *suttie clutto:* Scots 'sooty clout', soot-covered rag.

88 *oscularier:* this appears to be a misprint for the infinitive *osculare*.

91 *rasuinibus:* Scots 'rasuins' or 'raisins', grapes. *amaris:* this apparently means 'bitter' or 'unripe'.

92 *newbarmae:* the primary meaning here is 'of new barm', that is, new beer; but there may be also a pun on 'Newbarns', the local beer brewed on Newbarns farm.

93 *riftos:* Scots 'rift', a belch or fart, breaking wind.

94 *Barmifumi:* fuming with barm (beer). The correct Latin form here would be *barmifumosi*; this may well be another misprint, similar to *saltpannifumos* (line 76).

96 *ribauldis:* Scots 'rebald', low fellow.

97 *goulaeam:* Scots 'gully', a large knife.

98 *ad pellmellia:* Scots 'at pell-mell', in headlong disorder, utter confusion. *fleidos:* Scots 'fleyd', frightened or put to flight.

101 *thrapellum:* Scots 'thrapple', throat, windpipe, neck.

102 *rivabo:* Scots 'reeve', tear, rip. *luggas:* Scots 'lugs', ears.

105 *dirtfleyda:* Scots 'dirt-fleyed', frightened to such an extent as to suffer an involuntary bowel evacuation.

107 *Middini:* Scots 'midden', dung pile, rubbish heap.

108 *fleuram:* Scots 'fleur', smell, from OF 'fleur'. *gustasses:* should be *gustavisses*, perhaps another misprint.

109 *muckcreillius heros:* this appears to be a reference to Geordie Akinhead, the Scotstarvit foreman.

111 *shoollare:* Scots 'shool', to shovel. *dirta:* Scots 'dirt', dung.

112 *feire fairie:* Scots 'fery fary', state of confusion.

113 *breickas:* Scots 'breeks', trousers.

116 *yerdae:* Scots 'of yird', of earth, ground.

120 *scaldaverat:* Scots 'scaulded', scolded.

121 *gutture:* Scots 'gutter', mire, mud.

122 *Perlineasque:* Scots 'perling', lace of thread or silk used for trimming garments.

123 *Vasquineamque:* Scots 'vasquine', petticoat, from F. 'vasquine', from Sp. 'Vascuna', the people of the Basque country. *mucksherdo:* Scots 'sherd', or 'shard', a patch or cake of cow-dung; *muck* means dung here also, so that the compound noun *mucksherdo* is humorously redundant. *begariavit:* Scots 'begarie', to variegate with streaks of colour, hence to bespatter in this context; from F. 'bigarrer'.

128 *girnavit:* Scots 'girn', to snarl.

129 *Bublentem:* Scots 'bubbly', snotty. *bardum:* most likely this is a misprint for *beardum* (see note on *bardo* in line 84), so that the phrase means 'gripping his snotty beard'. An alternative reading, less probable in the context, would be 'gripping the snotty fool'.

131 *Herculeo:* 'like Hercules'. Kastner's text reads 'cum gerculeo', but this is a simple printer's error, no doubt perpetuated from the first printing of the

poem. In the seventeenth century, of course, typesetting was wholly manual, with the craftsman working from a tray with sets of letters arranged alphabetically, so that the 'g's would be next to the 'h's. One can easily imagine a stupefied or half drunken typesetter reaching for an upper case 'H' and picking up instead a lower case 'g'. Kastner was apparently baffled by 'gerculeo' since he passed over this difficulty in silence. *Gilliwyppum:* a severe blow, from Scots 'wipe' or 'wype', a blow, with 'Gilly' as an intensive.

132 *sherdam:* Scots 'sherd', or 'shard', a patch of cow-dung.

133 *gash-beardum:* Scots 'gash-beard', protruding beard or chin.

134 *sneezing:* Scots 'sneeshin', or 'sneezin', snuff.

135 *swingere:* Scots 'swinger', rascal, rogue.

136 *Gilliwamphra:* as Kastner suggests, 'wamphra' is probably an error for Scots 'whample', a blow, with 'Gilli' as an intensive. *nevellam:* Scots 'nevell', a blow.

139 *bumbasedus:* Scots 'bumbased', confused, perplexed.

141 *nizavit:* Scots 'neese', to sneeze or snort.

142 *Disjunium:* Scots 'disjune', breakfast, from OF 'desjeun', and F. 'déjeuner'.

143 *Lausavit:* Scots 'lowse', loosen or let loose.

145 *gimpare:* Scots 'gymp', to taunt or scoff (see *EDSL*).

149 *Monsmegga:* 'Mons Meg', the enormous historic cannon then, and now, located in Edinburgh Castle, possibly forged at Mons, Belgium, in 1476. Its huge barrel, made of thick iron staves welded together and held in place by iron hoops, was naturally susceptible to cracking apart under explosive pressures, and this possibility is humorously alluded to here. Ironically enough, in 1680, some thirty-five years after the approximate date of composition of this poem, Mons Meg did in fact crack open while firing a salute in honour of the visit to Edinburgh of James, Duke of York, who was soon to become King James II of England and James VII of Scotland in 1685. On the other hand, if this is a reference to the actual 'cracking' of Mons Meg in 1680, we are left with two possibilities: (a) the poem is not by Drummond but by some other poet writing between 1680 and 1684; or (b) the reference was inserted into Drummond's text by someone else. The latter explanation seems more probable since Kastner's variant readings include two examples of such interpolations – that is, lines not found in the 1684 printing but included in Bishop Gibson's edition of 1691.

150 *quaccare:* to 'quake' or tremble with fear.

153–155 A reference to the failed attempt by the Spanish army of King Philip II, under the Marquis of Spinola, to retake the town of Sluys in 1604.

155 *dingasset:* Scots 'ding', to smash down, batter.

156–158 Another mock-heroic reference, this time to the unsuccessful siege of the Huguenot town of Montauban in Gascony by the King of France, Louis XIII, in 1621.

158 *yerdam:* Scots 'yerd', earth, ground.

159 *wracco:* Scots 'with wrack', that is, with rubbish or perhaps destruction.

161 *wirriabo:* Scots 'worry', strangle.

162 *seustram:* Scots 'sewster', seamstress. *broddatus:* Scots 'broddit', pricked.

163 *stobbatus:* from Scots 'stob', to pierce with a pointed instrument. *greittans:*

Scots 'greeting', weeping.

164 *Barlafumle:* a call for a truce in fighting or playing; the first part of the compound is from French 'parlez!' and is still in use in Scotland in some children's games in the form of 'Barley!' The expression occurs also in 'Christis Kirk', line 158.

165 *guisa:* Scots 'gyse', an affair, masquerade, frolic, from F. 'guise'.

166 This last satiric line was very probably suggested by the final line (68) of Lindsay's 'Justing': 'Lovyng to god, that day was sched no blude'.

8. Anon., *The Blythsome Wedding, c.* 1680

TEXT: The two earliest surviving texts of this song are those printed by John Watson in *A Choice Collection of Comic and Serious Scots Poems, Both Ancient and Modern*, Part I, Edinburgh, 1706, pp. 8–10; and by Allan Ramsay in his first, one-volume edition of *The Tea-Table Miscellany*, Edinburgh, 1724. These texts are abbreviated below as 'W' and 'R'; both were undoubtedly derived from slightly different printed broadside texts of the song that have been lost. Since W is the oldest version, and seems textually at least as sound as R, I have used it here as the copy-text. It should be noted, however, that the title in R (which became standard in most later printings) is given as 'The Blythsome Bridal'. The more important of the many variant readings in R are recorded below.

9–44 The list of clownish rustics in these lines is a burlesque of the roll call of heroes in classical epic poetry, and is clearly derived as a satiric method from Drummond's 'Polemo-Middinia' ('P–M') which contains similar lists, including some ten of the same names (Maggie, Jockie, Willie, Tom, Andrew, Robbie, Katie, Wat, Geordie, Nansie), sometimes with the same epithet attached to the same name. See Allan H. MacLaine, 'Drummond of Hawthornden's "Polemo-Middinia" as a Source for "The Blythsome Bridal"', *Notes and Queries*, New Ser. 1 (Sept., 1954), 384–86.

18 *plouckie fac'd Wat:* cp. 'P–M', 38, 'plouky-fac'd Wattie'.

22 For this line R has: 'Wha in with black Bessie did mool'.

24 For this line R has: 'The lass that stands aft on the stool', i.e., the stool of repentance in the church – here, presumably, for sexual transgressions.

29–30 For these lines R has: 'And there will be gleed Geordy Janners, / And Kirsh wi' the lilly-white leg'.

31–32 Cp. 'P–M', 149. The allusion here is to Mons Meg, the huge cannon forged in the fifteenth century and used as one of the defences of Edinburgh Castle until its barrel accidentally burst in 1680 while firing a salute to the Duke of York. The joke here relates to the common folk notion that Meg was so enormous that a couple seeking privacy in crowded Edinburgh could actually make love inside the barrel. There is a witty pun on 'breeding' in two senses: cultivated manners and reproduction. The reference to going 'to the south' to Edinburgh suggests that the song's locale was somewhere to the north of that city. The same joke on Mons Meg is alluded to in the sixth stanza of Robert Fergusson's 'The King's Birth-Day in Edinburgh'.

35   *Gillie-Whimple:* this name seems to result from a misreading of 'P–M', 131, 136, where Drummond uses two rare common nouns – 'Gilliwyppum' and 'Gilliwamphra' – both capitalised and both meaning 'a heavy blow'. The poet here has mistaken these words for character names, and has included 'Gillie-whimple' among his rustic clowns.

35–36 For these lines R has: 'Wi' flae-lugged sharney-fac'd Lawrie, / And shangy-mou'd haluket Meg' – that is, 'With flea-eared dung-faced Lawrie, / And thin-mouthed half-witted Meg'.

37   *happer-ars'd Nanzie:* cp. 'P–M', 39, 'heavi-arstus homo'.

39   *Gleed Kettie:* cp. 'P–M', 85, 'gliedamque Ketaeam'. For this line R has: 'Muck Madie and fat-hippit Grify'.

47–68 In these lines (also 5–8) the poet gives an extended list of the foods and drinks available at the wedding, almost all of which are inexpensive items such as would in fact be parts of the ordinary fare of the peasantry. Most of the foods, for example, involve oatmeal, cabbage, fish, and animal viscera; there is no solid meat. The drinks (with the exception of brandy) are also plebeian. The entire menu, however, is described as though it were a list of luxurious gourmet treats, and this is an essential part of the total burlesque method in this song. It should be noted, also, that three of the fishes – 'skate', 'haddocks', and 'flouks' – had also been featured in 'P–M', 3–4, as 'sketta', 'haddocus', and 'fleuca'.

49   R reads: 'And there will be fadges and brachan'.

55   *haggize:* normally spelled 'haggis', a traditional Scottish meat pudding made of the heart, liver, and lungs of a sheep, minced and mixed with oatmeal, onions, and spices, boiled in the sheep's stomach.

57   W has a comma after 'milk', but this must be a misprint since the phrase clearly means cheeses made from curdled milk, 'lapper'd milk kebbucks'. R has 'And there will be lapper'd milk kebbocks' for this line, and in some ways this seems a better reading; the version in W, however, parallels the pattern in the opening line (49) of the previous stanza, and works just as well with a slight reordering of the rhythm with heavy stresses on 'be' and on the first syllables of 'lapper'd' and 'kebbucks'.

58   *farles:* W has 'fardles', a misprint.

58–59 *sowens ... swatts:* W has 'swaets', certainly a misprint for 'swatts'. The two terms – 'sowens' and 'swatts' – are closely related, as explained in *SND* under 'sowans': 'A kind of flummery; husks or seeds of oats, together with some fine meal, steeped in water for about a week until the mixture turns sour, then strained and the husks thoroughly squeezed to extract all the meal, when the jelly-like liquor is left for a further period to ferment and separate, the solid glutinous matter which sinks to the bottom being *sowans*, and the liquid, *swats*. *Sowans* are usu. prepared by boiling with water and salt, and are eaten like porridge'. The word 'swatts' is also used to signify a newly-brewed weak beer (*SND*), but in this context it surely means the liquid by-product of 'sowens' used as a drink.

62   *skink:* this is a problematic noun in this context. It can mean the meat from an ox-shin, or soup made from boiled shin of beef; here, however, it more likely signifies drink in general, especially an alcoholic drink (such as weak beer) of a wishy-washy kind.

9. Allan Ramsay, *Christ's Kirk on the Green*,
Cantos II and III, 1715, 1718

TEXT: With the kind permission of the editors the text used here is that published in *Longer Scottish Poems*, Vol. II, edited by Thomas Crawford, David Hewitt, and Alexander Law (Edinburgh: Scottish Academic Press, 1987), pp. 18–30, a slightly modernised version – that is, with normal capitalisation – of the text printed in *The Works of Allan Ramsay*, Vol. I, edited by Burns Martin and John W. Oliver, Scottish Text Society, Third Series, 19 (Edinburgh and London: Blackwood, 1945), pp. 66–82, which itself reproduces Ramsay's own edition in *Poems by Allan Ramsay* (Edinburgh, 1721). Ramsay's headnotes for both cantos are included in the present text, while his textual notes are printed in full below in quotation marks preceded by the symbol [R]. References to the copy-text or notes in *Longer Scottish Poems* are abbreviated as *LSP.*

Canto II

5 *Braith:* The context here implies that 'Braith' was the name of a farm or small village. I have been unable to identify such a place, however, either in the vicinity of Leslie, Fife, or elsewhere. It may well be that Ramsay simply fabricated 'Braith' to provide a convenient rime with 'skaith', 'death', and 'aith'. The specific suggestion may have come from one of the corrupt broadside versions of the original 'Christis Kirk', derived from the manuscript text in the Laing Ms (L), where 'The black suter of bray' is mentioned in stanza 19.

7 *Came bellyflaught:* [R] 'Came in great haste, as it were flying full upon them with her arms spread, as a falcon with expanded wings comes soussing upon her prey.'

8–9 *Be...fast:* [R] 'Desist immediately.'

15 *Lets...rows:* [R] 'A bowling-green phrase, commonly used when people would examine any affair that's a little ravel'd.'

19 *Hutchon:* this name, repeated in line 200, was clearly derived by Ramsay from the original 'Christis Kirk', line 151, where it appeared as 'Heich Hucheoun'. Ramsay also incorporated several other characters from the older poem: Lawrie (line 60 and 200) from CK 101 'Lowry'; Willie (line 101) from CK 28; Jock (line 122) from CK 31 'Jok'; Tam Lutter (line 127) from CK 41 'Thome Lular'; Touzie (line 190) from CK 44 'Towsy'; and Dick (line 199) from CK 221 'Dik'. Steen (line 118) probably also comes from CK 51 'Stevin'.

56 *Did...birle:* [R] 'Contributed for fresh bottles.'

64 *Half and Half:* [R] 'half fuddled.'

68 *He...hight:* [R] 'So high as his head could strike the loft, or joining of the couples.' The 'bawk' here would be the tie beam or collar beam connecting the bottom ends of each set of rafters or couples, a ceiling joist.

75 *Falkland bred:* [R] 'Been a journey-man to the King's taylor, and had seen court-dancing.' In his note to the original 'Christis Kirk', Canto I, line 6, Ramsay says that the church of that name was probably the one in the village of Leslie in Fife, which was only seven miles from the site of the royal palace of Falkland. 'They' in this line would be the ordinary folk of

Leslie making fun of the pretensions of a young man who imitated the court dancing at Falkland, and 'danced by the book'.

77–81 This joke at the expense of tailors reflects a common prejudice against these tradesmen as infested with fleas or lice. Traditionally they were called 'Prick-the-louse' (as in Dunbar's 'Justis', line 5) or 'Jag-the-flae'. The same stigma was sometimes transferred to other cloth workers such as the weavers in the opening line of Burns's 'The Ordination' – 'Kilmarnock wabsters, fidge an' claw'.

92   *Glowming hous'd them:* [R] 'Twilight brought them into the house.'

94   *bade: LSP* has 'blade' here, a misprint.

107   *Cuttymun,* &c: [R] 'A tune that goes very quick.'

132   *His...moon:* [R] 'Round, full and shining. When one is staring full of drink, he's said to have a face like a full moon.'

136   *The...rhime:* [R] 'The reader or church precenter, who lets go, i.e. gives out the tune to be sung by the rest of the congregation.'

141   *Baith...read:* [R] 'A rarity in those days.'

143   *Keek on a bead:* [R] 'Pray after the Roman Catholick manner, which was the religion then in fashion.'

147   *Frae...creels:* [R] 'From turning topsy turvy.'

152   *rix-dollar:* a silver coin of high value (about 3 pounds Scots in 1694), current from late 16th to mid 19th centuries in various European countries, including Holland, Germany, Austria, Denmark, Sweden, and Scotland. See *DOST* under 'rex-dollor'. Cognate forms of the noun include Dutch 'rijksdaalder', Swedish 'ricksdaler', and German 'reichsthaler'.

161   *To Brownies:* [R] 'Many whimsical stories are handed down to us by old women of these Brownies: they tell us they were a kind of good drudging spirits, who appeared in shape of rough men, would have lyen familiarly by the fire all night, threshen in the barn, brought a midwife at a time, and done many such kind offices. But none of them has been seen in Scotland since the Reformation, as saith wise John Brown.'

178–79 *A...sheaf:* [R] 'A cheese full of crawling mites crown'd the feast.'

182   *Her...flung:* [R] 'The practice of throwing the bridegroom or the bride's stocking when they are going to bed, is well known: the person who it lights on is to be next married of the company.'

208–9 These lines are obviously modelled on the pattern of the original 'Christis Kirk', lines 1–2.

Canto III

1   *East...Fife:* [R] 'Where day must break upon my company if as I have observed, the scene is at Lesly church.' The 'East Neuk of Fife' was, and is, the colloquial term for the eastern peninsula of Fife, jutting into the North Sea. For discussion of Ramsay's error in locating the scene at Leslie in Fife, see my note on the original 'Christis Kirk', line 6.

13   *Their...pay:* [R] 'Payment of the drunken groat is very peremptorily demanded by the common people next morning; but if they frankly confess the debt due, they are passed for two-pence.' The 'groat' was a silver coin amounting to fourpence Scots, commonly imposed by kirk sessions as the fine for drunkenness.

16   *Rake their een:* [R] 'Rub open their eyes.'

19 *Fair foor days:* [R] 'Broad day light.'

23 *Aboon the claiths:* [R] 'They commonly throw their gifts of household furniture above the bed-cloaths where the young folks are lying.'

42 *Word...kanny:* [R] 'It was reported she was a witch.'

48 *Had...test:* [R] 'I do not mean an oath of that name we all have heard of.' Ramsay's note is a facetious reference to the British Test Act of 1673, requiring all public office holders to take an oath of allegiance to the Crown and to receive the sacraments of the Church of England.

53 *Charge of horning:* [R] 'It is a writ charging to make payment, declaring the debitor a rebel. N.B. It may be left in the lock-hole, if the doors be shut.' Ramsay's note makes it clear that he intended this as a sexual joke, a 'change of horning' being comparable to a deposit of seminal fluid resulting in a pregnancy.

68 *Mount the creepy:* [R] 'The stool of repentance.' This was the low stool or 'cutty stool' at the front of the church where those guilty of fornication had to sit to be publicly berated by the minister for three Sundays in a row.

75 *Coost a legen-girth:* [R] 'Like a tub that loses one of its bottom hoops.' That is, like a woman who gives birth to an illegitimate child.

94 *Fill...fou:* [R] ''Tis a custom for the friends to endeavour the next day after the wedding to make the new married man as drunk as possible.'

100 *A creel, &c:* [R] 'For merryment, a creel or basket is bound, full of stones, upon his back; and if he has acted a manly part, his young wife with all imaginable speed cuts the cords, and relieves him from the burthen. If she does not, he's rallied for a fumbler.'

118 *The souter, &c:* [R] '*Vide* Canto II. Line 177.' In this text, line 199.

128 *Skin and birn:* [R] 'The marks of a sheep; the burn on the nose, and the tar on the skin. i.e. She was sure it was him, with all the marks of her drunken husband about him.'

134 *Wind...pirn:* [R] 'It is a threatning expression, when one designs to contrive some malicious thing to vex you.' A 'pirn' was the spool or bobbin of a spinning wheel on which the spun yarn was wound.

141 *this:* *LSP* reads 'his', a misprint.

161–2 *Rade...her:* [R] 'The riding of the stang on a woman that hath beat her husband, is as I have described it, by one's riding upon a sting, or a long piece of wood, carried by two others on their shoulders, where, like a herauld, he proclaims the woman's name, and the manner of her unnatural action.'

172 *fou:* 'foo' as an adverb meaning 'hoo' or 'how', as in this case, is found nowhere else in Ramsay's work, being a pronunciation normally limited to Northern and Insular Scots. It is common, for example, in Aberdeenshire dialect where many initial consonant sounds usually pronounced as 'h' are sounded as 'f'. The same form may be seen in John Skinner's 'The Christmas Bawing of Monimusk',. line 113, a poem that is set in Aberdeenshire.

177 *Tane the sturdy:* [R] 'A disease amongst sheep that makes them giddy, and run off from the rest of the herd.'

10. John Skinner, *The Christmass Bawing of Monimusk*, 1739

TEXT: With the kind permission of the editors, the text reproduces that of *Longer Scottish Poems*, eds. Thomas Crawford, David Hewitt, and Alexander Law (Edinburgh: Scottish Academic Press, 1987), II, 103–114, which is based on the earliest known printing of the poem in the *Caledonian Magazine* for September 1788. Since Skinner tells us that he composed this work in 1739, the poem apparently remained in manuscript for almost half a century before its first publication in 1788. 1788, however, was a banner year for publication of Scots verse by minor poets riding on the coattails of Robert Burns, following the huge success of the first Edinburgh edition of Burns's poems in 1787. Burns's Ayrshire friends John Lapraik and David Sillar each published a volume of Scots poetry in 1788, as did Ebenezer Picken and others.

1–315 The general note in *LSP* on the custom of village games at Christmas is so helpful and well phrased that I quote it in full: 'Nearly every district in Scotland had its annual bawing at Christmas, New Year or Fastern's eve (Shrove Tuesday). The custom still continues in Jedburgh. Sometimes one part of a parish played another; sometimes whole parishes opposed each other. The rules were various but it was standard that in football no handling was permitted and in handball no kicking. In Monymusk, the game was football. It appears that the pitch is the churchyard and one of the goals is in the park, i.e., in the grounds of Monymusk House. It is permissible to trip, kick, fell and otherwise incapacitate opponents. There are spectators but it is part of the game to "involve" them from time to time and to lower the dignity of the schoolmaster and his like by tackling or by inducing falls in the mud. One goal constitutes a win in this game, but it might have continued had there been light enough.'

10–11 These lines echo Ramsay, 'Christ's Kirk', III, 166 – 'Like bumbees frae their bykes' – and Skinner's couplet, plus his 'fyke' rime in line 16, in turn influenced Burns in 'Tam o' Shanter', 11. 193–194: 'As bees bizz out wi' angry fyke, / When plundering herds assail their byke'.

19 *Rob Roy:* Skinner undoubtedly carried this name over from 'Robene Roy' of the original 'Christis Kirk', line 61. Several other character names derive from this same source or from Ramsay's two cantos of sequels to it; e.g., Geordy (21) from Ramsay, III, 183; Tammy (50) from 'Tammie' (Ramsay, III, 76); Steen (73) from 'Stevin' (CK 51) and 'Steen' (Ramsay II, 118); Hutchin (181) from 'Heich Hucheon' (CK 151) and 'Hutchon' (Ramsay II, 19); and Davy Don (259) from 'Donald Don' (Ramsay II, 170). Other names are simply alliterative, but some seem so specific and non-traditional that they may well refer to actual individuals in the parish of Monymusk whom Skinner knew personally: e.g., Francy Winsy (46), Leitch (91), Cowley (100), and Davy Mair (169).

47 *sauchin slav'ry slype:* this is an example of three notable stylistic tendencies in this poem: (a) the use by Skinner of fairly heavy alliteration as well as rime, as in the original 'Christis Kirk' but not attempted in Ramsay's sequels; (b) the use of extremely colloquial idioms for antiquarian or picturesque effect, more so here than in Ramsay; and (c) the use of dialectal forms peculiar to Aberdeenshire, Skinner's home territory.

Further examples of these usages may be seen, for instance, in *bleed* (55) for 'blood', *grunshy* (94), *rammage glyde* (106), *lang tripal* (203), *stiblart gurk* (221), and *derf dawrd* (259); there are many others.

63 *And made me blae:* this is the first variation on the pattern of 'that day' taglines in the poem; others occur in the final lines of stanzas 23, 26, 27, 30, and the final stanza, but all of these variations end with an '-ay' rime.

75 *doyt:* a small copper coin of Dutch origin, equal to one twelfth of an English penny; it had unofficial currency in Scotland in the early 18th century. Here the term is used as a symbol of worthlessness.

82 *inset dominie:* this character is probably the poet himself, presented with humorous self-deprecation, since Skinner was in fact serving as assistant schoolmaster at Monymusk in 1739.

102 *He stenn'd bawk-height:* compare Ramsay, II, 68: 'He lap bawk-hight'.

113 *fow:* this is Aberdeenshire dialect for 'hoo' (how); compare Ramsay, II, 172, where the identical form occurs, a form that would have been natural for Skinner but not for Ramsay.

145 *neipor:* this is a phonetic spelling of the Aberdeenshire pronunciation of 'neighbour'.

161 *fou'd be:* this is an obscure phrase in which the first syllable means 'hoo' or 'how' (see *fow* in line 113). The idiom seems to mean 'however it be (was)'; see *SND* under 'Foo'.

185 *seek his lare:* another obscure phrase in which 'lare' is probably used in the sense of 'learning' or 'enlightenment', so that the whole phrase means 'to seek enlightenment' or simply 'to think'.

199 *town sutor:* this identical phrase had appeared in the original 'Christis Kirk', line 171. *Laury:* a common Scots diminutive form for 'Lawrence', also used as a generic name for the fox, as in several of Robert Henryson's *Moral Fabillis* (where it is spelled 'Lowrence').

298–9 *Monimuss:* this spelling no doubt represents the actual local pronunciation of the name of the village of Monymusk, located about eighteen miles west of Aberdeen. These two lines together are obviously modelled on the famous opening of the original 'Christis Kirk', line 1–2.

11. Robert Fergusson, *Hallow-fair*, 1772

TEXT: With the kind permission of the editors, the text here reproduces that of *LSP*, II, 138–141, which is a slightly modernised version (with normalised italics and capitalisation) of the standard scholarly edition, *The Poems of Robert Fergusson*, ed. Matthew P. McDiarmid, Scottish Text Society, 2 vols. (Edinburgh and London, 1954, 1956), II, 89–93. The poem was first published by Fergusson in *The Weekly Magazine or Edinburgh Amusement* for 12 November 1772.

1. *Hallowmas:* All Saints Day, or All Hallows, a church holiday on November 1. The fair was held annually just outside of Edinburgh, during the first week of November.

28 *chapman billies:* this phrase certainly suggested the opening line of Burns's 'Tam o' Shanter': 'When chapman billies leave the street'.

37–45 In this stanza Fergusson skilfully reproduces in his spellings the forms and sounds of Aberdeenshire dialect (the speech of his father): *fa* for 'wha'; *guid*, pronounced 'gweed', for 'gude'; *protty* for 'pretty'; *weyr* for 'wire'; *leem* for 'loom'; *forseeth* for 'forsooth'; and *teem* for 'tume' or 'toom'. At the fair Sawney sells stockings, a product for which Aberdeen was famous in the 18th century.

56 *The serjeant:* an army recruiting sergeant at the fair who offers 'two guineas and a crown' (that is, two pounds and seven shillings, a considerable sum in those days) as a bribe for enlisting – plus a large quantity of strong drink.

73 *Phoebus:* god of the sun in Greek mythology. *Thetis:* a Nereid or sea nymph, mother of Achilles. From the Scottish perspective the sun would set each night into the western ocean, so that Phoebus would sink into the lap of Thetis.

79 *Lochaber aix:* the standard and formidable weapon of Edinburgh's City Guard, a much hated police force recruited mainly from invalid members of Highland regiments. It had a long wooden handle with an axe and hook at the end.

93–96 Fergusson is here satirising the heavy Gaelic accents and idioms of the Highlanders in the City Guard. *She maun pe see our guard* (94) means 'He (Jock Bell) must be seen by our guard' for disciplinary action.

98 *drunken groat:* a fine of fourpence Scots for drunkenness. See Ramsay, 'Christ's Kirk', III, 13.

12. Robert Fergusson, *Leith Races*, 1773

TEXT: With the kind permission of the editors, the text here reproduces that of *LSP*, II, 163–169, which is a slightly modernised version (with normalised italics and capitalisation) of the standard scholarly edition, *The Poems of Robert Fergusson*, ed. Matthew P. McDiarmid, Scottish Text Society, 2 vols. (Edinburgh and London, 1954, 1956), II, 160–167. The poem was first published by Fergusson in *The Weekly Magazine or Edinburgh Amusement* for 22 July 1773.

1–45 This entire opening section, featuring the mythical character of 'Mirth', obviously gave Burns the idea for the personification of 'Fun' in 'The Holy Fair'. M.P. McDiarmid, II, 293, also notes similarities to passages in William Dunbar's 'The Thrissil and the Rois' and in the ballad of 'Thomas the Rhymer'.

1 The Leith Races were an annual horses-racing event held for several days on the sands at Leith, the port of Edinburgh, around July 20, sponsored by the Town Council of Edinburgh with a 'purse' of 100 guineas for the winner of the races.

11 *sud musand:* these are Middle Scots verb forms used to achieve a deliberately old-fashioned effect.

25 *Hebe:* goddess of youth and spring in Greek mythology, daughter of Zeus and Hera, and wife of Hercules.

29 *Land o' Cakes:* Scotland, where oatcakes are a national speciality. Compare

Burns's use of the same phrase in 'On the late Captain Grose's Peregrinations thro' Scotland', lines 1–2: 'Hear, Land o' Cakes, and brither Scots, / Frae Maidenkirk to Johny Groats!'

31 *late-wakes:* M.P. McDiarmid, II, 293, has an interesting note on the mixture of dancing and drinking with mourning in Scottish funerals in the 18th century.

52 This homely metaphor – to crow in someone else's crop – is interpreted in *LSP*, II, 375, and in McDiarmid, II, 294, to mean that she will be painfully remembered by him; but the alternate gloss – she will triumph over him – seems to make at least as good sense in this context (see *SND* under 'crap').

73–83 In these lines the poet is laughing at the Gaelic accents of the City Guardsman: *hafe* for 'have', *marsh* for 'march', *Her nanesel* ('her own self') for 'we', and *pe* for 'be'.

80 *birth-day wars:* attacks on the City Guard during celebrations of the King's Birthday on June 4; see Fergusson's poem 'The King's Birth-Day in Edinburgh'.

84 *baxter lads:* a baker had recently died of a fractured skull at the hands of the City Guard, and his fellow tradesmen had vowed revenge. See the note in McDiarmid, II, 294.

91 *Bow:* the ancient steep street called the West Bow, ascending from the Grassmarket to the Lawnmarket, where the tinsmiths (*tinkler billies*) had their shops.

95 *Leith-walk:* the main road connecting Edinburgh with its port, Leith.

113 This line may be understood as follows: 'If the good Lord allows many of them to live until the next day'.

118–121 *Buchan:* the far northeast part of Aberdeenshire. *Geed* and *fa* are Buchan dialect for 'good' and 'wha'.

119 *Findrums:* These were small haddocks, split and smoked, called 'speldings'. McDiarmid, II, 294, thinks they were so-named from the village of Findhorn on the Moray Firth; the editors of *LSP*, II, 376, on the other hand, say they originated at Findon in Kincardineshire; on the whole, the latter seems more likely.

127 *rowly powl:* a game in which a stick is thrown at small pegs topped with cakes of gingerbread; the player who knocks down a peg gets to eat the cake. See the detailed note in McDiarmid, II, 294.

129–130 As McDiarmid explains (II, 294), these lines mean 'such games proved as treacherous (financially) to the players, as walking on ice'.

142 *Dian:* Diana, Roman goddess of chastity.

145 *The Lyon:* the Lord Lyon King of Arms, the Scottish officer regulating heraldic coats of arms; he can prosecute wearers of unregistered arms.

149 *Jamie's laws:* a law of 1592, in the reign of James VI, authorising punishment of those bearing false arms.

152 *Whigs:* members of a political party, but here used as a derisive term for any unruly or radical persons who would be likely to reject the authority of the Lyon King and wear unrecognised arms. See McDiarmid, II, 295.

163 *Robinhood:* a popular debating society in Edinburgh.

172 *hale the dools:* score a goal and win the game in football, here used in a general sense – to celebrate enthusiastically. Cp. Skinner, 'Christmass Bawing', stanza 32, and the original 'Christis Kirk', line 217 and note.

13. Robert Fergusson, *The Election*, 1773

TEXT: With the kind permission of the editors, the text here reproduces that of *LSP*, II, 169–173, which is a slightly modernised version (with normalised italics and capitalisation) of the standard scholarly edition, *The Poems of Robert Fergusson*, ed. Matthew P. McDiarmid, Scottish Text Society, 2 vols. (Edinburgh and London, 1954, 1965), II, 185–190. The poem was first published by Fergusson in *The Weekly Magazine or Edinburgh Amusement* for 16 September 1773.

Motto: This macaronic couplet (Latin mixed with Scots) says: 'Now is the time for drinking, and to drain the big bowl; beware of the City Guard, especially Dougal Ged and Dougal Campbell'.

7 Deacons were a feature of the incredibly complicated elections for the Town Council of Edinburgh in the 18th century, a system devised to ensure the perpetuation of political power in the hands of a few, resulting in massive corruption. The Council had twenty-five members, comprising seventeen merchants and eight tradesmen or deacons. Each year deacons were elected by each of the fourteen incorporated trades in the city. First, each trade would submit a list of six potential nominees for the position of deacon; this was called 'the lang leet' (a Scots word derived from the French 'élite' – the chosen). The outgoing Town Council would then reduce this list to three candidates, 'the short leet', and the trade would elect the deacon from these. The fourteen trades would then get together for a celebratory banquet with the outgoing Council members, at which the Council would select six of the fourteen new deacons to serve as Council deacons, together with two deacons held over from the old Council. In this game of musical chairs, the same group of 'reliable' members would be regularly re-elected on a rotating basis, and any troublesome or radical nominees could easily be excluded.

18 All public office holders were required by the Test Act to swear a formal oath of loyalty to king and established church.

43 *Walker's:* a tavern in the High Street where the City Chambers are now located; this was the site of the annual banquet for the tradesmen on this occasion.

61–2 I have corrected the punctuation and capitalisation in these lines. In the original printing in the *Weekly Magazine* and in all subsequent editions the text reads: Quod Deacon let the toast round gang, / 'Come, etc.'

66 *handsel-Teysday:* first Tuesday of the New Year.

74 *lamps:* special decorated lamp posts used to be set up in front of the houses of Edinburgh's magistrates.

81 *that night:* this is a variation on the usual 'that day' tag-line; it recurs in stanzas 10, 11, 12, and 15, and may well have been suggested by the similar shift in Alexander Scott's 'Justing and Debait' where he moves from the refrains 'Up at the Drum that day' and 'Up at Dalkeith that day' to 'Within the toun that nicht'.

82 *souter Jock:* this phrase probably suggested to Burns his 'souter Johnny' in 'Tam o' Shanter', line 41.

94 *'Gin ye man reel my pirny':* in this context this spinning metaphor (wind

my bobbin) clearly means 'If you must do my work for me' (with my wife). The note on this point in *LSP*, II, 377, seems off the mark.

111–116 These elections were notoriously corrupt; the furtiveness of these bribes is deftly suggested by the recipients' reluctance to check the gold guineas for exact weight.

120–121 These lines certainly gave Burns the hint for his couplet in 'The Twa Dogs', 147–48: 'Wha, ablins thrang a parliamentin, / For Britain's guid his saul indentin –.'

123 *protests:* this apparently means objections to some parts of the incredibly complicated election procedures.

124 *Sandy Fife:* possibly the town bell-ringer.

125 *Clout the caudron:* a traditional folk tune (repair the pot). Burns was to use the same tune for the Caird's Song (Song 5) of 'Love and Liberty'; see lines 165–180 and the note on this song in Burns's cantata.

134 *lang leet:* see note on line 7; this is a brilliant stroke by Fergusson, expressing the deacons' mortality by way of a technical term in the election.

14. John Mayne, *Hallowe'en*, 1780

TEXT: For the text of this rare piece I have used that of George Eyre-Todd, ed., *Scottish Poetry of the Eighteenth Century* (London and Edinburgh, n.d. [1890s]), II, 162–64. The poem was first printed in Ruddiman's *Weekly Magazine or Edinburgh Amusement* for November 1780, where it would have been accessible to Burns, and was reprinted by Mayne together with *The Silver Gun* in a separate publication in Glasgow by the Foulis Press in 1783.

2 *Frae Handsel-Monday till New-Year:* since Handsel-Monday is the first Monday in January, from then until New Year's Day would comprise an entire year, all year long.

3–6 Mayne's rhetorical pattern here seems to be based on that of Fergusson's 'Hallow-fair', 5–9.

7–10 The mildly anti-Catholic sentiment here is similar to that of Ramsay's 'Christ's' Kirk', II, 143.

27–29 Cp. Ramsay's delightful drinking song, 'Up in the Air', 3–4: 'In glens the fairies skip and dance, / And witches wallop o'er to France'.

45–48 Mayne's imagery here clearly suggested that of Burns in 'Halloween', stanzas 11–12.

57 *saw hempseed:* cp. Burns, 'Halloween', 147.

70 *steek their e'en:* cp. Burns, 'Halloween', 30.

72 Mayne's trick of working his own name into the rime scheme of the final stanza of this poem surely gave Burns the hint for the closings to several of his verse epistles where this same technique is used; see, e.g., 'To William Simson, Ochiltree', 108; 'Third Epistle to John Lapraik', 54; 'Letter to James Tennant of Glenconner', 71; and 'To Mr. Gavin Hamilton, Mauchline', 42.

15. John Mayne, *The Siller Gun*, Canto I, 1808

TEXT: With the kind permission of the editors, the text here reproduces that of *LSP*, II, 176–183, which itself is based on the version of *The Siller Gun* in four cantos published in Glocester [*sic*] in 1808. Mayne worked on this poem off and on through most of his long lifetime, publishing no fewer than six versions of it, as follows: (1) the first brief version in twelve stanzas written in Dumfries when the author was eighteen and deeply impressed by the poems of Robert Fergusson whom he had met four years earlier during Fergusson's visit to that town; (2) an expanded version in two cantos published in 1779; (3) a longer text in three cantos published in Ruddiman's *Weekly Magazine or Edinburgh Amusement*, beginning 19 June 1780, the same periodical where Fergusson's work had first appeared in the early 1770s; (4) a version in three cantos enlarged from the 1780 text and published, together with Mayne's 'Hallowe'en', in Glasgow by the Foulis Press in 1783; (5) an extended four-canto version published in Glocester [*sic*] in 1808; and finally (6) a five-canto text published in London in 1836, the year of Mayne's death. In the first four of these versions the title is given as *The Silver Gun*, but this was Scotticised to *The Siller Gun* in the 1808 and 1836 editions.

2 *Dumfries:* an important provincial town on the River Nith in southwestern Scotland, where Burns lived in the last few years of his life and where he is buried. At the time of Mayne and Burns, Dumfries had a population of about 10,000 – now about 30,000.

4 *the sev'n trades:* these were the seven incorporated trades in Dumfries: 'hammermen' (blacksmiths), 'squaremen' (carpenters), tailors, weavers, shoemakers, skinners, and 'fleshers' (butchers). Each trade elected a 'deacon' annually, and the seven deacons elected one of their number as 'convener of trades' – all with seats on the town council of Dumfries.

5 *siller gun:* this famous trophy was a silver tube about ten inches long, given to the town of Dumfries by King James VI in 1617 to encourage good marksmanship through periodic muster of local volunteer companies of soldiers (the seven trades) for a shooting competition or 'wappenshaw'.

8 *the King's birth-day:* Mayne's note tells us that the 'wappenshaw' in Dumfries was held sporadically rather than every year, but invariably on the birthday of the reigning monarch. The birthday of George III was celebrated on the fourth of June, as depicted in Fergusson's 'The King's Birth-Day in Edinburgh', a poem that surely helped inspire Mayne's opus.

39 *James M'Noe:* this was a real person, as were two others named in this canto and identified in the notes in *LSP*, II, 378. M'Noe was the town drummer; Geordy Smith (line 94) was an old soldier who had been a sergeant in the Black Watch; and Robin Tamson (line 156) was deacon of the blacksmiths and 'convenor of trades'.

92 *the Sands:* a flat sandy beach on the bank of the River Nith near the centre of Dumfries; the town is seven miles north of the mouth of the Nith where it reaches the sea in the Solway Firth.

100 *side coats, and dockit:* as the note in *LSP*, II, 378, points out, these were contrasting styles in coats according to social class: greatcoats for the gentry, and shorter (*dockit*) ones down to the hips for working folk.

123 *Prestonpans:* the battle of 21 September 1745, when the Highland army of Prince Charles Edward Stuart defeated the English under General Cope, near Edinburgh.

147 *The Craigs:* cliffs on the Nith about a mile from central Dumfries, where the shooting match was held.

216 *Maids catch the stocking:* an old-fashioned Scottish marriage custom, whereby the bride throws her left stocking at the crowd of well-wishers in the bridal bedchamber; the girl on whom it falls or who catches the stocking is supposed to be the next to be married. The same practice is referred to in Ramsay's 'Christ's Kirk', II, 182.

16. Robert Burns, *A Mauchline Wedding*, 1785

TEXT: As copy-text I have used Burns's letter to Mrs Dunlop, dated from Mauchline, 21 August 1788, as printed from the Lochryan MS for the first time in W.E. Henley and T.F. Henderson, eds., *The Poetry of Robert Burns,* (Edinburgh, 1896), II, 42–44. Nearly identical texts of the poem may be found in *The Letters of Robert Burns*, ed. J. De Lancey Ferguson (Oxford, 1931), second ed. by G. Ross Roy (Oxford, 1985), and in *The Poems and Songs of Robert Burns*, ed. James Kinsley (Oxford, 1968). All of Burns's own glosses and comments on the poem are given below, preceded by the symbol [B].

Intro. In these remarks Burns, with his characteristic succinctness and vigour, placed Mrs Dunlop in command of the facts necessary to an understanding of the poem.

3 *rolling:* in the texts edited by Ferguson, Roy, and Kinsley this word is given as 'rotting'.

10 *Blacksideen:* [B] 'a hill.'

10–13 The picture of young girls getting up and dressing in finery very early on the big day is common in poems of the *Christis Kirk* genre – as in Fergusson's 'Hallow-fair', stanza 2, or 'Leith Races', stanza 6; this tradition goes all the way back to the prototype 'Peblis to the Play', stanzas 2–4.

12 *Nell and Bess:* [B] 'Miller's two sisters.' Nell Miller appears as 'Miss Miller' in Burns's early song often called 'The Belles of Mauchline', beginning, 'In Mauchline there dwells six proper young Belles'; Bess was Elizabeth Miller (with whom the poet was temporarily infatuated) who appears in the same song as 'Miss Betty' and was also the heroine Eliza in another of Burns's early songs, beginning, 'From thee Eliza I must go'. *got:* texts edited by Ferguson, Roy, and Kinsley read 'get'.

26–27 The two missing lines here were left out purposely by Burns, probably not 'in deference to Mrs Dunlop' as James Kinsley in *The Poems and Songs of Robert Burns* (Oxford, 1968), 1125, would have it, but rather to allow Mrs Dunlop the added pleasure of filling them in for herself. The lady, after all, though highly respectable, was no prude and would have enjoyed a joke of this kind, happily providing 'gawn up' to rime with 'drawn up'.

29 *silken:* [B] 'The ladies' first silk gowns, got for the occasion.' Cp. 'The

Holy Fair', 60.

34 *grieve:* texts edited by Ferguson, Roy, and Kinsley read 'grave'. Either word makes sense in the context, but 'grieve' provides the internal rime that Burns is using in the tetrameter lines of this stanza.

37 *Sandy:* [B] 'Driver of the post chaise.'

41 *John:* [B] 'M–'s father.'

41–45 These lines were clearly affected by Fergusson's 'The Election', 10–13:
> Haste Epps, quo' John, an' bring my gizz!
> Tak tent ye dinna't spulzie;
> Last night the barber ga't a friz,
> An' straikit it wi' ulzie.

45 At the end of this fragment Burns explained to Mrs Dunlop why he left off: 'Against my Muse had come thus far, Miss Bess & I were once more in Unison, so I thought no more of the Piece. – Tho' the folks are rather uppish, they are such as I did not chuse to expose so I think this is about the second time I ever scrawled it.'

17. Robert Burns, *Halloween*, 1785

TEXT: With the kind permission of the editors the text here reproduces that of *LSP*, II, 221–28, which itself is based on Burns's Kilmarnock edition of 1786, slightly modernised. The poet's own extensive notes on the poem are all given below, again slightly modernised in terms of capitalisation, italics, etc., and preceded by the symbol [B]. For other annotations the editor is especially indebted to the excellent 'Commentary' by James Kinsley in volume 3 of his edition of *The Poems and Songs of Robert Burns*, Oxford English Texts, 1968 (abbreviated as K), as well as to the notes in *LSP*, II, 386–88.

Motto: these lines are quoted from Oliver Goldsmith's *The Deserted Village*, 251–54.

1 *that night:* [B] 'is thought to be a night when witches, devils, and other mischief-making beings, are all abroad on their baneful, midnight errands: particularly, those aerial people, the fairies, are said, on that night, to hold a grand anniversary.' Halloween is the eve of All Saints Day or Hallowmass (1 November), a night traditionally notorious for anti-Christian frolics of witches, fairies, and devils. Burns's rimes and phrasing here (1–4), owe something to Mayne's 'Halloween', 25–30, and perhaps also to Ramsay's 'Up in the Air', 1–4.

2. *Cassilis Downans:* [B] 'Certain little, romantic, rocky, green hills, in the neighbourhood of the ancient seat of the Earls of Cassilis.' These hills are just outside of the village of Kirkmichael, three miles west of Maybole, eight miles south of Ayr. Since the eighteenth century the house of the Earl of Cassillis has been associated in folk tradition with the exploits of Johnny Faa, the hero of several versions of the ballad of 'The Gypsy Laddie', no. 200 in *The English and Scottish Popular Ballads*, ed. Francis J. Child.

5 *Colean:* Culzean Castle, on the Ayrshire coast about ten miles south of Ayr, in the parish of Kirkoswald. It was the stronghold of the Earls of Cassillis.

7 *Cove:* [B] 'A noted cavern near Colean-house, called the Cove of Colean;

which, as well as Cassilis Downans, is famed, in country story, for being a
favourite haunt of Fairies.'

11 *Doon:* A river immortalised by Burns in 'Tam o' Shanter' and other works;
it runs northwest, reaching the sea about two miles south of Ayr, and
formed the boundary between the ancient districts of Kyle and Carrick.

12–13 *Bruce:* [B] 'The famous family of that name, the ancestors of Robert the
great deliverer of his country, were Earls of Carrick.' *Carrick* is the
southern part of Ayrshire lying south and west of the River Doon.

23 *wooer-babs:* these were special garters knotted below the knee with two
loops to signify the wearer's intention to propose marriage.

29–45 *stocks:* [B] 'The first ceremony of Halloween, is, pulling each a *stock*, or
plant of kail. They must go out, hand in hand, with eyes shut, and pull the
first they meet with: its being big or little, straight or crooked, is prophetic of
the size and shape of the grand object of all their spells – the husband or
wife. If any *yird*, or earth, stick to the root, that is *tocher*, or fortune; and the
taste of the *custoc*, that is, the heart of the stem, is indicative of the natural
temper and disposition. Lastly, the stems, or to give them their ordinary
appellation, the *runts*, are placed somewhere above the head of the door; and
the christian names of the people whom chance brings into the house, are,
according to the priority of placing the *runts*, the names in question.'

47–54 *stalks o' corn:* [B] 'They go to the barn-yard, and pull each, at three
several times, a stalk of oats. If the third stalk wants the *top-pickle*, that is,
the grain at the top of the stock, the party in question will want the
maidenhead.'

53 *fause-house:* [B] 'When the corn is in a doubtful state, by being too green,
or wet, the stack builder, by means of old timber, &c. makes a large
apartment in his stack, with an opening in the side which is fairest exposed
to the wind: this he calls a *fause-house.*'

55 *nits:* [B] 'Burning the nuts is a favourite charm. They name the lad and lass
to each particular nut, as they lay them in the fire; and according as they
burn quietly together, or start from beside one another, the course and issue
of the courtship will be.' The 'guidwife' with her nuts had been featured in
Mayne's 'Halloween', 19–20: 'Placed at their head the gudewife sits, / And
deals round apples, pears, and nits.'

98 *blue-clue:* [B] 'Whoever would, with success, try this spell, must strictly
observe these directions. Steal out, all alone, to the kiln, and, darkling,
throw into the pot, a clew of blue yarn: wind it in a new clew off the old
one; and towards the latter end, something will hold the thread: demand,
wha hauds? i.e. who holds? and answer will be returned from the kiln-pot,
by naming the christian and sirname of your future spouse.' Mayne, in
'Halloween', 45–48, had recorded the same ritual.

111 *eat the apple:* [B] 'Take a candle, and go, alone, to a looking glass: eat an
apple before it, and some traditions say you should comb your hair all the
time: the face of your conjugal companion, *to be*, will be seen in the glass,
as if peering over your shoulder.'

123–4 Compare Burns's phrasing here with Fergusson's 'Hallow-fair', 75:
'Great cause he had to rue it'; and Ramsay's 'Christ's Kirk', II, 3: 'And
mony a ane had gotten his death'.

127 *the Sherra-moor:* a partly phonetic rendering of Sheriffmuir, site of a

famous battle in 1715, near Dunblane, between the Hanoverian army under
the Duke of Argyll and the Jacobite forces under the Earl of Mar.

139 *Achmacalla:* Kinsley is surely right in suggesting that this place-name was
'concocted' by Burns to make the rime.

140 *hemp-seed:* [B] 'Steal out, unperceived, and sow a handful of hemp seed;
harrowing it with any thing you can conveniently draw after you. Repeat,
now and then, "Hemp seed I saw thee, Hemp seed I saw thee; and him (or
her) that is to be my true-love, come after me and pou thee". Look over
your left shoulder, and you will see the appearance of the person invoked,
in the attitude of pulling hemp. Some traditions say, "come after me and
shaw thee", that is, show thyself; in which case it simply appears. Others
omit the harrowing, and say, "come after me and harrow thee".'

182 *three wechts:* [B] 'This charm must likewise be performed, unperceived
and alone. You go to the barn, and open both doors; taking them off the
hinges, if possible; for there is danger, that the Being, about to appear, may
shut the doors, and do you some mischief. Then take that instrument used
in winnowing the corn, which, in our country-dialect, we call a *wecht;* and
go thro' all the attitudes of letting down corn against the wind. Repeat it
three times; and the third time, an apparition will pass thro' the barn, in at
the windy door, and out at the other, having both the figure in question and
the appearance or retinue, marking the employment or station in life.'

201 *stack:* [B] 'Take an opportunity of going, unnoticed, to a bearstack [barley
stack], and fathom it three times round. The last fathom of the last time,
you will catch in your arms, the appearance of your future conjugal yoke-
fellow.'

212 Burns repeated this line almost verbatim in 'Tam o' Shanter', 93: 'And
thro' the whins, and by the cairn'.

214 *three...burn:* [B] 'You go out, one or more, for this is a social spell, to a
south-running spring or rivulet, where "three lairds' lands meet", and dip
your left shirt-sleeve. Go to bed in sight of a fire, and hang your wet sleeve
before it to dry. Ly awake; and sometime near midnight, an apparition,
having the exact figure of the grand object in question, will come and turn
the sleeve, as if to dry the other side of it.' This was a superstitious ritual
widespread in Scotland, but Burns apparently gave it a very specific and
local Ayrshire application; A.L. Taylor in 'Tam's Road and Leezie's Pool',
an amazingly detailed and knowledgeable article in *Ayrshire in the Time of
Burns,* ed. John Strawhorn (Kilmarnock, 1959), 211–19, has identified the
burn and 'pool' (232) as part of Riddick's Moss Burn where the lands of
three lairds met – Mount Oliphant (Doonholm estate), Broomberry
(Rozelle), and Pleasantfield – a stream that the poet would have known
intimately from his early years at Mount Oliphant farm.

217–225 This charming stanza certainly gave Tennyson the germ of his idea for
'The Song of the Brook'; see Allan H. MacLaine, 'Some Echoes of Burns
in Tennyson', *Studies in Scottish Literature,* 14 (1979), 249–52.

236 *luggies:* [B] 'Take three dishes; put clean water in one, foul water in
another, and leave the third empty: blindfold a person, and lead him to the
hearth where the dishes are ranged; he (or she) dips the left hand: if by
chance in the clean water, the future husband or wife will come to the bar
of matrimony, a maid; if in the foul, a widow; if in the empty dish, it

foretells, with equal certainty, no marriage at all. It is repeated three times; and every time the arrangement of the dishes is altered.'

240 *Mar's-year:* according to K 1124 this was 1715, when the Jacobite rebellion under the Earl of Mar took place.

248 *butter'd so'ns:* [B] 'Sowens, with butter instead of milk to them, is always the halloween supper.' For a precise definition of *sowens* or *sowans* see note on 'The Blythsome Wedding', 58–59

18. Robert Burns, *The Holy Fair*, 1785

TEXT: With the kind permission of the editors, the text here reproduces that of *LSP*, II, 201–208, which itself is based on Burns's Kilmarnock edition of 1786, slightly modernised, with two corrections (see notes on lines 86 and 103) from the poet's later editions. All proper nouns, often reduced to asterisks or initials and asterisks in the Kilmarnock volume, are spelled out in full.

Motto: This stanza is quoted by Burns from a rather obscure satiric dialogue on Jeremy Collier by Thomas Brown (1663–1704), entitled *The stage-beaux toss'd in a blanket; or, Hypocrisie alamode* (London: J. Nutt, 1704).

5 *Galston muirs:* moorlands west of the village of Galston, located four miles west of Kilmarnock and six miles north of Mauchline, hence visible on a fair day to an observer at Burns's farm of Mossgiel on the north side of Mauchline.

15 *lyart lining:* this would be the mantle of Hypocrisy; the one whose cloak is wholly black is Superstition, whereas Hypocrisy, being two-faced, has black on the outside, grey on the inside.

37 *Fun:* this amusing pseudo-mythological figure is obviously based on Fergusson's portrait of 'Mirth' in the first five stanzas of 'Leith Races', though Burns's *Fun* is noticeably earthier in style, closer to the spirit of a lively, frank, warm-hearted country girl.

41 *Mauchline:* this small rural town (about ten miles east of Ayr) was Burns's home during his most creative years from 1784 to 1786, when he lived at Mossgiel Farm just a mile north of the town centre. A 'holy fair' was held in the kirkyard of Mauchline church in August of 1785, an occasion that no doubt provided many of the realistic details in this poem.

60 *scarlets:* a woman's best cloak was usually coloured scarlet (note in *LSP*, II, 382), and would only be worn on such special occasions.

75 *racer Jess:* this was a real person, the half-witted daughter of George and Agnes ('Poosie Nansie') Gibson, the proprietors of the disreputable tavern in Mauchline, where she served as part-time barmaid and part-time prostitute. She was called 'racer Jess' because she was remarkably fast on her feet. She appears again as 'hav'rel [simpleton] Jenny' in Burns's poem 'Adam Armour's Prayer', line 31.

86 *chosen:* in Burns's first published volume (Kilmarnock, 1786) the adjective is 'elect', but the poet changed this to the smoother 'chosen' in all subsequent editions. The reference is to the doctrine of Election, the belief that certain souls are predestined by God for salvation through Christ. These are the elect of God, the chosen people blessed by the special grace

of God. This doctrine is part of the official creeds of many Protestant churches (including the Church of England), but it was and is especially prominent in Scottish Presbyterianism. The belief was open to gross distortions, such as the idea that worldly prosperity was a sure sign of election. The 'chosen swatch' here are fanatics who are wholly convinced that they are among God's elect.

87   *grace-proud faces:* in the doctrine of Election the chosen are saved by God's grace and are therefore 'grace-proud', arrogantly flaunting their spiritual superiority over the ordinary people. John Calvin in his original *Institutes* taught that the elect had a duty to lead holy and selfless lives in order to 'illustrate' the grace of God within them; but this concept was often lost sight of in Burns's Scotland. In this stanza the phrases 'chosen swatch' and 'grace-proud faces' have the force of devastating satire on hypocrisy and self-righteous fanaticism.

91   This line in Burns's daring parody of a well known line in the Scottish Metrical Version of Psalm 146, verse 5: 'O happy is that man and blessed/ whom Jacob's God doth aid'.

102   *Moodie:* the Reverend Alexander Moodie of Riccarton (1722–1799), a fanatical representative of the 'Auld Licht' party in the Church of Scotland, the 'evangelicals' who stressed the doctrines of original sin, election, and justification by faith, as opposed to the 'New Lichts' or 'Moderates' (generally favoured by Burns) who emphasised morality, good works, and common sense. The Auld Lichts held that ministers should be democratically elected by congregations, whereas the New Lichts supported the legal rights of landlords to appoint clergy. Moodie served as minister of Riccarton, adjacent to Kilmarnock, from 1761–1799, and was noted for his hysterical preaching style. With the Reverend John Russell of Kilmarnock (see stanza 21) he was one of the 'heroes' of Burns's 'The Holy Tulzie' or 'The Twa Herds', a hilarious satire on a vituperative dispute over parish boundaries heard before the Presbytery of Ayr. Moodie also appears in Burns's 'The Kirk of Scotland's Garland' or 'The Kirk's Alarm', line 30, where he is called 'Singet Sawnie'.

103   *tidings o' damnation:* in the Kilmarnock volume this phrase was 'tidings o' salvation', but Burns changed it to 'damnation' in all subsequent editions. This felicitous change was suggested to him by Dr Hugh Blair, professor of rhetoric in the University of Edinburgh, who more often gave Burns bad advice.

116   *cantharidian plaisters:* Thomas Crawford in *Burns* (Edinburgh and London, 1960), 71–72, explains that 'cantharides, or "Spanish fly", is a blistering agent if taken externally, an aphrodisiac if swallowed'; Burns here brilliantly suggests both effects – Moodie's words are blistering, but they may also stimulate sexual feelings internally.

122   *Smith:* The Reverend George Smith (1748–1823), the 'New Licht' minister at Galston from 1778 to 1823. The characterisation of Smith in lines 122–123 and 127–137 was intended not as adverse criticism of the man, but should be read as Burns's satire on the Auld Lichts' *objections* to Smith: he was far too rational and cultivated for them.

131   *Socrates:* ancient Greek philosopher (470–399 BC). *Antonine:* Marcus Aurelius Antoninus, Roman emperor AD 161–8, and stoic philosopher.

138 *Peebles:* The Reverend William Peebles (1753–1826), an Auld Licht who became minister of Newton-upon-Ayr in 1778. The church is near the mouth of the river Ayr – hence, Peebles is 'frae the water-fit'. He featured in two other of Burns's poems: as 'Poet Willie' in 'The Kirk of Scotland's Garland', or 'The Kirk's Alarm' (lines 34–37); and as 'Peebles shawl' (shallow) in 'The Holy Tulzie', or 'The Twa Herds' (line 56). Peebles was terrified of Burns's satiric pen, and cowardly enough to attack him in 1811, long after the poet's death, in an anonymous diatribe called *Burnomania; the Celebrity of Robert Burns considered in a Discourse addressed to all real Christians of every Denomination,* where he stigmatised Burns as an 'irreligious profligate' writing 'vile scraps of indecent ribaldry'.

142 *common-sense:* this is a personification of Burns's friend Dr John Mackenzie (d. 1837), a Moderate who was present at the Holy Fair in August of 1785, but left when the fanatic Peebles began to preach. Here and elsewhere Burns uses the term 'common-sense' to sum up the rational principles of the New Licht or Moderate party.

143 *Cowgate:* this was and is the name of a street in central Mauchline, running southward from Loudon Street (the main east-west thoroughfare), with its opening just opposite the entrance to Mauchline kirkyard where the Holy Fair was held.

145 *Wee Miller:* The Reverend Alexander Miller (died 22 December 1804). According to a note in Burns's hand in the British Library copy of his Kilmarnock ed. (1786), at the time (autumn, 1785) Miler was 'the assistant minister at St Michael's'. I am deeply indebted to Dr John Strawhorn of Mauchline, Ayrshire, for the identification of this church together with other interesting side-lights on 'Wee Miller'. 'St Michael's' was the pre-reformation name for the church in Burns's own parish of Mauchline. Dr Strawhorn cites Andrew Edgar, *Old Church Life in Scotland* (1885), I, 360, who quotes from the Chartulary of Melrose Abbey (which held Mauchline parish), a document from the reign of William the Lion (1165–1214): 'Territorium de Mauchelin et ecclesiam Sancti Michaelis in eo sitam'. Such old Catholic names for churches sometimes lingered on for centuries in popular usage. In actual fact Miller was officially the assistant minister not in Mauchline but in the small parish of Auchinleck just to the south of Mauchline, where he served under the minister, the Rev. John Dun, from 1780 to 1787. He was also employed as the tutor to the children of the biographer James Boswell whose ancestral home was in Auchinleck. In addition to these duties, Miller apparently also preached occasionally in Mauchline Kirk to help out the Rev. William Auld, the ageing minister of that parish who was 76 in 1785. At any rate, Burns implies in this stanza that Miller was actually fairly liberal but pretended to be an Auld Licht conservative in order to get a parish ('a manse') of his own. Apparently this hypocritical strategy was successful, since Miller was ordained as minister of Kilmaurs in May 1788. His ordination had been delayed since August 1787 in the face of violent opposition, a ruckus partly caused, Miller later alleged, by Burns's debunking stanza.

151 *carnal wit an' sense:* 'carnal' was a cant term in Auld Licht preaching, used to discredit the idea that a man could earn salvation through his own 'fleshly' good works and moral behaviour. Here it has the force of

withering irony.

163–171 Matthew Arnold in his famous essay on 'The Study of Poetry' (1880) quoted this stanza and totally misinterpreted it. He saw this passage as 'bacchanalian poetry', that is, poetry in praise of strong drink, and found it 'unsatisfactory' and 'poetically unsound' because lacking sincerity! Burns, however, is not praising drink here at all; rather he is making fun of the way a few drinks will make a relatively ignorant person suddenly an expert in any field (especially theology). Arnold took the stanza out of its context and misread it grotesquely.

181 This line is another Biblical echo: see Isaiah. xviii. 3 and xxvii. 13. In Christian tradition generally the trumpet will herald the last judgement.

184 *Black Russel:* the Reverend John Russel or Russell (1740–1817), minister of the High Kirk in Kilmarnock from 1774 until 1800, a staunch Auld Licht preacher, famous for his tremendously powerful voice. He appears in four other of Burns's kirk satires: as 'wordy Russel' in 'The Holy Tulzie' or 'The Twa Herds' (see lines 13, 37–48); in 'The Ordination' (line 13); as 'Black Jock' in 'Epistle to John Goldie' (lines 9–10); and as 'Rumble John' in 'The Kirk of Scotland's Garland', or 'The Kirk's Alarm' (lines 22–25).

185–6 *His piercin words:* this image is closely modelled on Hebrews. iv. 12: 'For the word of God is quick, and powerful, and sharper than any two-edged sword, piercing even to the dividing asunder of soul and spirit, and of the joints and the marrow.'

188 *'Sauls does harrow':* this phrase is presented as a direct quotation, but it is actually a distortion of a well-known passage in the ghost's speech in Shakespeare's *Hamlet*, I, v, 15–16: 'I could a tale unfold whose lightest word / Would harrow up thy soul, freeze thy young blood.'

217 *Waesucks!* etc: Cp. Fergusson's 'Braid Claith', I. 13: 'Waesuck for him wha has nae fek o't!'

232 *faith an' hope, an' love:* Burns is here engaging in daring word play with St Paul's three theological virtues – faith, hope, and love (charity); see I Corinthians, xiii. 13: 'And now abideth faith, hope, charity, these three; but the greatest of these is charity.'

237–8 In these lines the poet is playing upon yet another Biblical text; see Ezekiel. xxxvi. 26: 'A new heart also will I give you, and a new spirit will I put within you; and I will take away the stony heart out of your flesh, and I will give you a heart of flesh.'

19. Robert Burns, *The Ordination*, 1786

TEST: For the copy-text of this poem I have used the poet's first printing of it in the first Edinburgh edition of 1787, slightly modernised in terms of normal capitals, italics, etc., and with all names spelled out in cases where Burns supplied only asterisks or initials or dashes or a combination of these. The handful of Burns's own notes and references are all reproduced below, preceded by the symbol [B]. The present editor is indebted to James Kinsley's very helpful notes in *The Poems and Songs of Robert Burns* (Oxford, 1968), 1164–67.

Motto: This couplet is of Burns's own composition as attested by the fact that in one of the two surviving manuscripts of the poem the motto is signed 'Ruisseaux', the poet's facetious rendering of his own surname in French ('ruisseaux' means 'brooks' or 'burns'). He used the same playful device in the poem entitled 'Elegy on the Death of Robert Ruisseaux'.

1–4 In Burns's time the two most important trades in the town of Kilmarnock were those of the weavers (flea-bitten) and leather workers (tanners and shoe-makers).

 5 *Laigh Kirk:* this was the principal church for the parish of Kilmarnock, a parish divided into two main districts or 'charges', each with its own congregation and minister. In addition, there was a separate church or 'chapel of ease', called the High Kirk, with its own congregation and minister, but also belonging to Kilmarnock parish. Of the six preachers referred to in this poem, Robertson (73) was the minister of the 'first charge'; Lindsay (see Lauder, 11), Mutrie (82) and Mackinlay (14) successively of the 'second charge'; and Oliphant (12) and Russell (13) successively of the High Kirk.

 7 *Begbie's:* a tavern (later the Angel Hotel) in Market Street, Kilmarnock, directly across the Marnock Water from the Laigh Kirk, whence it was accessible by a foot bridge so narrow that folk had to walk in single file, *in a raw.*

10 *Common-sense:* a quality much admired by the New Licht clergy, detested by the Auld Lichts; see Burns's 'The Holy Fair', 142–44.

11 *Maggie Lauder:* [B] 'Alluding to a scoffing ballad which was made on the admission of the late Reverend and worthy Mr. Lindsay to the Laigh Kirk.' In a note in an early manuscript version of this poem Burns added the following information: 'I suppose the author here means Mrs Lindsay, wife of the late Reverend and worthy Mr. Lindsay, as that was her maiden name, I am told. N.B. – He got the Laigh Kirk of Kilmarnock.' The Reverend William Lindsay (*c.* 1725–1774) was a Moderate or New Licht minister who had been presented to the second charge of the Laigh Kirk by the Earl of Glencairn in 1762, but not actually ordained (in the teeth of fierce Auld Licht opposition) until 1764. The 'scoffing ballad' on his wife Margaret Lauder was modelled on the bawdy seventeenth-century folk song of 'Maggie Lauder'.

12 *Oliphant:* the Reverend James Oliphant (*c.* 1734–1818) had been the Auld licht minister of the High Kirk, Kilmarnock, from 1764 to 1773.

13 *Russell:* the Reverend John Russell (1740–1817) another Auld Licht minister who succeeded Oliphant in the High Kirk from 1774 until 1800. See note to Burns's 'The Holy Fair', 184.

14 *Mackinlay:* the Reverend James Mackinlay (1756–1841), an Auld Licht minister who was presented to the second charge of the Laigh Kirk by the Earl of Glencairn in August 1785, on the death of John Mutrie (see note on line 82). Owing to opposition by the New Lichts in Kilmarnock Mackinlay's ordination was actually delayed until 6 April 1786, so that Burns's poem (apparently written in January or early February of 1786) was composed in anticipation of the ceremony. Later, in 'The Kirk of Scotland's Garland' or 'The Kirk's Alarm', Burns devoted a satiric stanza (lines 26–29) to Mackinlay, where he is called 'Simper James', and where the poet alludes to

the minister's overly zealous enthusiasm for 'the fair Killie dames'.

16–18 *shangan:* this refers to a cruel and mischievous game played by children, whereby a 'shangan' or 'shangie', a cleft stick, is fastened to a dog's tail and the poor, tormented beast is then pelted with refuse.

19 *turn King David owre:* this means to choose one of the Psalms of David for singing in church.

21 *double verse:* in the Scottish *Metrical Psalms* each stanza normally consisted of two quatrains, called 'double verse'.

22 *Bangor:* the name of a favourite Psalm tune.

28 *proper text:* with conscious irony Burns presents in stanza 4 three minor incidents from the Old Testament that are especially gross or violent – 'improper' texts, calculated to deepen the impression of the speaker's vulgarity.

30 *Ham:* [B] 'Genesis, ch. ix. vers. 22.'

31 *nigger:* in the 1787 Edinburgh edition this noun is spelled 'niger', but this seems to be an error – perhaps by contamination from *tiger* (line 35) – since the context here and in Genesis clearly tells us that the meaning intended is 'slave', and since Burns makes it rime phonetically with *vigour* and *rigour* (29, 33).

32 *Phineas:* [B] 'Numbers, ch. xxv. vers. 8.'

34 *Zipporah:* [B] 'Exodus, ch. iv. vers. 25.'

39 *carnal weed:* a fleshy luxury (like tobacco); 'carnal' is here used satirically as a cant term in Auld Licht preaching. See note on Burns's 'The Holy Fair', 151.

46–54 In this stanza Kilmarnock is hilariously personified as a cow, now looking forward to ample and delicious fodder

55–58 Burns is here echoing the opening of Psalm 137: 'By the rivers of Babylon, there we sat down, yea, we wept, when we remembered Zion. We hanged our harps upon the willows in the midst thereof.' The speaker is comparing the plight of parishioners of the Laigh Kirk under the recent Moderate ministers to that of the Israelites in foreign captivity.

64–72 In this stanza the fanatical speaker contrasts the situation in two Ayrshire parishes, Fenwick and Kilmarnock. At Fenwick the selection of a minister (William Boyd) through 'Patronage' by the Earl of Glasgow resulted in disaster, since Boyd was a Moderate opposed by the majority of parishioners who barricaded the church in 1780 rather than accept him. The dispute was finally resolved by the General Assembly with the ordination of Boyd in 1782. At the Laigh Kirk in Kilmarnock, on the other hand, patronage by the Earl of Glencairn ('a godly, elect bairn') has resulted in the ordination of a popular Auld Licht minister, without the kind of ruckus experienced at Fenwick.

73 *Robertson:* the Reverend John Robertson (1733–1799), the New Licht minister of the first 'charge' or district of the Laigh Kirk since 1765.

75–76 *Ayr:* in the warped view of the Auld Licht speaker the town of Ayr was 'wicked' because it was dominated by New Lichts.

79 *Netherton:* the carpet-weaving district of Kilmarnock.

82 *Mu'trie:* the Reverend John Multrie (1745–1785), the previous New Licht minister of the second charge of the Laigh Kirk since 1775, whose death in June 1785 created the vacancy that was filled by the ordination of Mackinlay.

Kinsley (1164) is mistaken in calling Multrie an 'evangelical'; he was a New Licht, as Burns makes clear by pairing him with Robertson ('We never had sic twa drones', 83) who was certainly a New Licht or Moderate.

98   *Jamie Beattie:* Dr James Beattie (1735–1803) was a minor Scottish scholar, poet, and philosopher much admired by Burns (see 'The Vision', 171–174, and 'Epistle to John Lapraik', 21–22). He was the best Greek scholar of his class at Marischal College, Aberdeen, where, after a few years as a schoolmaster in secondary schools, he became Professor of Moral Philosophy in 1760. In that same year Beattie published his *Original Poems*, followed by his most celebrated poem, *The Minstrel*, in two parts in 1771 and 1774. In 1770 appeared his extremely popular prose work, *Essay on the Nature and Immutability of Truth*, attacking the ideas of David Hume.

120 *New Light:* [B] 'New-light is a cant phrase, in the West of Scotland, for those religious opinions which Dr Taylor of Norwich has defended so strenuously.'

20. Robert Burns, *Love and Liberty*, 1785–86

TEXT: With the kind permission of the editors, the text here reproduces that of *LSP*, II, 229–239, itself based on the manuscript version in the Burns Cottage Museum, Alloway, except that I have omitted the 'Merry-andrew' section from the text and relegated it to the note on line 80 below. The textual history of the cantata is exceedingly complicated and full of uncertainties, since Burns never published the work during his lifetime. A few basic facts, however, are fairly clear. Burns conceived the idea of the cantata and produced some kind of first draft in the autumn of 1785, shortly after dropping in at Poosie-Nansie's with his friends John Richmond and James Smith to observe a company of ragged beggars in the midst of a hilarious drinking party. Sometime during 1786 he subjected the cantata to extensive revisions, deleting several characters from the earlier version (including a sailor, a sweep, a quack doctor, and probably Merry-andrew), adding others, and reworking the whole thing. Though Burns omitted 'Love and Liberty' from the Kilmarnock volume, together with 'Holy Willie's Prayer' and other potentially offensive or dangerous pieces, he certainly intended the cantata for publication and seriously considered including it in his first Edinburgh edition of 1787. There is evidence that he was dissuaded from doing so by Dr Hugh Blair and no doubt other conservative friends.

Of the three surviving manuscripts of the whole work the Alloway version is certainly the latest and the best. However, it includes an interpolated sheet, between the second and third sheets of the original MS, with the 'Merry-andrew' section – on different paper, with different ink, certainly written at a different time. John C. Weston, in his most thorough study of all these matters – see 'The Text of Burns' "The Jolly Beggars"', *Studies in Bibliography*, 13 (1960), 239–247 – argues convincingly that 'Merry-andrew' was left over from an earlier draft and has no place in Burns's final version of the cantata. Apart from this article, Weston provides full and useful notes in his separate edition of *Robert Burns: The Jolly Beggars, A Cantata*, Northampton, Mass.: The Gehenna Press, 1963. James Kinsley, to whose notes in *The Poems and Songs of*

Robert Burns, 3 vols. (Oxford, 1968), III, 1148–1162, I am also heavily indebted, agrees with Weston's judgement. The most compelling reason for this conclusion is that 'Merry-andrew' simply does not fit into the dramatic structure of 'Love and Liberty': he is uniquely unconnected with the other characters, and his song interrupts the natural flow, blurring the fact that the female pickpocket's song of bereavement is a dramatic response to the doxy's song of joyous reunion with her old lover. To preserve the superb dramatic force of the cantata in Burn's final version I have omitted 'Merry-andrew' from the text. Nevertheless, since the piece is certainly by Burns and has interesting satiric themes in its own right, I have provided the full text of the 'Merry-andrew' section in these notes. Additionally, I have supplemented the text with panels of musical notation (melody lines only) for all of the songs, reproduced from James C. Dick's invaluable work, *The Songs of Robert Burns* (London, 1903), as reprinted in facsimile by Folklore Associates, Hatboro, Pa., 1962. In all other respects the text of 'Love and Liberty' in *LSP* has been followed precisely.

1 The verse form of this opening is the complex and distinctively Scottish 14-line stanza made famous by Alexander Montgomerie in his love allegory of *The Cherrie and the Slae* [Sloe], *c.* 1580, a form to which Burns returns at the end of the cantata in his Recitativo 7. He had already experimented (successfully) with this lively but difficult stanza in 'Epistle to Davie, a Brother Poet' in January 1785.

9 *Poosie-Nansie's*: the disreputable tavern and inn for vagrants in Mauchline. It still exists as a pub on Loudon Street at the corner of the Cowgate, directly across the street from Mauchline church and churchyard (the site of 'The Holy Fair'). Poosie-Nansie was Agnes Gibson who, with her husband George and her half-witted daughter Janet ('Racer Jess' of 'The Holy Fair', 75), operated this primitive 'howf'. The soubriquet of 'Poosie' by which she was popularly known in Mauchline is, as Kinsley (1153) says, Burns's spelling of 'pussie' or 'puss' – 'a pejorative term for a woman' in the eighteenth century. It also has sexual connotations.

29 The verse form of this song is incredibly complex and demanding, including internal rimes and a refrain in the following pattern:

      1———A———A
      2———A———B
      3———C———C
      4———C———B

It should be noted that the final phrase, 'at the sound of the drum', acts as a refrain in all five stanzas, and that the B rime of this refrain is repeated in the second and fourth lines throughout. The tricky sound effects of the words are a perfect complement to the bold and lively tune of 'Soldier's joy'.

34 *the heights of Abram:* the battlefield of the Plains of Abraham just west of the old walls of Quebec city where, in September 1759, a British army under General Wolfe defeated the French under Montcalm, a victory that ultimately resulted in British control of all of eastern Canada. James Wolfe ('my leader', 33) died on the field of battle.

36 *the Moro:* the fortress guarding the harbour of Santiago, Cuba, stormed by the British in 1762.

37 *Curtis:* Admiral Sir Roger Curtis, who destroyed the *floating batt'ries* of the French and Spanish forces who were besieging British Gibraltar in 1782.

39 *Elliot:* General George Augustus Elliot (1717–1790), a governor of Gibraltar, who held the British fortress against a long siege by the French and Spanish from 1779 to 1783. Since the ex-soldier tells us that this was his last engagement (line 37), he was presumably discharged in 1783 and had thus been a vagabond for two years by 1785.

49–56 This recitativo is in the *Christis Kirk* stanza without the final tag-line or 'bobwheel'. The imagery in the first quatrain (49–52) is a brilliant parody of Milton's *Paradise Lost*, I, 541–43:

> At which the universal host upsent
> A shout that tore hell's concave, and beyond
> Frighted the reign of Chaos and old Night.

Kinsley (1154) suggests a much less striking parallel with Dryden's *Fables*, 'The speeches of Ajax and Ulysses', lines 197–200, 587–9.

73 *the Peace:* the Peace of Versailles, 1783.

74 *Cunningham fair:* Cunningham or Cunninghame is the northern district of Ayrshire, lying north of the River Irvine.

80 The 'Merry-andrew' section was interpolated here, the only place it could logically fit in at all. For reasons given above in the note on the *TEXT*, it has been removed from the text of the cantata, but it seems worthwhile to present the section here in its entirely. The recitativo and song of Merry-andrew read as follows:

Poor Merry-andrew, in the neuk,	clown; corner
Sat guzzling wi' a tinkler-hizzie;	tinker wench
They mind't na wha the chorus teuk,	not who; took
Between themsels they were sae busy:	
At length wi' drink an' courting dizzy,	
He stoiter'd up an' made a face;	staggered
Then turn'd, an' laid a smack on Grizzie,	kiss
Syne tun'd his pipe wi' grave grimace.	Then

SONG

AIR

Tune: *Auld Sir Symon.*   [*Pills to Purge Melancholy*, 1719, iii. p. 143.]

Andante

1   Sir Wisdom's a fool when he's fou; Sir Knave is a fool in a ses-sion, He's

4   there but a prentice I trow,   But I am a fool by pro - fes - sion.

Sir Wisdom's a fool when he's fou;	drunk
Sir Knave is a fool in a session,	law court
He's there by a prentice, I trow,	apprentice
But I am a fool by profession.	

My grannie she bought me a beuk,	book
An' I held awa' to the school;	went away
I fear I my talent misteuk,	mistook
But what will ye hae of a fool.	have

For drink I would venture my neck;	
A hizzie's the half of my craft:	wench
But what could ye other expect	
Of ane that's avowedly daft.	crazy

I, ance, was ty'd up like a stirk,	once; bullock
For civilly swearing and quaffing;	
I, ance, was abus'd i' the kirk,	
For towsing a lass i' my daffin.	rumpling, frolicking

Poor Andrew that tumbles for sport,	
Let nae body name wi' a jeer;	
There's even, I'm tauld, i' the court,	told
A tumbler ca'd the premier.	called

Observ'd ye yon reverend lad	
Mak faces to tickle the mob;	Make
He rails at our mountebank squad,	
It's rivalship just i' the job.	

And now my conclusion I'll tell,	
For faith I'm confoundedly dry:	
The chiel that's a fool for himsel,	fellow
Guid Lord, he's far dafter than I.	Good; crazier

The main satiric theme of Merry-andrew's song is similar to that of John Gay's *The Beggar's Opera* (1728), namely, that in actual practice the morals of the ruling class are identical to those of the criminal class. Gay's Peachum, the master criminal and receiver of stolen goods, is called the 'prime minister' of the London underworld. Burns follows this line in stanzas 5 and 6 of the song where Andrew castigates both political and spiritual leaders – 'A tumbler ca'd the premier' and 'yon reverend lad' – as gross hypocrites. Burns certainly knew *The Beggar's Opera*, and he may also have been influenced here by Jonathan Swift's *Gulliver's Travels*, Part I – specifically by the passage in Chapter 3 describing Flimnap, the chief minister of Lilliput, and the political game of jumping on the tight rope as qualification for high government office.

81–88 This recitativo is in another traditional Scots verse form, the octosyllabic couplet, going back to Barbour's *Bruce* (c. 1375). Burns himself used it in two others of his major poems, 'The Twa Dogs' and 'Tam o' Shanter'.

86 *weary fa' the waefu' woodie:* this was a traditional formula for cursing the gallows. Literally, *woodie* or 'widdie' is the Scots spelling of the English noun 'withy', meaning a tough, slender twig of willow; withies were often twisted together to make a rope, including (as in this context) a hangman's rope or noose. By extension *woodie* was sometimes used as a term for the gallows.

99 *trepan:* ensnare, a term from underworld jargon, probably suggested to Burns by John Gay's use of it in *The Beggar's Opera* (1728), II, xiii: 'Force or cunning / Never shall my heart trepan'.

101 *from Tweed to Spey:* the Tweed is a southern river partly forming the boundary with England, whereas the Spey is a northern river in the Highlands emptying into the Moray Firth; the phrase, therefore, means from the south to the north of Scotland.

117–128 The fourth recitativo is in Burns's favourite form, the six-line 'Habbie' stanza made famous by Robert Sempill of Beltrees in his comic elegy 'The Life and Death of Habbie Simson' (*c.* 1640). This verse form was the most widely used in the Scots poems of both Ramsay and Fergusson, and is also the stanza of both of Mayne's *Christis Kirk* poems.

125–28 Burns's amusing use of Italian musical terms embedded in the 'braid Scots' texture of his verse here was surely suggested by the following passage in Ramsay's 'Elegy on Patie Birnie', 50–54:

> Jove's nimble son and leckie snell [keen servant]
> Made the first fiddle of a shell,
>   On which Apollo,
> With meikle [great] pleasure play'd himsel
>   Baith jig and solo.

130 This seems to be an ironic echo of the famous opening line – 'Come live with me and be my love' – of Christopher Marlowe's 'The Passionate Shepherd to his Love'. The burlesque effect is similar to that of the Miltonic echo already noted in lines 49–52. Kinsley (1157) also suggests a source in a couplet in the *Westminster-Drollery*, I (1671), 16–17: 'Come live with me, and be my Whore, / And we will beg from door to door'.

132 *whistle owre the lave o't:* this famous refrain traditionally had sexual undertones implying fornication or copulation; the idea is that the words to this part of the song are too coarse or offensive to be spelled out, so that we must 'whistle over the rest of it'. Burns's use of the formula, however, is notably flexible, depending on the context. In this line, for example, and again in lines 140 and 148, the expression simply means 'go to the devil' in a general sense of reckless abandon, with no explicitly bawdy connotations; whereas in lines 136 and 144 the traditional sexual suggestion is clearly present.

145 *heav'n o' charms:* a common euphemism for the female genitals, the pudendum.

146 *kittle hair on thairms:* a brilliant sexual *double entendre* in which the primary meaning is to play the fiddle (*hair* being the horsehair of violin bows and *thairms* the dried animal intestines or 'guts' used for violin

strings), and the secondary is to indulge in sex play or intercourse.

149–164 This recitativo is written in a modified form of the *Christis Kirk* stanza without the final 'tag line', as in Song 5 (165–180) that follows. To this pattern Burns added internal rimes in the tetrameter lines of the second stanza of the recitativo, and throughout the song.

165–180 The caird's song belongs to a popular tradition of tinker-songs (see the note in Kinsley 1158). For centuries tinkers were notorious as sexual adventurers (like friars in earlier times and travelling salesmen more recently), wandering about the countryside and calling on lonely women to offer more than one kind of service. The tune to which this song is set – 'Clout the Caudron' (mend the pot) – was traditionally connected with words that could be understood in two ways, but Burns resists that temptation here and gives his tinker a straightforward work song.

169–172 Tinkers were also notorious for cheating the government by enlisting in the army, accepting the standard bribe of golden guineas (see Fergusson's 'Hallow-fair', stanza 7), and then promptly deserting to return to their vagabond lives as tinkers.

178 *keilbaigie:* a kind of whisky, distilled at Kilbagie near Clackmannan, that was popular throughout the Lowlands of Scotland in the eighteenth century.

181–207 Recitativo 6 is in the *Christis Kirk* verse form, with feminine rimes in the trimeter lines of the second and third stanzas. The tag-line ending in 'that night' was probably suggested by Fergusson's use of the same device in the later stanzas of 'Hallow-fair' and 'The Election'.

183–184 The superbly witty contrast in these lines recalls the similar effect in 'The Holy Fair', 239–240: 'There's some are fou o' love divine; / There's some are fou o' brandy'.

192 *rak'd her, fore and aft:* this is naval jargon – to 'rake' a ship is to sweep it with cannon fire. There is evidence that in an early draft the cantata included a sailor who was later deleted, and this expression is more probably a vestige of that version. Another example of nautical jargon – 'clear the decks' – appears in line 230.

195 *the spavie:* the spavin, a disease of the hock joint of horses, causing a limp.

197 *shor'd them Dainty Davie:* offered them the folk song of 'Dainty Davie'; this is a complex allusion to the 17th-century song celebrating the exploit of the Covenanting minister David Williamson being saved from capture by brutal dragoons through the quick wit of Lady Cherrytrees, who put a woman's night-cap on him and slipped him into bed with her daughter. The daughter, of course, became pregnant as a result of this adventure, and shortly became the third of Williamson's series of seven wives. The allusion to this particular song here is appropriate for two reasons: (a) Williamson was noted for sexual vigour, and his nickname of 'Dainty Davie' was used in bawdy versions of the song as a euphemism for the male organ itself, as in the text apparently by Burns in *The Merry Muses of Caledonia*, eds. James Barke and Sydney Goodsir Smith (Edinburgh, 1959), p. 74, where the hero 'produc'd a dainty Davie'; and (b) the episode involves the willing giving of a woman to a man, as the Bard is doing in this situation.

209 *an' a' that:* the implication here, and also in lines 217, 221, 225, and 229, is

'and all that sort of nonsense'.

212 *For a' that:* the meaning of this phrase here and also in the refrain lines throughout, is 'In spite of all that'.

216–19 The hilarious classical allusions here to the Muses, Castalia, and Helicon recall Fergusson's 'The King's Birth-Day in Edinburgh', stanza 3:

> O *Muse*, be kind, and dinna fash us
> To flee awa' beyont Parnassus,
> Nor seek for Helicon to wash us,
>   That heath'nish spring;
> Wi' Highland whisky scour our hawses,
>   And gar us sing.

226 *the flie:* sexual desire, probably alluding, as Kinsley (1161) suggests, to the aphrodisiac 'Spanish fly'. Burns had used a related image in 'The Holy Fair' ('cantharidian plaisters'); see note on 'The Holy Fair', line 116.

228–29 These are sexual *double entendres* as Kinsley (1161) notes: *put me daft* means 'distracted me' and 'driven me wild with excitement'; *ta'en me in* means 'deceived me' and 'admitted me sexually'.

234 *dearest bluid:* an amusing euphemism for semen.

247 *twa Deborahs:* this is an ironic Biblical reference, comparable to 'the proper text' in 'The Ordination' (stanza 4); Deborah was an heroic Hebrew prophetess and singer in Judges, 4–5, here equated with the singing Bard's two remaining sluts.

Selected Bibliography

Note: Under *General Commentaries* are included specific studies of the genre, and the more useful histories of Scottish literature and critical studies of individual poets that deal with these poems, or some of them – arranged alphabetically by author. Under *Texts of Individual Poems* are the most important editions listed chronologically, with the copy-texts used in this edition marked with asterisks.

General Commentaries on the Genre

Bentman, Raymond, *Robert Burns*, Boston, 1987

Craig, Cairns, gen. ed., *The History of Scottish Literature*, II, ed. Andrew Hook, Aberdeen, 1987 (see especially essays by A.M. Kinghorn and Alexander Law and by Carol McGuirk)

Crawford, Thomas, *Burns: A Study of the Poems and Songs*, Stanford, 1960

Daiches, David, *Robert Burns*, New York, 1950

—, *Robert Fergusson*, Edinburgh, 1982

Freeman, F.W., *Robert Fergusson and the Scots Humanist Compromise*, Edinburgh, 1984

Henderson, Thomas F., *Scottish Vernacular Literature*, Edinburgh, 1910

Jack, R.D.S., and Andrew Noble, eds. *The Art of Robert Burns*, London, 1982 (see especially the essays by John C. Weston and Robert P. Wells)

Jones, George F., '"The Christ's Kirk", "Peblis to the Play", and the German Peasant-Brawl', *PMLA*, 68 (1953) 1101–1125

Kinghorn, Alexander M., 'The *Christ's Kirk* Tradition' in editor's 'Introduction' to *The Middle Scots Poets*, 13–16, London, 1970

Kinsley, James, ed., *Scottish Poetry: A Critical Survey* (essays by various hands), London 1955

Lindsay, Maurice, *History of Scottish Literature*, London, 1977

Low, Donald A., *Robert Burns*, Edinburgh, 1986

—, ed., *Robert Burns: The Critical Heritage*, London, 1974

MacLaine, Allan H., 'The *Christis Kirk* Tradition: Its Evolution in Scots Poetry to Burns', *Studies in Scottish Literature*, II (1964–65), 3–18, 111–124, 163–182, 234–250

—, *Robert Fergusson*, New York, 1965

—, 'Radicalism and Conservatism in Burns's *The Jolly Beggars*', *Studies in Scottish Literature*, 13 (1978), 125–43

—, *Allan Ramsay*, Boston, 1985

Masson, David, *Drummond of Hawthornden*, New York, 1873

Millar, James Hepburn, *A Literary History of Scotland*, London, 1903

Simpson, Kenneth, *The Protean Scot*, Aberdeen, 1988

Smith, Sydney Goodsir, ed., *Robert Fergusson, 1750–1774: Essays by Various Hands to Commemorate the Bicentenary of his Birth*, Edinburgh, 1952

Watson, Roderick, *The Literature of Scotland*, London, 1984, New York, 1985

Wittig, Kurt, *The Scottish Tradition in Literature*, Edinburgh, 1958

Texts of Individual Poems

1. Anon., *Peblis to the Play, c.* 1430–50

*Maitland Folio MS (*c.* 1570–1585) in Pepys Library, Magdalene College, Cambridge, England; ed. William A. Craigie, *The Maitland Folio Manuscript*, II, Edinburgh, 1927
John Pinkerton, ed., *Select Scotish [sic] Ballads*, II, Edinburgh, 1783
William Tytler of Woodhouselee, ed., *The Works of James I, King of Scotland*, Perth, 1783
James Sibbald, ed., *Chronicle of Scottish Poetry*, II, Edinburgh, 1802
George Chalmers, ed., *The Poetic Remains of Some of the Scotish [sic] Kings*, London, 1824
George Eyre-Todd, ed., *Scottish Poetry of the Sixteenth Century*, London, [1892]

2. Anon., *Christis Kirk on the Grene, c.* 1490–1510

*Bannatyne MS (1568) in National Library of Scotland, Edinburgh; ed. W. Tod Ritchie, *The Bannatyne Manuscript*, II, Edinburgh, 1928
Maitland Folio MS (*c.* 1570–1585) in Pepys Library, Magdalene College, Cambridge, England; ed. William A. Craigie, *The Maitland Folio Manuscript*, II, Edinburgh, 1927
Laing MS (*c.* 1640) in Edinburgh University Library; ed. Janet M. Templeton, 'Seventeenth-century Versions of *Christis Kirk on the Grene* and *The Wyf of Awchtirmwchty*', *Studies in Scottish Literature*, 4 (1966–67), 130–137
Edmund Gibson, ed., *Polemo-Middinia* ... [and] *Christ's Kirk on the Green* (tentatively attributed to James V), Oxford, 1691
James Watson, ed., *A Choice Collection of Comic and Serious Scots Poems*, Part I, Edinburgh 1706
Allan Ramsay, ed., *The Ever Green*, I, Edinburgh, 1724 (based on the Bannatyne MS)
William Tytler of Woodhouselee, ed., *The Works of James I, King of Scotland*, Perth, 1783
John Pinkerton, ed., *Ancient Scotish [sic] Poems*, I, Edinburgh, 1786
James Sibbald, ed., *Chronicle of Scottish Poetry*, II, Edinburgh, 1802
George Chalmers, ed., *The Poetic Remains of Some of the Scotish [sic] Kings*, London, 1824
George Eyre-Todd, ed., *Scottish Poetry of the Sixteenth Century*, London, [1892]
Earl F. Guy, 'Some Comic and Burlesque Poems in the Sixteenth Century Scottish Manuscript Anthologies', unpublished Ph.D. Thesis (Edinburgh University, 1952)
John MacQueen and Tom Scott, eds., *The Oxford Book of Scottish Verse*, Oxford 1967
Alexander M. Kinghorn, ed., *The Middle Scots Poets*, London, 1970
Christine Marie Harker, ed., 'Chrystis Kirk of the Grene: A Critical Edition', unpublished M.A. Thesis (University of Victoria, Victoria, B.C., Canada, 1990)

3. William Dunbar, *The Justis Betwix the Talyeour and the Soutar, c.* 1500

The Asloan Manuscript, A Miscellany in Prose and Verse, Written by John Asloan in the Reign of James the Fifth (1513–42), II, ed. William A. Craigie, Edinburgh, 1925
The Bannatyne Manuscript (1568), II, ed. W. Tod Ritchie, Edinburgh, 1928
The Maitland Folio Manuscript (*c.* 1570–85), II, ed. William A. Craigie, Edinburgh, 1927
W. Mackay Mackenzie, ed. *The Poems of William Dunbar*, London, 1933
James Kinsley, ed., *The Poems of William Dunbar*, Oxford, 1979

4. Anon., *Sym and his Bruder, c.* 1530

The Bannatyne Manuscript (1568), III, ed. W. Tod Ritchie, Edinburgh, 1928
James Sibbald, ed., *Chronicle of Scottish Poetry*, I, Edinburgh, 1802 (first seven stanzas only)
David Laing, ed., *Select Remains of the Ancient Popular and Romance Poetry of Scotland*, Edinburgh, 1825, re-edited by John Small, Edinburgh, 1885
—, ed., *Early Popular Poetry of Scotland and the Northern Border*, II, London, 1826, re-edited by W. Carew Hazlitt, London, 1895

5. Sir David Lindsay, *The Justing Betwix James Watsoun and Jhone Barbour, c.* 1539

The Works of Sir David Lindsay, Edinburgh, 1568, printed by John Scot for Henry Charteris
*Douglas Hamer, ed., *The Works of Sir David Lindsay of the Mount*, 4 vols., Edinburgh, 1931–34 (text in vol. I, notes in III)

6. Alexander Scott, *The Justing and Debait up at the Drum, c. 1560*

The Bannatyne Manuscript (1568), II, ed. W. Tod Ritchie, Edinburgh, 1928
James Sibbald, ed., *Chronicle of Scottish Poetry*, III, Edinburgh, 1802
James Cranstoun, ed., *The Poems of Alexander Scott*, Edinburgh, 1896
*Priscilla Bawcutt and Felicity Riddy, eds., *Longer Scottish Poems*, I, Edinburgh, 1987

7. William Drummond of Hawthornden, *Polemo-Middinia, c.* 1645

Polemo-Medinia, Edinburgh, 1684
Edmund Gibson, ed., *Polemo-Middinia: Carmen Macaronicum, autore Gulielmo Drummundo* ... [and] *Christ's Kirk on the Green*, Oxford, 1691
*L.E. Kastner, ed., *The Poetical Works of William Drummond of Hawthornden*, II, Manchester, 1913

8. Anon., *The Blythsome Wedding, c.* 1680

*James Watson, ed., *A Choice Collection of Comic and Serious Scots Poems*, Part I, Edinburgh, 1706

Allan Ramsay, ed., *The Tea-Table Miscellany*, Edinburgh, 1724
James Paterson, ed., *The Poems of the Sempills of Beltrees*, Edinburgh, 1849

9. Allan Ramsay, *Christ's Kirk on the Green*, Cantos II and III, 1715, 1718

Allan Ramsay, ed., *Poems by Allan Ramsay*, Edinburgh, 1721
Burns Martin and John W. Oliver, eds., *The Works of Allan Ramsay*, I, Edinburgh, 1945
*Thomas Crawford, David Hewitt, and Alexander Law, eds., *Longer Scottish Poems*, II, Edinburgh, 1987

10. John Skinner, *The Christmas Bawing of Monimusk*, 1739

The Caledonian Magazine, September 1788
Amusements of Leisure Hours, or Poetic Pieces ... by John Skinner, Edinburgh, 1809
H.G. Reid, ed., *Poems and Songs of the Rev. John Skinner*, Peterhead, Scotland, 1859
*Thomas Crawford, David Hewitt, and Alexander Law, eds., *Longer Scottish Poems*, II, Edinburgh, 1987

11–13. Robert Fergusson, *Hallow-fair*, 1772, *Leith Races*, 1773, and *The Election*, 1773

The Weekly Magazine or Edinburgh Amusement, published by Walter and Thomas Ruddiman, for 12 November 1772, 22 July 1773, and 16 September 1773, respectively
Poems on Various Subjects, Edinburgh, 1779
Alexander B. Grosart, ed., *The Works of Robert Fergusson*, London, 1851
Matthew P. McDiarmid, ed., *The Poems of Robert Fergusson*, II, Edinburgh, 1956
*Thomas Crawford, David Hewitt, and Alexander Law, eds., *Longer Scottish Poems*, II, Edinburgh, 1987

14. John Mayne, *Hallowe'en*, 1780

The Weekly Magazine or Edinburgh Amusement, published by Walter and Thomas Ruddiman, Nov. 1780.
*George Eyre-Todd, ed., *Scottish Poetry of the Eighteenth Century*, II, London and Edinburgh, n.d. [1890s]

15. John Mayne, *The Siller Gun*, 1808

The Weekly Magazine or Edinburgh Amusement, published by Walter and Thomas Ruddiman, in 3 cantos, beginning 19 June 1780
The Siller Gun, in 4 cantos, Glocester [*sic*], England, 1808
The Siller Gun, in 5 cantos, London, 1836
*Thomas Crawford, David Hewitt, and Alexander Law, eds., *Longer Scottish Poems*, II, Edinburgh, 1987 (based on Glocester ed.)

16–20. Five Poems by Robert Burns, 1785–86

James Kinsley, ed., *The Poems and Songs of Robert Burns*, Oxford, 1968

16. Robert Burns, *A Mauchline Wedding*, 1785

   *W.E. Henley and T.F. Henderson, eds., *The Poetry of Robert Burns*, II, Edinburgh, 1896

17, 18, 20. Robert Burns, *Halloween*, 1785, *The Holy Fair*, 1785, and *Love and Liberty*, 1785–86

   *Thomas Crawford, David Hewitt, and Alexander Law, eds., *Longer Scottish Poems*, II, Edinburgh, 1987

19. Robert Burns, *The Ordination*, 1786

   Poems. Chiefly in the Scottish Dialect, Edinburgh, 1787

THE ASSOCIATION FOR SCOTTISH LITERARY STUDIES

Annual Volumes

Volumes marked * are still available from the address given opposite the title page of this book.